For His glory,

The
Gospel Lens

Looking at Life
Through the Heart of Jesus

Jonathan C. Griffin

Published by Lucid Books in Houston, TX
www.LucidBooks.com

eISBN: 978-1-63296-548-6
ISBN: 978-1-63296-546-2 (paperback)
ISBN: 978-1-63296-547-9 (hardback)

Special Sales: Most Lucid Books titles are available in special quantity discounts. Custom imprinting or excerpting can also be done to fit special needs. Contact Lucid Books at Info@LucidBooks.com

In the narratives provided, some names have been changed to protect the identity and privacy of their families.

To:
My lovely bride, Kelley

Special Thanks

I first want to thank my Lord and Savior Jesus Christ for this book. *The Gospel Lens* is all about You, Jesus. I pray that You are honored and glorified through every word and page of this book.

Secondly, I want to thank my dad, whose constant encouragement to persevere, made this book possible. The hundreds of conversations, phone calls, texts, and emails we had about the book were indeed life-giving to me and spurred me on to finish what I started in June of 2020. Dad, I am deeply grateful for all the meticulous and tedious hours you spent editing and fine-tuning the book because you believed in me and the content I have written, all for the glory of Christ's name.

Thirdly, I want to thank all the people I interviewed for this book. I thank Nick, Clara, my wife (Kelley), Jos, Joseph, Ryan, Jordan, Amanda, Matt, Lindsey, Sean, Lisa, and Dad. My heart swells with gratitude toward each of you for allowing me to put your narratives into this book. I pray that people are blessed by your transparency and authenticity. Your stories provide an enriching vividness to each chapter.

I also want to thank my mom, Susan, my brother, Grant, and Nick for reading through the first draft chapters and providing much-needed encouragement along the way. Thank y'all so much.

Thank you to Pastor Thomas Weaver for offhandedly mentioning during one of your sermons that there are people in your congregation who have books in them to write. The Spirit took this word of encouragement and bore the fruit you now see.

And I would like to give a very special thanks to Carolina Weaver for her fantastic illustrations. Carolina, thank you for the many hours you spent capturing 27 different scenes and adding a vivid visual dimension to my writing. Wonderful job!

I believe huge thanks are in order to Dr. Timothy Keller whose preaching has greatly influenced me and inspired the contents of this book. Thank you for your Gospel in Life podcast and the years you labored in preaching at Redeemer Presbyterian Church in NYC.

I also want to thank Dr. Dane Ortlund whose book, *Gentle and Lowly: The Heart of Christ for Sinners and Sufferers*, has had a profound impact on my theology, thinking, and writing. Thank you, Dr. Ortlund, for helping me see the heart of Jesus clearly for the first time.

And a very special thanks to Jeff Vanderstelt whose book, *Gospel Fluency: Speaking the Truths of Jesus into the Everyday Stuff of Life*, has been especially formative for me in my faith journey. Jeff, I thank you for inspiring me and for discipling me from afar. Your writing inspired me to begin writing this book. Specifically, I need to give credit to when you wrote the following in *Gospel Fluency*: "I believe such fluency is what God wants his people to experience with the gospel. He wants them to be able to translate the world around them and the world inside of them through the lens of the gospel—the truth of God revealed in the person and work of Jesus[1]." This has been my aim as I, by the grace of Jesus, have addressed the various topics explored in this book. I see *The Gospel Lens* as a companion volume to *Gospel Fluency*.

I want to thank my beautiful bride, Kelley, again, who believed in me and stood by me as I endeavored such a colossal task of writing a book while raising three young children, with the eldest being 3 years old. Thank you so much for getting me the new laptop for the writing and completing of this book. Babe, I love you so much!

Lastly, again, I want to thank you, Jesus, my Lord, and Savior. You are so amazing and so wonderful. I pray that the words I have written make you smile, bring glory to Your name, and build up your bride, the church. All the glory evermore to You, Jesus!

---

1. Jeff Vanderstelt, *Gospel Fluency: Speaking the Truths of Jesus into the Everyday Stuff of Life*, (Wheaton, IL, Crossway, 2017), 41.

Contents

PART 6: The Gospel Lens and Suffering

PART 7: The Gospel Lens and the Heart of Jesus

Part 1

Introduction to The Gospel Lens

"And we all, with unveiled face,
beholding the glory of the Lord, are being
transformed into the same image . . ."
(2 COR. 3:18).

1

The Purpose and Premise

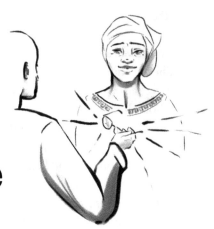

Her name is Esther.

She has walked six miles from her village in Tanzania, East Africa, to arrive at the Olorien Community Medical Clinic nestled amidst the verdant trees of Arusha. Although Esther has impaired vision, she has come for medical treatment for a completely different ailment. With sweat beading up on her brow from her long journey she sits down on a plastic armchair in the waiting area. Some forty other patients are there too, and many of them are her friends and neighbors. After twenty minutes of waiting, she perks up.

"Esther," one of the clinic nurses calls out smiling and waving her to come over to the examination room where her blood pressure and temperature will be checked.

A nervous excitement spreads through her as she walks into the room. After triage, Dr. Byemba, the clinic doctor, invites her into the exam room. He observes her squinting when looking at him, so he decides to check her eyesight. The test reveals she has a vision of 20/100 where even the big "E" at the top of the Snellen eye chart is fuzzy and the "F" and the "P" on the second line are indistinguishable. What Dr. Byemba does next for Esther will change her life.

"Here . . . put these on," Dr. Byemba says handing her a pair of bifocals. She puts on the glasses.

In a single moment, the world around her is suddenly transformed. Where once there was nothing but distorted shapes and blurry figures, now there is a beautifully clear array of distinguishable objects and textures surrounding her. She gazes at Dr. Byemba, wearing his white lab coat. She can now tell he is clean-shaven and wears a stethoscope around his neck framing a checkered tie. Sheer elation erupts in her chest and no light is needed in the room that morning because the brilliance of Esther's smile is bright enough to illuminate the whole clinic.

Now I want you to imagine that you are Esther before she receives the corrective lenses. Everything around you is distorted, blurry, and vague. A man stands before you and hands you a pair of glasses. You take them. As you bring them up to your face and peer through them your perception of the entire world is *transformed*.

What if we looked at all of life through the lens of the gospel? Imagine the good news of Jesus Christ as a pair of glasses. When you put the gospel glasses on and look through the lenses everything suddenly takes on a different color, a different contour, a different clarity, and consequently, a different meaning. The purpose of this book is to show you how to view all of life through the lens of the gospel, which is the heart of Jesus.

Scripture has a few different ways of talking about this concept. In 2 Corinthians 3:18, Paul shares, "And we all, . . . , beholding the glory of the Lord, are being transformed into the same image from one degree of glory to another." How does that happen? How can we be transformed into Christ's image from glory to glory? The Greek word for "transformed" here is where we get our English word "metamorphosis." Viewing life through the lens of the gospel is a transformative process that takes time. Consider this real-life scriptural example.

When Jesus calls Nathanael to be His disciple, He reveals supernatural knowledge of Nathanael's character when He has never even met him before (see John 1:48). Nathanael then declares Jesus to be "the Son of God" and "the King of Israel" (John 1:49). Jesus' response is very interesting once we understand the depth behind the Greek wording that He uses with Nathanael in John 1:50:

> Jesus answered him, "Because I said to you, 'I saw you under the fig tree,' do you believe? You will see greater things than these."

The word for "see" in Greek is *blepō* and this word refers to taking in optic information. However, this is not the Greek word used in John 1:50. Rather, the Greek word for "see" in verse 50 is *horaō*. This word means seeing with *spiritual insight* and *understanding,* and it appears twice in the verse. The first time refers to Jesus seeing Nathanael under the fig tree and secondly when Jesus declares the greater things that Nathanael will "see" (*horaō* in Greek).

Jesus is amazingly profound! Jesus *saw* Nathanael with a depth of insight and perception that could only lead to Nathanael confessing Jesus as the Son of God and the King of Israel. Then Jesus turns the tables on Nathanael and declares that *Nathanael* will see with the same insight and spiritual understanding. Jesus says Nathanael will perceive greater things than these because Jesus will give him the ability to truly see and perceive.

So, what are those greater things Jesus is referring to Nathanael seeing? Nathanael ". . . will see heaven opened, and the angels of God ascending and descending on the Son of Man" (John 1:51). This is a clear allusion to Jacob's dream in Genesis 28:12 where the angels of God were ascending and descending on a ladder set up on the earth reaching to heaven. Jesus is declaring right then and there that Nathanael will "see" how Jesus is the true access to the presence of God as He is God, the Word, become flesh to dwell among us (see John 1:14). When we rightly perceive Jesus by His grace we are transformed by the renewing of our minds. This is the lens of the gospel that we must look through to perceive all of life.

Let me explain this concept in another way. In Philippians 2:5 the Apostle Paul says, "Have this mind among yourselves, which is yours in Christ Jesus." The Greek word translated as "mind" here is a difficult word to translate in English, but this word is profoundly rich and packed with meaning. The Greek word is *phroneō*. If you have studied anatomy, you may recognize this word because it has the same root as the anatomical term "phrenic." The phrenic nerve innervates the diaphragm (the dome-shaped muscle below the heart that helps us breathe).

So, the Greek word *phroneō* has a visceral or emotive aspect as well as a cognitive meaning. Therefore, we are to have what is called the *phroneō Christō*, or the mind, attitude, and *heart of Christ*. This is the essence of peering through the gospel lens. You will see how Christ sees, think how Christ thinks, and empathize the way Christ empathizes. In other words, you will be emotively impacted the way Christ is impacted. This reality will transform you from the inside out. What do I mean by transformed?

Let's look at Jesus in Phil. 2:6–8:

"who, though he was in the form of God, did not count equality with God a thing to be grasped, but emptied himself, by taking the form of a servant, being born in the likeness of men. And being found in human form, he humbled himself by becoming obedient to the point of death, even death on a cross."

If we are to look through the gospel lens to view all of life, we will need the phroneō Christō by the power of the Holy Spirit. This will transform us by making us humble servants to become obedient to our Father's will at whatever cost.

The gospel lens also leads us to look beyond the present situation and fixate our minds on the exaltation of Christ and the glory of God the Father. In other words, we are lifted beyond the mire and drudgery of the temporal, so we can see *life in the light of eternity*. Look at the next verses in Phil. 2:9–11:

> Therefore God has highly exalted him and bestowed on him the name that is above every name, so that at the name of Jesus every knee should bow, in heaven and on earth and under the earth, and every tongue confess that Jesus Christ is Lord, to the glory of God the Father.

If we are looking through the gospel lens, our heartbeat will be the exaltation of Jesus. There is no way around this. Jesus is so incredible and so wondrous that we will simply long for His glory and not our own. He is the Servant King who captures our hearts with His heart, wins our affections, and triumphs through being shamed and dying for sinners like you and me on a Roman cross. He has the name above every name! Jesus Christ is Lord to the glory of God our Father.

So, what does this look like practically in real life? The remainder of this book will delve into answering the specifics, but for now, here is a practical example. The other day, my wife, Kelley, and I took our kids on a nature trail hike in the blazing heat of June in south Texas. We began walking the trail in the Judson Nature Preserve, which is rather shaded by beautiful trees and forest foliage. But before long, Kelley began to feel stuffy and miserable from the poorly circulating hot air in the forest. I could tell she was uncomfortable, but I persisted in wanting to continue the hike. The gospel lens I needed at that moment is found in Phil. 2:3, "Do nothing from selfish ambition or conceit, but in humility count others more significant than yourselves."

So, to view my wife and the situation at that moment through the gospel lens, through the heart of Jesus, I would *not only* turn around and take her home to get some ibuprofen and AC, but I would also *want* to do so. I would empathize with her uncomfortable state, show her compassion, and love her with the heart of Christ, as He loves the church.

Only when my own heart is melted by the compassion Jesus shows me in the gospel will I long to demonstrate the same compassion to my wife. She's an amazing woman so, of course, I had to insist that we stop the hike and return to the car. If I'm not peering through the gospel lens to see (horaō) her misery and discomfort I will not empty myself and serve her and count her as more significant than myself.

We will examine several different aspects of life through the gospel lens or through the heart of Jesus, but before we do so we need to define the gospel and our identity in Christ. I will rely on an in-depth look at Ephesians chapters 1 and 2 to do this.

Part 2

Building a Gospel Lens Foundation

"But God, being rich in mercy, because of the great love with which he loved us" (EPH. 2:4).

2

The Gospel: Our Radical Sin Nature

Her name is Mariam.

Like Esther, she also lives in Tanzania, East Africa. She has come to the Olorien Community Medical Clinic for treatment of her abdominal pain, but she also carries pain of a different sort in her body. She carries the weight of shame at the core of her being. She sits in a foldable white chair, talking with the clinic chaplain, Baba Bryan. Although she is physically unbound right now, she sits emotionally shackled by the shame of her past. She begins to tell her heart-wrenching story to the chaplain.

"I was married before to a monstrous man. At age 17, I was forced to become his wife and bear him three children. He was a devout Muslim, and so he tried to have me converted to Islam on numerous occasions. He would bring in an Islamic leader to try to convert me and teach me his religion. I was not convinced by anything the leader or my husband said. The suffering and strain on our marriage were too much for me to bear." Mariam wipes a tear away from her left eye as she recalls the emotional abuse she endured in her marriage.

She goes on, "So we finally separated and I went back to live with my parents."

The chaplain reaches out to touch her shoulder to comfort her gently. Baba Bryan then asks, "So, did you find a church of your own after you were free to choose for yourself?"

"No. I cannot bring myself to go to any church." Mariam now looks at the floor as if to avoid the chaplain's eye contact.

He realizes the utter shame weighing her down, drawing her gaze to the floor. With compassion and heartfelt tenderness, Baba Bryan reaches out and tilts her chin up so she can lock eyes with him.

"My dear child, what has happened to you?"

"I tried going to a church after I was divorced. But at this church, there was a red chair in the back, separated from the rest of the congregation, where 'sinners' had to sit if and when they returned to church. They told me I was one such 'sinner' because I had been forced into marriage and now was divorced."

Deeply grieved by what he has just heard, Baba Bryan brings two missionaries in the clinic, Lindsey, and Joseph, over to Mariam to provide care and support. After Mariam retells her story, Lindsey's eyes fill with tears and she becomes truly indignant. She thinks to herself, *how could the gospel of grace be so distorted?* She then reaches out to Mariam and wraps her in a warm embrace.

With tears flowing down her cheeks and her voice quivering with empathy, Lindsey tells her, "Mariam, if there is a 'red chair' apart from the others that one must sit in to soak in their shame and be mocked and humiliated, then we are all deserving of such a chair . . . every chair in the church should be red. But thanks be to Christ whose blood covered over the red chair and ran freely over us, cleansing us for all eternity of past, present, and future shame."

Lindsey thinks to herself of the irony of the chair being red and she is reminded anew of the blood that Jesus spilled.

She goes on, "Jesus actually invites us into the 'throne of grace' to come before the very throne room of God anytime we want to have a rich, abiding relationship with the Father."

Baba Bryan then adds, "Mariam, no such red chair exists at our church, and you are welcome anytime. You will be welcomed in love and acceptance."

My prayer is that the gospel of Jesus Christ and His heart will grip you and captivate you through this chapter. I also pray that your heart will be melted by the grace of God toward us in Jesus Christ. Only when your heart is melted by the beauty of Jesus and what He has done for you will you long to view all of life through the lens of the gospel. There are no red chairs here. There is only grace and truth.

So, before we understand our identity in Christ, we need to define and examine the gospel more closely. To do this, let's explore Eph. 2:1–10. I will define the gospel by breaking these 10 verses up into four different sections:

Our Radical Sin Nature

Let's look at Eph. 2:1–3 first:

> And you were dead in the trespasses and sins in which you once walked,
> following the course of this world, following the prince of the power
> of the air, the spirit that is now at work in the sons of disobedience—
> among whom we all once lived in the passions of our flesh, carrying
> out the desires of the body and the mind, and were by nature children
> of wrath, like the rest of mankind.

In just 3 verses the Apostle Paul, through the Holy Spirit, delivers a stunning wallop of conviction to the human race. In verse 1, he tells the saints of Ephesus that they were dead in their sins. Likewise, in our natural sin state, we also are dead before God. Pulseless. Lifeless. Unresponsive. Airless. Breathless. Motionless. Dead.

The Greek word for "dead" in Eph. 2:1 is *nekros.* This is where we get our English word "necrosis." This word appears in the medical science field and often refers to necrotic or decomposed human tissue which is repulsive by nature.

Here in this verse, Paul is telling us that the human heart is riddled with necrosis due to sin. Our disease of sin is humanly incurable. This is why we can only be saved by the sheer grace of Jesus (Eph. 2:8, 9). Dead people do not respond to external stimuli. They are unfeeling, stiff, and cold. *Nekros* can also be translated as "corpse." To view ourselves through the gospel lens means we must abandon every false notion of self-salvation and every false pretense of innate human goodness. "None is righteous, no, not one; no one understands; no one seeks for God" (Romans 3:10, 11).

For we have all fallen into the quicksand pit of our sin. And the harder we kick our legs and flail our arms of self-righteousness the farther we sink toward the suffocating reality of eternal separation from God. We desperately need the gracious and strong nail-scarred hands of Jesus to pluck us out of the miry bog of our depravity. And then, we will know that we are saved by His grace alone.

Eph. 2:1, "And you were dead," brings us back to what God promised Adam and Eve if they disobeyed Him, "but of the tree of the knowledge of good and evil you shall not eat, for in the day that you eat of it you shall surely die" (Gen. 2:17). Sin entered into the world through one act of disobedience and brought death. "For the wages of sin is death," (Rom. 6:23). I believe this death is both spiritual and physical in nature. The immediate effect is spiritual deadness before God, and the end result is physical death. In defining the gospel, we must come to a profound understanding of the depth of our sin and deadness before God, who is completely holy and pure.

In verse 2 Paul brings more conviction in stating that apart from Christ we were followers of Satan: "following the prince of the power of the air." In context, this would have resonated loudly with the Ephesian church. The cultural and historical perspective of first century Ephesus reveals that the city was completely caught up in pagan worship of the goddess Artemis (see Acts 19). In fact, one of the Seven Wonders of the World, the temple of Artemis, was located in Ephesus.

Acts 19 demonstrates for us just how much the civic, economic, and cultural pride of the people all hinged on the worship of this pagan goddess. You may recall how the people rushed into the amphitheater and shouted for two hours, "Great is Artemis of the Ephesians!" (Acts 19:34). So, in Eph. 2:1–3 Paul is drawing the Ephesians' minds back to what their identity was before Christ: "following the prince of the power of the air."

Acts 19:18–20 also shows us how prevalent the practice of magic was in Ephesus:

"Also many of those who were now believers came, confessing and divulging their practices. And a number of those who had practiced magic arts brought their books together and burned them in the sight of all. And they counted the value of them and found it came to fifty-thousand pieces of silver. So, the word of the Lord continued to increase and prevail mightily." It's noteworthy to mention that fifty-thousand pieces of silver are equivalent to $6 million U.S. dollars in today's currency. That's a lot of spell books and sorcery paraphernalia!

These cultural details are important because the Ephesian Christians still lived their lives embedded in a culture overrun and influenced by "the prince of the power of the air" (Eph. 2:2). So, Paul is reminding the Ephesians that they used to be just as dead and just as overrun by Satan as their very countrymen and neighbors.

When Jesus took hold of my wife, Kelley, He revealed Himself through the book of Ephesians to her in profound ways. As Kelley read the beginning of chapter two, she realized she, herself, was dead in her sins. She also realized that everywhere she went she was amongst dead people walking and living their lives held captive to Satan.

In our culture, we may not worship a pagan goddess or practice magic, but we do worship a host of other false gods. Make no mistake; our culture does follow the prince of the power of the air. The only difference is, that Satan's tactics here are insidiously subtle rather than his glaringly obvious strategies in first-century Ephesus. In the U.S. we are prone to worship the self, our comfort, romance, our smartphones, television, entertainment, wealth, material possessions, status, prestige, the American dream, family, social media, human approval, and our individuality. To begin to realize your very own deadness before God and your tendency to follow Satan is to begin to grasp the richness of the gospel. But Paul's not finished with his indicting statements.

In Eph. 2:3 he reveals that we all lived in the lusts and passions of our flesh. The word translated as "passions" is the Greek word *epithumia*. The prefix "epi" is an intensifier of the root word *thumia* which means "desire." So *epithumia* could also be translated as over-desire or inordinate desire.

In other words, Paul states that humans not only naturally commit sin, but we also *long* to commit sin with a passionate or inordinate desire. We cannot water our sin down or distance ourselves from the guilt we incur. We cannot fluff it off by chalking our sin up to: "Oh I was just in the wrong place at the wrong time." Or, "Oh I was just going along with what everyone else was doing."

No. The Scripture is abundantly clear that apart from Christ's saving grace, we all lust after sin. We must own our sin, claim it, confess it, and experience gospel-led desperation for the Savior.

Eph. 2:3 ends with a terrifying statement. Paul explains that the Ephesians "were by nature children of wrath, like the rest of mankind." This verse poignantly states that all of humanity deserves the wrath of God. The Greek word for "wrath" in verse 3 does *not* denote a sudden outburst of anger or capricious divine rage. So, what does this word mean?

Actually, the word picture connoted by God's wrath is His divine retribution building up like water behind a dam. The book of Revelation reveals that there will come a Judgment Day when the dam will collapse and the torrent of

God's wrath will be poured out on sinful humanity (see Rev. 20:11–15). This speaks to the holiness and justice of God.

Ultimately, we deserve God's wrath because we have sinned against Him and Him alone (see Psalm 51:4). We have offended the Most High. We have trampled over His heart. We have broken His perfect law. We have spit in His face. And this is why a gnawing conviction echoes in the recesses of every human heart—accusing, condemning, and consigning us to guilt, shame, fear, darkness, and death.

We naturally, apart from Christ, are dead in our sins, following Satan, disobedient, inordinately longing to sin, and deserving of God's wrath. Wow! Our radical sin nature is so devastating and so depressing. This reality is almost too much to bear and too much to behold.

But what if I told you there is a reality more powerful than our depression, greater than our guilt, stronger than our shame, more dominant than our fear, overpowering Satan, destroying sin, delivering from darkness, and defeating death? What is this reality? It's the gospel! It's the good news of Jesus Christ. It's the Father's rich mercy, great love for you, and lavish grace poured out on undeserving sinners.

3

The Gospel: The Father's Rich Mercy, Great Love, and Lavish Grace

Eph. 2:4–7:

> "But God, being rich in mercy, because of the great love with which he loved us, even when we were dead in our trespasses, made us alive together with Christ—by grace you have been saved—and raised us up with him and seated us with him in the heavenly places in Christ Jesus, so that in the coming ages he might show the immeasurable riches of his grace in kindness toward us in Christ Jesus."

Let's look at the first two words: "But God . . ." These two words are absolutely pivotal. These two words serve to fundamentally and completely change the direction and destination of the whole passage. We were hell-bound in verses 1–3, and now in verse 4, we are soaring heavenward. "But God" reorients us, raises us from the grave of our depravity, lifts us to unforeseen heights, and is the exact impetus for our spiritual hearts to start beating. "But God" takes our eyes off of our sinful state and locks our gaze onto God the Father and His transformative mercy and power to resurrect those dead in their sins.

The gospel lets us accurately see how sinful and depraved we are but at the same time shows us how powerful God is, how merciful He is, how kind He is, and how gracious He is *toward us*. In the spring of 2009, at the University of Texas in Austin, I witnessed the "But God" reality happen to an actual person in real-time.

His name is Nick.

He grew up in a Catholic background, but around the time he was about to start studying at university he was not even sure if God existed.

He now sits in his room, struggling with doubts, feeling an abyss of emptiness in his chest, and wondering if there is any point at all to the universe. He mutters a dangerous prayer, "God, if you're real then show me."

The first day of class arrives for Nick. It's 8 a.m. and the lecture hall is abuzz with students chatting and filing in to take their seats for Sociology 301. I am one of those students. Nick takes his seat near the middle of the row and close to the back of the lecture hall. He listens to the opening lecture from the professor who then asks the class to partner up with someone next to them and begin asking questions to get to know their fellow classmate.

Nick begins talking with a student named Eric and asks the usual preliminary questions. The activity ends quickly, and the professor makes a sociological connection by observing that the class followed cultural norms in the types of questions asked during the activity. For example, she remarks, "I bet no one asked if the classmate you met goes to church." This was to imply that such a question is out of bounds for a brief, first-time meeting.

After her first lecture, the professor dismisses the class. Nick and Eric stand up from their seats. I am sitting in the row in front of them, gathering my belongings and putting them in my backpack. I stand up and meet Nick and Eric for the first time.

Eric casually offers, "Hey, what do you guys think of forming a study group?"

Nick and I agree.

Within a week, we find ourselves at the Perry-Castañeda Library, or "PCL" for short. We begin studying sociology, and before long we find ourselves neck-deep in a spiritual discussion courtesy of Eric's catalytic remarks. Coming to the discussion with an atheistic worldview, Eric tells of how the existence of God cannot be proven. I counter with the necessity of faith in God and open my Bible and read from Hebrews 11:1. All the while Nick remains quiet, but he seems to be siding with me as he watches a verbal ping pong match ensue for another hour or so.

Exhausted, all three of us then leave the library. Eric still strongly holds his position, and I still resolutely hold mine. But Nick is somewhat of a mystery.

I want to get to know him better, so we talk about hanging out sometime. We both like racquetball, so we agree to meet up one evening for a game or two at the rec center.

On the racquetball court, he tells me of his Catholic background and then describes how he had recently started attending a non-denominational church with his mom. Nick reveals nothing to me about the prayer he prayed before the start of the semester. After we finish our game, I ask if I can pray over him and he agrees. As we are walking back from the rec center I can tell he is spiritually hungry.

So I nonchalantly challenge Nick to start reading the gospel of John in the New Testament. At the time, I think nothing of this.

Within a week or so Nick comes back to me and says, "Okay I've read John. What do I read now?"

I suggest, "Read the other gospels: Matthew, Mark, and Luke."

Nick begins to voraciously consume the beginning of the New Testament. Within a couple of weeks or so he calls me on the phone.

"Jonny, I read Matthew, Mark, Luke, and I also reread John. Bro, Jesus is amazing!"

With passion and awe in his voice, Nick relates to me how Jesus has become real to him. He has met Jesus. He is astounded by the miracles and the deity of Christ. The phone call feels like a moment of worship. Jesus has taken hold of Nick's life profoundly.

I have just witnessed the reality of "But God" in someone else's life.

In the next year, Nick becomes my roommate, and in the following semester, he meets his future wife. He becomes a leader in our dorm pointing young men to Jesus and even starts a Bible study group called Moore-Hill More Hope. The women in the dorm become inspired by this group and start their own as a result. This Christ-centered group goes on for years even after Nick has graduated from UT. At the time of this writing, Nick now serves as a leader with the youth at his church and teaches high schoolers to follow Jesus. Christ has transformed this once timid college student into a mature leader whose heart beats for his Savior to be glorified. The theme of the youth ministry he leads is, "Jesus is better."

Looking back eleven years later on the whole train of events, Nick and I marvel at how Jesus used an atheist to suggest that we start the study group in the first place. And Jesus also used an atheist as the catalyst for the spiritual conversation in the library that later led to pivotal interactions with Nick. Jesus is so amazing! "But God, being rich in mercy . . ."

God *is* "rich in mercy" (Eph. 2:4). The magnitude of God the Father's rich mercy on us is underscored by how much mercy we need due to our sinful state. There are two equal and opposite errors that we can make regarding the richness of God's mercy. On the one hand, we can conceive of ourselves as naturally good, and therefore the richness of God's mercy would not mean much at all to us.

And on the other hand, we can conceive of ourselves to be so utterly sinful that we would dare to think that God's mercy could never be rich enough to cover the immensity of our sins. These superiority and inferiority complexes respectively have no place in the gospel. In other words, we are both dead in our sins without any hope of self-salvation, *and* the Father's mercy is truly rich enough to completely cover all the atrocities we have or will ever commit. This is indicative of the Father's lavishly generous and merciful character.

The Greek word for "rich" means wealthy or abounding. This word carries with it the notion of never running out or being lavishly stocked. Do you see God as rich in mercy toward you? An easy litmus test to find out is to ask yourself, "How quick am I to show mercy when wronged or snubbed? How quick am I to take offense and harbor a grudge?"

The degree to which you show mercy when wronged is the degree to which you have received God's rich mercy. After unfolding the parable of the two debtors to a Pharisee, Jesus tells him, "Therefore I tell you, her sins, which are many, are forgiven—for she loved much. But he who is forgiven little, loves little" (Luke 7:47). The good news of God's great love for sinners continues in the next part of Eph. 2:4.

". . . because of the great love with which He loved us, even when we were dead in our trespasses, [God] made us alive together with Christ—by grace you have been saved—" (Eph. 2:4, 5). The Greek word for "great" in this verse is where we get our English word "poly," and it means numerous or vast in quantity. A diamond is polygonal which means it has many sides. A diamond is beautiful because it has multifaceted brilliance. God's love for you is also multifaceted. His love is so vast for you! What is the magnitude of God's love for you?

The magnitude is such that it will take us all eternity to fully plumb the depths, scale the heights, and explore the vastness of the Father's love for us in Christ Jesus. "For God so loved the world, that He gave His only Son, that whoever believes in Him should not perish but have eternal life" (John 3:16). It's one thing to read this statement, but it's quite another to have His love for you shed abroad in your heart . . . envelop your thoughts . . . and captivate your being.

The Father's love for you is demonstrated by the infinite cost He paid to open the door of salvation to have you as His own. In other words, when the Father gave His only Son, Jesus, He was giving what was most precious to Him. 1 Peter 2:4 says this about Jesus: "As you come to him, a living stone rejected by men but in the sight of God chosen and precious . . ." Jesus is infinitely precious to the Father, but the Father gave up the One most precious to Him so He could have you.

The Greek word for "love" in Eph. 2:4 and John 3:16 is *agapé*. This kind of love is choice-based and comes from the will but by no means excludes deep affection and feeling. *Agapé* has nothing to do with our goodness or loveliness but everything to do with the Father's sovereign choice and extravagantly loving character. He is so awesome!

What are the implications of God's staggering love for us in Christ Jesus? The implications are limitless. Let me ask you a question, "What motivates you to obey Jesus? Why do you obey Him?"

If you were to ask me this question some time ago, I would have said, "I obey Him because I love Him." But now I answer the motivation question differently. It is not my love for Jesus that motivates me to obey Him but rather *His love for me*. My love for Jesus is subject to ebb and flow like the ocean's tide, but His love for me is constant, steadfast, never changing, unstoppable, immovable, rock-solid, and a firm foundation (see Matthew 7:24, 25).

When you intimately and personally know the love of Jesus, you will be utterly freed from the rat race of seeking human approval. You will be transformed to serve and love others without ulterior motives. You will no longer see people as means to an end. You will not make your conversations about yourself anymore. You will be given a blessed self-forgetfulness. You will turn the focus onto Jesus. When you experientially know the love of Jesus you will smile more, weep more, laugh more, hug more, cry more, empathize more, confront injustice more, sing more, pray more, show more gratitude, serve more, listen more, and forgive more. His love will be the reason you get out of bed in the morning. Jesus will become the reason for everything you do.

How do we come to experience the Father's love for us in Jesus? Have you ever tried starting a fire without a match, lighter, or lighter fluid? You need friction and lots of it over a sustained length of time. You also need kindling and oxygen for the sparks to catch fire. The gospel friction that will heat the base of your heart with the love of the Father is sustained meditation and prayer through the truths and beauty of Jesus. The oxygen or wind that makes the heat become a roaring fire is the Holy Spirit. His presence is mediated through "the word of Christ dwell[ing] in you richly" (Colossians 3:16).

Eph. 2:5 says even when we were dead in our sins by His power the Father resurrected us and "made us alive together with Christ."

God the Father supernaturally imparts new life to us in Jesus! We become "born again" (John 3:3). And we become a "new creation" in Christ (2 Cor. 5:17). This is such good news! Now, what does this verse tell us about Jesus? As much as this verse speaks of our resurrection it also speaks of Christ's resurrection. If Christ has been raised from the dead then He has also lived a life perfectly acceptable to God the Father. Jesus' resurrection is proof that the Father has accepted His atoning sacrifice for our sins.

In other words, by implication, verse 5 tells us that Jesus lived a sinless life submitted to God, perfectly fulfilling the law. Jesus declared, "Do not think that I have come to abolish the Law or the Prophets; I have not come to abolish them but to fulfill them" (Matt. 5:17). The gospel necessarily includes the perfect life, righteousness, and sacrificial death of Jesus. You may recall that the sacrificial Passover lamb in Exodus 12 had to be a lamb *without blemish* for God to spare the firstborn and pass over the household with the blood of the lamb smeared over and around the doorframe.

God said, "The blood shall be a sign for you, on the houses where you are. And when I see the blood, I will pass over you, and no plague will befall you to destroy you, when I strike the land of Egypt" (Ex. 12:13). Jesus is "the Lamb of God, who takes away the sin of the world!" (John 1:29).

Now please don't miss the phrase "together with Christ" in Eph. 2:5. The Father "made us alive together with Christ." What does this phrase tell us about true followers of Jesus? This speaks to our *union* with the resurrected Christ. We now identify with His death and resurrection. Whatever is true of Jesus is now true of us. This is amazing news!

If Christ has been crucified then our old sinful nature has also been crucified with Him (see Galatians 2:20). If Christ has been made alive, then we also have been made alive in Him. If Christ is counted as perfectly righteous before God the Father, then we also are counted as perfectly righteous before God the Father. This is because the righteous record of Jesus has been credited to our account. When the Father declares, "You are my beloved Son; with

You I am well pleased" (Luke 3:22b), He is also declaring His delight over us because of our union with Christ.

Here's the gospel: on the cross, Jesus bore *all* our sins, so that He could in turn give us His perfect righteousness. He took the wrath of God, so we could have the grace of God. This is called the Great Exchange, and it's nothing short of amazing! It's not a coincidence that the Greek word for "reconciliation" also means "exchange."

Paul poignantly puts the Great Exchange this way, "For our sake he made him to be sin who knew no sin, so that in him we might become the righteousness of God" (2 Cor. 5:21).

Wow! How amazing is our Father and our Savior Jesus Christ? We are now ministers of "the message of reconciliation" or the Great Exchange (2 Cor. 5:19). We are now "ambassadors for Christ" (2 Cor. 5:20). Our union with Christ gives us a new identity!

In Eph. 2:5, 6 notice how the phrase "with Christ" or "with Him" appears three times consecutively: God "made us alive together *with Christ* . . . and raised us up *with Him* and seated us *with Him* in the heavenly places in Christ Jesus" (emphasis mine). This is such good news. We get to be *with Jesus*! He is our treasure, our eternal joy. He is so good.

Jesus is also the fulfillment of all Scripture. Remember how Jesus declares in Matt. 5:17 that He came to fulfill the law *and* the prophets. This means He fulfilled the entire Old Testament.

In the Old Testament book, 1 Samuel, Hannah's prayer is uncannily similar to Eph. 2:5, 6. She prays, "The Lord kills and brings to life; he brings down to Sheol and raises up . . . He raises up the poor from the dust; he lifts the needy from the ash heap to make them sit with princes and inherit a seat of honor." (1 Sam. 2:6, 8).

The similarities between this passage and Eph. 2:5, 6 are striking. The "Lord . . . brings to life" corresponds to "made us alive together with Christ." "He brings down to Sheol and raises up" corresponds to "and raised us up with him." Elevating "the needy from the ash heap to make them sit with princes and inherit a seat of honor" corresponds to "and seated us with him in the heavenly places in Christ Jesus."

Jesus is the Prince of all princes.

By God's grace, we who were dead in our trespasses and sins can be seated with Jesus, the Prince of Peace, to inherit a seat of distinct honor. Do you remember how Mariam was shamed by the red chair designated for her in the back of the church? We all deserve this red chair, but in Christ, we are raised up to be seated with Him in the heavenly places! As Paul is declaring this to the Ephesians, he is speaking to a people in a shame-honor culture. The place of honor at the table has critical importance in such cultures.

Jesus highlights this importance when He says, "But when you are invited, go and sit in the lowest place, so that when your host comes he may say to you, 'Friend, move up higher.' Then you will be honored in the presence of all who sit at the table with you. For everyone who exalts himself will be humbled, and he who humbles himself will be exalted" (Luke 14:10, 11).

In the gospel, we humble ourselves before Jesus. We turn to Him and confess our deadness in sin and desperate need for Him to save us. And the Father in His power and grace makes us alive together with Christ. He raises up with Him, and seats us with Jesus in a place of astounding honor, in the heavenly places. The gospel is life-transforming news!

What are the implications of being seated with Christ in the heavenly places? If you are seated with Christ, you can take criticism without becoming offended. If you are seated with Christ, you are not inordinately concerned about the opinions of others. If you are seated with Christ, you are secure in who you are and what you do. If you are seated with Christ, you look to bestow honor on others because you have been shown so much undeserved honor in Christ.

Eph. 2:4–6 describes our present reality in Christ. In other words, the verses we have been examining indicate our present position with Christ in the sight of God the Father. Notice the past tense of "made alive together with Christ," "raised up with Him," and "seated with Him." Our newfound reality in Christ is breathtaking compared to our radical sin nature described in verses 1-3.

But Eph. 2:7 now gives us a foretaste of what our future reality will be in Christ:

"so that in the coming ages He might show the immeasurable riches of His grace in kindness toward us in Christ Jesus."

God the Father seats us with Christ so that in the coming ages we may taste the surpassing riches of His grace and kindness toward us in Jesus.

Do you see God from that perspective right now in your life? The gospel puts the very goodness of God on display for all eternity. To look at life through the gospel lens graciously gives us an eternal mindset rather than a temporal one; a God-centered and Christ-exalting framework and focus from which to work (see 2 Cor. 5:14, 15).

Let me drive this point home. You're alive for trillions and trillions of years after your life on earth. Comparatively, our time on earth is shorter than a blink of an eye in light of eternity. What are you doing in this life that will echo into eternity? Only what we do through Jesus and for Jesus will last forever. Everything else we do and hold onto will perish and be burned up. Let us not build with wood, hay, or straw but with the lasting gospel materials of gold, silver, and precious stones (see 1 Corinthians 3:10–15).

Quite frankly, our ambitions and expectations are way too small compared to the eternal purpose for which we were designed. We were designed to be seated with Jesus in the heavenly places "so that in the coming ages he might show the immeasurable riches of his grace in kindness toward us in Christ Jesus . . ." (Eph. 2:7).

The word for "immeasurable" in this verse means "to throw beyond." God the Father's grace and kindness expressed to us in Christ exceeds our greatest expectations, surpasses all our earthly dreams and transcends our deepest longings.

Our God is so kind and so gracious to us. For those in Christ, the best is yet to come! So how do we receive the grace of Jesus? What does this look like practically, in real life? By God's grace, I had the distinct and unique opportunity to watch the grace of Jesus invade the life of a colleague of mine in the workplace.

4

The Gospel: Receiving Grace

Her name is Clara.

From childhood, she viewed God as distant and far away from her. She felt she had to be very good to gain His favor. God was not a loving Father to her. She felt He was on a different planet from her. She regularly attended Catholic Church, practiced repetitious prayers, and read from the catechism. But none of this was real to her. She would stare at the body of Jesus on the crucifix and become acutely aware of just how far she was from Him. She sought to be perfect and attain "good girl" status to gain her mother's approval.

In her freshman year of high school, she began what would become a 14-year-long battle with anorexia and bulimia. For Clara, to be beautiful was to be thin. This became an obsession. The number on the scale became the carrot on the stick; the shadow she could never catch. This struggle spanned across high school, college, graduate school, and throughout her dating relationship into marriage. Again, she hid all of this from her friends, co-workers, and the public eye to maintain the righteous image demanded and expected of her since childhood.

She became possessive, controlling, and extremely jealous with her boyfriend, Josue. She became verbally abusive to him. She would bring him down and criticize what he would do. She became judgmental of him and angry if something good was happening in his life. Arguments would include Clara shouting, "I hate you and want you to die." I have to add a brief sidebar here:

the Clara I know would never be capable of such behavior. I was astounded when I heard this part of her story.

As she relayed this part she became choked up and said, "I'm surprised he stayed with me. I can't believe he stayed with me through all of this. He stayed."

She told me this through tears as she realized the grace of God shown to her in Josue. Anxiety was also an issue for Clara. She became very dependent and clingy to Josue. She would use him to fill a void, get her fix, and for her own means. But through it all, he still stayed.

The anxiety she felt with Josue was also felt toward God. She was deathly afraid of going to hell. Her anxieties were further exacerbated when she and Josue unknowingly joined a cult when they were students at Baylor during their undergraduate studies. The cult reinforced Clara's greatest fears. She was led to focus on her sin and to change her behavior patterns through sheer willpower. The cult was all about changing yourself through good works. This was very familiar to Clara from her religious upbringing. She even became guilty of dating Josue at the time, so she broke up with him for a couple of days.

She would cry to herself and say, "I failed again and again and I'm unable to truly change myself."

Their cult involvement lasted for six months.

Clara and Josue got married in 2015 and encountered marital issues. She even threatened divorce and to cheat on him. But through it all, he stayed with her. They both began to feel a deep need for God . . . a conviction that something was not right. Clara felt that God was the only one who could give her peace.

So, in 2017 they left the Catholic Church, and in January of that year, they both resolved to grow closer to God. They started going to a Pentecostal church, which she found placed a huge emphasis on emotional spirituality. But in 2018 she started attending a Bible study at work. During this time there came a night when Clara prayed a dangerous prayer like my friend, Nick.

❧

She kneels to pray on the carpet in her room. Inexplicably she begins to experience the presence of God entering her bedroom. She starts reading Scripture. She begins to cry and then she prays, "God, I'm Yours. Can You do something with me? Do whatever You want with me. Use me. I put myself in

Your hands." She begins worshipping the Lord. She later would describe the experience as the Lord doing a "deep tissue massage" on her soul.

After this experience, Clara still did not understand that you are saved by grace. The whole bit about Jesus dying on the cross for her did not make sense or click for her. So, she regularly attended the Bible study at her work. My supervisor, David, and I would lead this time in teaching and praying with our co-workers.

We find ourselves sitting in a windowless conference room on the third floor of the John Hornbeak building. We sit with the chairs and tables forming a semi-circle so we can all see one another. We begin with a prayer like any other Bible study, but what is about to happen in the room is not like any other Bible study we've had.

I open our time by reviewing the gospel message of Jesus Christ. I had not planned to do this, but as I continue to speak the age-old truths of the good news, I begin to witness the power of the Spirit in the room. The rich meaning of Jesus dying to forgive us of *all* our sins (past, present, and future) becomes alive as I speak the words. The Spirit takes the words, and He ministers to Clara's heart.

I see the expression on her face begin to change. A dawning of comprehension appears like bright illumination from a flood light showering a building. I witness the "aha moment" of the Spirit making Jesus real to Clara. Like scales falling from her eyes, she once was blind, but now she sees.

She would later describe the experience as a switch turning on and light coming into her and filling her being. She would also describe the Holy Spirit rushing through her. In that room, on that day, and for the first time, Clara understood that salvation is through Jesus alone.

The Bible study ends and I walk over to her. She's crying and weeping because of the beauty of Jesus and the gospel. We talk about how the scales fell from her eyes just moments ago. She explains that she now understands that Jesus has forgiven her of *all* her past, present, and future sins. She is overjoyed by the work of grace Christ has done in her.

After receiving the grace of Jesus, Clara begins to have a passionate desire to be with Jesus and to get to know Him. She begins reading Scripture with her husband regularly. Her marriage relationship with Josue completely transforms after this. She apologizes to him for all the wrong she has done to him over the years, and he forgives her.

Josue tells Clara, "The Lord has already forgiven you."

Josue immediately notices a dramatic change in his wife. She now greatly desires to respect and honor him as her husband.

Clara's view of God also changes. He was so distant and far away before Jesus came to her, but now she sees Him as Father and she as His daughter. She once lived her life riddled with fear and anxiety over losing her salvation and going to hell, but now she knows she is sealed with the Holy Spirit (see Eph. 1:13, 14). Jesus is now the hope and anchor for her soul. She now knows she could never do anything to earn salvation because Jesus poured His grace out on her. "For by grace you have been saved through faith;" (Eph. 2:8a).

Now let's examine the next two verses in our text:

"For by grace you have been saved through faith. And this is not your own doing; it is the gift of God, not a result of works, so that no one may boast" (Eph. 2:8, 9).

You can see through Clara's story how she came to grasp the reality of these verses. The word for "grace" in verse 8 is *charis*. This word means a freely given, unmerited favor from God. Eph. 2:1–3 shows us that this gift is undeserved and unmerited.

So what is the grace or the gift and favor God has given us? Actually, this verse indicates two gifts: salvation from the wrath our sin deserves *and* the faith necessary to take hold of this salvation. The Greek word for "faith" here is *pistis* and it means confidence, trust, and being fully convinced of the truth. In His grace, the Father imparts faith as a gift through Jesus to those whom He chooses.

This is why Heb. 12:2 encourages us, "looking to Jesus, the founder and perfecter of our faith, who for the joy that was set before him endured the cross, despising the shame, and is seated at the right hand of the throne of God." The Greek word for "founder" in this verse can also be translated as "pioneer," "leader," "originator," or "author."

The Greek word for "perfecter" in Heb. 12:2 can also be translated as "consummator," "finisher," or the one who brings something to completion.

If you have faith in Jesus right now, it is because Jesus has *authored* and *originated* that faith for you.

The good news is that He will also bring your faith to completion, "And I am sure of this, that he who began a good work in you will bring it to completion at the day of Jesus Christ" (Phil. 1:6). By God's *grace*, He gives us *both* salvation and faith through Jesus Christ and His Spirit!

Jesus illustrates what grace is in the parable of the two debtors, "A certain moneylender had two debtors. One owed five hundred denarii, and the other fifty. When they could not pay, he canceled the debt of both. Now which of them will love him more?" (Luke 7:41, 42).

What strikes me about this illustration is that Jesus skillfully shows us that we are unable to pay our debt if our debt is huge *or even* if our debt is small. Both the woefully sinful *and the extremely religious* are unable to pay. Jesus also shows us God's lavish grace in choosing to graciously forgive both debtors. The one who owed five hundred denarii had debt equivalent to roughly $100,000 in today's terms. The one who owed fifty denarii had roughly $10,000 of debt in today's terms.

Both debtors were unable to pay, had fallen short, and were in desperate need of the moneylender's grace to cancel their debts. The gospel of grace says you are woefully unable to pay your debt before God, but Jesus Christ has graciously paid *all* your debts for you with His death on the cross. He has purchased salvation for us through His perfect life, sacrificial atoning death, and triumphant resurrection over sin, Satan, and death!

This is why Eph. 2:8a declares, "For by grace you have been saved . . ."

The verb tense in Eph. 2:8a where it says, "you have been saved", indicates a completed and irrevocable action. In other words, nothing can take away our salvation. The saving work of Christ on our behalf cannot be undone. This is amazing news for those in Christ! Once He has saved you, He has also sealed you and secured you with His Holy Spirit (see Eph. 1:13, 14).

Eph. 2:9 emphasizes the concept of grace by underscoring that our salvation is "not a result of works, so that no one may boast." God does it all! We can take zero credit for beginning, maintaining, or finishing our faith in Jesus. We have no room to boast if we are saved by the lavish grace of Jesus. This also means that we can cease the endless, exhausting battle of trying to prove ourselves before God and other people. I have spent the better part of my life trying to prove myself to gain God's acceptance and approval. It has been so exhausting and so empty.

But the gospel of grace stops me dead in my tracks in this futile pursuit and allows me to rest in Christ and obey Him out of loving thankfulness for all He has done for me. If I'm going to boast, I must boast in Him and Him alone,

"But far be it from me to boast except in the cross of our Lord Jesus Christ, by which the world has been crucified to me, and I to the world" (Gal. 6:14).

Our Savior Jesus is so amazing. I'm overwhelmed by His lavish grace, steadfast love, and radical kindness expressed to me when I deserved death and His wrath. "But God, being rich in mercy . . . " (Eph. 2:4).

What is the fruit or the result of this gospel of grace? The next chapter will answer this question as we look at Clara's life after she met Jesus. We will see how Jesus used her uniquely in the workplace when a patient in the Intensive Care Unit (ICU) was in dire need of God's grace.

5

The Gospel's Transformative Purpose: God's Plan

Clara continued to grow in her faith in Jesus. God gave her a new way to look at the work she was doing as a speech therapist in the hospital. She began to pray with her patients so that she could address not only their physical healing but also their spiritual needs. One day she was assigned to a patient in the ICU who had suffered a hemorrhagic stroke, which is bleeding in the brain. Unfortunately, the patient had now incurred a second brain bleed at the brainstem (a part of the brain responsible for vital respiratory function).

Clara and her student-in-training enter through the opened sliding glass doors of the ICU room to ask Sarah, the patient's nurse, if they can do any speech therapy with him.

Sarah informs Clara, "I think you better hold off for now. The patient is declining rapidly, and he has no swallowing function at this time."

The nurse steps out of the room to go check on her other patient. Clara and her student are about to do the same, but suddenly Clara is inexplicably drawn to stay in the room. She feels the weight of her long list of patients she has yet to see. A decision has to be made. Does she move on quickly to the next patient for productivity's sake, or does she listen to the Holy Spirit?

Not audibly, but in her spirit, she senses the Holy Spirit urging her, "Don't go. Don't go. Just go talk to him and greet him."

She walks over to the patient. He's an African American man lying in the bed with multiple IV lines and tubes connected to his body. Clara looks at the heart rate monitor and notices the patient is having short runs of ventricular tachycardia (a deadly heart rhythm). His breathing is shallow and very rapid. The man's condition seems utterly hopeless.

Clara thinks to herself, *this man is going to die soon.*

"Hi, sir," Clara begins somewhat timidly. The conversation at this point can only be yes/no questions as the man is unable to speak but can only nod or shake his head. He is still coherent and communicative.

Clara thinks to herself, *does this man know Jesus?*

The Holy Spirit reveals the eternal significance of the conversation she's about to have with this man in desperate need. *I know why I'm here now.*

"Sir, do you know about the grace of Jesus?"

The man looks at Clara with piercing eyes.

Nudged forward by the Spirit's leading Clara tells him, "Jesus died on that cross for the forgiveness of our sins, even if we have done something really bad."

Tears begin to stream down the man's face.

"Sir, the only way to heaven is through Jesus. Do you repent of all your sins?"

The man nods and blinks through the tears.

"Do you want to receive Jesus into your life?"

He squeezes her hand tightly and finally let's go.

The patient stops breathing.

"Sir! Are you okay? Are you okay?"

Clara shakes the man forcefully four times.

With heart pounding from the gravity of the moment, she calls out to the man, "Sir, Jesus loves you! I will see you again in heaven."

The respiratory rate monitor is alarming rapidly at this point. The nurse rushes in and observes the man's apneic (breathless) state. She places him on a BiPap ventilator to provide artificial breathing for the patient. He passes away before dawn later that night.

⁂

A man on death's doorstep was ushered into eternal life because Jesus used one of His followers as a faithful witness to the gospel. What I love about Jesus is that He pursues us and pursues us up until the final moments of our life here on earth. All the moments in that man's life led up to this last moment when

Jesus took hold of him on his deathbed. All of his failures and all of his sins were redeemed through a single encounter with Christ.

Our Savior is relentless in His pursuit of undeserving sinners. And you know what's amazing? Jesus reaches the lost through ordinary people He has already redeemed from their sin . . . people like Clara. His relentless pursuit of sinners comes through those who belong to Him.

Remember how Clara prayed, "God, I'm yours. Can you do something with me? Do whatever you want with me. Use me."

God indeed did answer that prayer. He made Clara a new creation in Christ Jesus. He made her His workmanship to do good works which He prepared in advance so that she would walk in them.

This brings us to the gospel's transformative purpose and God's plan:

"For we are his workmanship, created in Christ Jesus for good works, which God prepared beforehand, that we should walk in them" (Eph. 2:10).

The previous verses (8, 9) told us we are saved by the sheer grace of Jesus and have no good works of our own to boast about with regards to our salvation. Verse 10 reveals the result and purpose of this gospel of grace. Remember we started our passage in Ephesians 2 by highlighting how we were dead in our sins, following Satan, enslaved to our lusts, and deserving of God's wrath. But verse 10 reveals there is a Grand Canyon of difference between our former identity and our new identity in Christ.

Eph. 2:10 tells us the amazing result of the gospel: those saved by God's grace are now "His workmanship." What does this word mean? The Greek word for "workmanship" is *poiéma* and this is where we get the English word for "poem." This word can also be translated as "masterpiece." Let that sink in for a moment. Did you wake up this morning feeling like a masterpiece? If your faith is in Jesus, you *are His* masterpiece. The life you now live puts on real-life display the gracious and masterful work God has done for you in Christ.

Our new purpose because of the gospel is seen in the phrase: "created in Christ Jesus for good works." As new creations in Christ, we cannot remain solely consumers of the gospel message, but we must also declare the message with our lips and lives. The gospel never remains static in you but is forever a living and dynamic process transforming you to serve like Jesus, love like Jesus, listen like Jesus, come alongside like Jesus, and see the world like Jesus. The essence of doing good works is when God's masterpiece created in Christ brings the gospel to bear on any given situation. The above real-life story where Clara listened to the Holy Spirit is one such example of the gospel being brought to bear on one man's hopeless situation.

With her busy schedule, she could have easily justified moving on to the next patient without saying a word to the dying man.

But Jesus had other plans.

Jesus had eternal plans for this man, and He slowed down Clara from her busy schedule to carry out those plans through her. Jesus is never in a hurry. We see His unhurried pace in the New Testament gospel accounts because He always submitted to the Father's perfect plan and timing.

Eph. 2:10 truly frees us from the burden and drudgery of trying to run ourselves ragged by doing what we think are good works in our own timing, plan, and strength. This verse shows us that God is the ultimate Planner, and we simply get to walk in the good works He has already planned out and pre-pared for us in advance. This means we have to release our plans, schedules, and timing to Him.

We need to slow down as Clara did in that ICU room. We need to let go of the frenzied and frenetic schedules of our culture. Only then can we participate in the work He's going to do through us. He graciously lets us be a part of His work of redemption in a dying world. Our God is so awesome!

Not only does the nature of God as the ultimate Planner free us from self-driven futility, but we are also freed by our two-fold identity found in Eph. 2:10. What is our identity according to this verse? As stated earlier we are the Father's masterpiece, and we are His new creations in Christ. Take note that this passage tells us our identity comes from what Jesus has done and not from anything we have done. Therefore, we have nothing to boast about (see verse 9). Our identity in Christ as masterpieces and new creations leads to the good works we do and not the other way around. Our culture gets this completely reversed.

Generally, a person's career choice determines their identity. In other words, what someone does is who they are. One of the first questions we ask new people we meet is what they do for a living. We get to know who people are by asking about their careers or life's work.

But verse 10 outlines a completely different order.

The gospel order is God makes us who we are because of what Jesus has done for us, and this leads us to do the good works He has already prepared in advance for us. In other words, He makes us His masterpiece and entirely recreates us in Christ, and therefore we obey.

In our culture, you are continually trying to prove your worth to others and attain masterpiece status through what you do. This worldview is enslaving and exhausting, whereas the gospel worldview is utterly exhilarating. In the gospel, you get to see the glory and work of God in who He has made you to be and what He has already prepared for you to do.

So how do we respond to all of the glorious truth of the gospel found in Eph. 2:1–10? Jesus Himself gives us the answer in Mark 1:14, 15:

"Now after John was arrested, Jesus came into Galilee, proclaiming the gospel of God, and saying, 'The time is fulfilled, and the kingdom of God is at hand; repent and believe in the gospel.'"

According to Jesus, our response is summed up in two words: "repent and believe."

The Greek word "repent" means a fundamental change in heart and life trajectory. Simply put, this entails turning away from our sin and self-righteousness to instead turn to Jesus and receive His righteousness. Moreover, in Mark 1:15 Jesus tells us the kingdom of God has drawn near. How could that be? The kingdom of God is at hand because King Jesus has come. When Jesus becomes your King, the kingdom of God has come into your life. He is the one who brings true repentance and change in us. What change does the gospel produce in us?

Eph. 2:1–10 is like a beautiful bouquet of flowers, with each set of verses like a flower in full bloom. Eph. 2:1–3 reveals our radical sin nature including our being dead in sin and deserving of God's wrath. Eph. 2:4–7 reveals God's rich mercy, staggering love for us, and lavish grace He pours out on us by bringing us out of death into life through Jesus and His perfect work on our behalf.

Instead of receiving God's wrath we receive His grace and are seated with Jesus in the heavenly places. Eph. 2:8, 9 tells us that we are saved by the sheer grace of Jesus when we put our faith in Him, and we therefore having nothing to boast about. Eph. 2:10 reveals the complete reorienting of our life's trajectory so we may do good works because God has made us His masterpiece and new creation in Christ.

The other response word in Mark 1:15 is "believe." Believe what? Repent *and believe in the gospel.* The Greek word for "believe" means to completely entrust and put your confidence in something. Have you done so with Jesus and the good news He freely offers you? Have you stopped looking to yourself and your good work as a means of salvation? Instead, are you convinced that God will accept you based on the perfect record, sacrificial death, and triumphant resurrection of Christ?

The King is calling you if you have not yet trusted in Jesus for salvation. He is so good and so loving. He will not enslave you to the bondage of this world, but He brings liberty to the captives and freedom to those who are oppressed. Repent and believe in the gospel. You can simply pray:

"Lord Jesus, I turn from my sin and self-righteousness. Instead, I turn to You for salvation. I ask You to save me and forgive me of all my sins by Your grace. My trust is in You and You alone for salvation. I confess You as Lord and King and believe that God raised You from the dead."

If you just trusted in Christ for salvation, I'm so thrilled for you! It's important that you tell someone about what God has done in you if this truly is the case. A local pastor at a Bible-believing church is a good person to speak with about your salvation in Christ. You now have received a new identity in Jesus!

In the next chapter, we will delve deeper into our identity in Christ by examining Eph. 1:3–8.

6

Riches in Christ: Our identity in Christ

His name is Roger.

With bloodshot eyes, he stares at his computer screen riddled with anxiety. Moments ago his landlord, Sarah, gave him the ultimatum that if he does not pay rent by tomorrow he and his family will be evicted, no ifs or buts. Roger's bank account statement stares daggers back at him in the darkened room where he sits despairing in his office chair. The available account balance reads $26 and the rent due is $900.

In the dim computer light glow, he runs his calloused hands through his hair and lets his head hang downward. *What am I going to do?* he thinks to himself. His body is completely exhausted. He has been working overtime in his construction job but with little to nothing to show for the grueling hours of manual labor. His wife, Kasey, is also exhausted as she has been caring nonstop for their two daughters, ages four and two.

What am I going to tell Kasey? We're completely broke! The shame, guilt, and fear of the moment grip him like a vice, and do not let go. He feels like a failure; not only as a husband but also as a father and provider for his family. He sits shackled to the chair with an enormous weight of anxiety perched on his chest like an elephant.

Suddenly, Roger glances to the far-right upper corner of his computer desk. A stack of long-forgotten discarded mail catches his eye. As if by divinely guided impulse, Roger begins feverishly rummaging through the envelopes. The first three envelopes he sees are from Capital One, Progressive auto insurance, and Jiffy Lube respectively. He rifles through more mail until an official-looking eight by eleven sized manila packet stops him cold. The cover reads, Open Immediately, and is addressed to a Mr. Roger Latimer.

He tears open the top of the envelope and plucks out the first of many pages within the packet. Two scales of justice are printed on the upper right and left corners forming the letterhead of the legal document. The words "REGISTERED MAIL" are on the first line under the letterhead. The next several lines state "Roger Latimer, 1424 Lancing Avenue Apt #1212, Conroe, Texas, 77301." All of the information is correctly addressed to him. The next line takes his breath away.

The letter reads: "*TO THE HEIR OF HENRY LATIMER.*" Roger's face goes numb and tingly. Nervous shivers shoot up his spine to the base of his skull. He reads on. "I, Scott Muccino, Chief Legal Executor of Mr. Henry Latimer's estate and assets hereby notify you, Mr. Roger Latimer, of the final distribution of Henry Latimer's estate. The final distribution to you, the sole heir, is a total of $6 billion US Dollars."

Is this some sort of scam? he immediately wonders after reading and reread-ing the first paragraph. He then reads the following: "The final accounting and inventory of Henry Latimer's estate are enumerated and detailed in the following documents within this estate distribution packet."

Roger's mind begins whirling. *Is this real? Why did Uncle Henry choose me to be his sole heir?* He remembers his uncle passing away three months ago but he did not have the time or money to fly to Atlanta for the funeral with all the economic hardship he and his wife are going through. Roger thumbs through the remaining enclosed documents to verify the claims of the letter. The more he reads the more assured he becomes that these documents are, indeed, legitimate. He feels a thrill of hope ripple through his being.

This changes everything, Roger thinks to himself as he leaps to his feet and runs to the living room where Kasey is lounging with their youngest daughter on the couch.

"Babe! Babe! Babe! I've gotta tell you something big!"

☙

In the gospel, we have been given far more than Roger Latimer ever inher-ited from his late uncle. The vast repository of our riches in Christ goes far beyond any earthly inheritance, wealth, or assets. The purpose of these next 3 chapters is to plumb the depths of the spiritual riches and blessings enumerated in Eph. 1:3–8 for those in Christ.

We will see that the ultimate purpose of these blessings is "to the praise of [God's] glorious grace" (Eph. 1:6). Our Father is so amazing. He is so generous, so kind, and so gracious towards undeserving sinners like you and me. We will divide this passage up into three different sections:

1. We are chosen (Eph. 1:4)
2. We are adopted (Eph. 1:5)
3. We are redeemed (Eph. 1:7)

Knowing your identity in Christ is foundational to viewing all of life through the gospel lens. We daily need to be reminded of who Jesus is, what He has done, and who we are in Him. Our culture tells us what we need to strive to be successful, wealthy, busy, and well-liked. But Jesus frees us from that rat race and speaks identity into us.

We are Chosen

Let's first examine Eph. 1:3, 4 to understand the identity God speaks over us:

> "Blessed be the God and Father of our Lord Jesus Christ, who has blessed us in Christ with every spiritual blessing in the heavenly places, even as he chose us in him before the foundation of the world, that we should be holy and blameless before him."

Eph. 1:3 begins with the phrase "Blessed be the God and Father." Paul erupts with praising God when he starts to think about enumerating all that God has done to make us who we are in Christ. He introduces a critical aspect of the character of God: He is Father. What comes to mind when you think of the term father? Maybe you have a very loving father or an abusive or absent one. Whatever the case, this verse has good news for you. God is the perfect Father. His great love for you is boundless. His affection for you is sweet. God's father-heart is so tender.

Look at Hosea 11:1–4, "When Israel was a child, I loved him, and out of Egypt I called my son. The more they were called, the more they went away;

they kept sacrificing to the Baals and burning offerings to idols. Yet it was I who taught Ephraim to walk; I took them up by their arms, but they did not know that I healed them. I led them with cords of kindness, with the bands of love, and I became to them as one who eases the yoke on their jaws, and I bent down to them and fed them."

These verses are dripping with honey sweetness and the paternal tenderness of a dad overflowing with love and kindness for His wayward son. When Hosea 11:3 says, "I taught Ephraim to walk," you can picture a dad standing behind his one-year-old son holding his hands out above him and letting his son grasp his index and middle fingers while teaching him how to walk. Is that the picture you have of God when you think of Him?

He is "the God and Father of our Lord Jesus Christ." This tells us two things about Jesus: He is the divine Son of God the Father and He is Lord. The Greek word for "Lord" is *kurios,* and this word means "master" or one with complete authority and ownership. We see the lordship of Jesus when He declares, "All authority in heaven and on earth has been given to me" (Matt. 28:18). Who can say that? Nobody on earth has that kind of power or authority. Jesus is the Lord of lords and the King of kings (see Rev. 19:16).

Eph. 1:3 declares that God the Father "has blessed us in Christ with every spiritual blessing in the heavenly places." The tender love of the Father and the absolute authority of the Son indicate these spiritual blessings come with great love and power to those in Christ. The spiritual blessings we have in Christ are melt-in-your-mouth encouraging and unstoppably irrevocable. The word "spiritual" indicates that these blessings come from the Holy Spirit. The three Persons of the Godhead are in view here: God the Father, God the Son, and God the Holy Spirit.

The word for "blessing" in the phrase "every spiritual blessing" is the Greek word *eulogia,* and this is where we get the English word "eulogy." Eulogies are given at funerals so mourners can speak a good word over the dead. But here God the Father speaks a better word over those who *were dead* in their sins but now have been "made alive together with Christ" (Eph. 2:5).

The eulogy at a funeral is spoken by a man or woman, but the spiritual eulogy of Eph. 1 is spoken *by God* over those in Christ. The praise and spoken word of man can be comforting and reassuring for a time, but the word spoken *by God* over you lasts forever. If you are alive in Christ, do you know what that better word He speaks over you is?

You are chosen.

"Even as he chose us in him before the foundation of the world, that we should be holy and blameless before him" (Eph. 1:4).

❦

Her name is Kelley.

She finds herself at a packed house for the birthday party of her friend, Amy. She goes to the kitchen and opens the fridge to get a drink. I am also at this party. I see the fridge door open and my view of Kelley is partially obstructed for a moment. Underneath the door, I notice she's wearing a pair of red Chuck Taylor sneakers (Converse shoes). For some reason, they suit her persona well. She closes the door, and it's then that I see her. I immediately notice how beautiful she is. As if being drawn by a magnetic attraction, my legs walk me over to her.

"Hi, I'm Jonny. It's nice to meet you."

"My name's Kelley. Good to meet you too."

She smiles warmly, steps closer to me, and extends her hand. We shake hands. Seeing her up close is delightful. She's so beautiful. Her smile and greeting are so kind. I hear country music begin to play in the garage.

I tell her, "Hey, I'll be right back."

I go to the garage to scope out the situation, and a bold idea ignites in my mind like the striking of a match. I have to figure out a way to spend the rest of the party with her. I want to get to know all about her. I return to Kelley in the kitchen.

"Hey Kelley, would you like to dance with me?"

She replies in an affirming tone, "Sure."

I'm elated by her response. We go to the open garage together and music fills the night air. I take her by the hand and lead her onto the makeshift dance floor. Although we have just met, conversation flows easily. The chemistry between us is electric. I ask her question after question to get to know her story.

I find out she's a doctor and currently doing a hospital fellowship in pediatric medicine. She is very intelligent but does not come off as pretentious in the slightest. I learn that she loves Jesus and is seeking Him passionately.

She asks, "What about you? I don't know anything about you."

I begin to tell her my story.

Before we know it, we have danced for about an hour. We become fast friends. I decided to teach her a new dance move. She initially struggles with the turn.

"Come on!" I tease her.

"Oh, stop being so dramatic," she chides.

After a couple more tries, we nail it. At this point, my friend, Jordan, enters the garage as he's been wondering where I've been all evening. He's looking for me because he and his wife, Amanda, took me to the party. He sees me with Kelley and a huge grin forms on his face. He leaves us to continue dancing.

After the party ends, Jordan and Amanda, take me back to my car at their house. The whole car ride I cannot stop talking about this girl named Kelley I just met. Amanda can tell how smitten I am with her. She takes a picture of me because she wants to capture the moment and the glowing effect Kelley is having on me.

A little over a year later this photo ends up on several different tables . . . tables at a wedding reception because that night at Amy's birthday party I met my wife.

What follows is Kelley's story about how she came to know the better word her heavenly Father speaks over her: He chose her in Christ before the foundation of the world.

Like Clara, Kelley grew up seeing God as distant. She thought that if you were a good person and believed God was real then you would go to heaven. She believed that as long as you ask for forgiveness then you're good with God and can live how you want to live. She did not understand grace and had no personal relationship with God.

Her upbringing led her to focus on achieving and being successful because she grew up in poverty. Her mom was left to provide and care for the household as a single mother. Kelley grew up without a father figure in her life.

So, she studied hard and got into medical school. Her identity was primarily found in her performance as a successful medical student. This led to anxiety and the exhausting battle of always striving to prove herself to others. One accomplishment was never enough, and she was continually comparing herself to her classmates and dealing with the stress of measuring up to her peers in med school and residency.

She began a dating relationship that eventually ended because of betrayal. This experience was jarring and shook her identity at its core. She was reeling from the pain. Finding identity in a career and success was never enough, and now her identity in a romantic relationship was shattered. The pain was almost too much to bear and had to be dealt with on a deeper level. So Kelley turned to reading Scripture in search of comfort.

She now sits on her couch in the early morning hours with her two-toned brown Bible open on her lap being bathed by the lamplight in her single-bedroom apartment. She turns to Eph. 2:1 (NIV) and reads, "As for you, you were dead in your transgressions and sin . . . ." For the first time, this verse becomes real to her. She suddenly realizes that she, herself, is dead in her sins. She realizes everything she's reading is the truth. This dawning comprehension opens her soul to the healing process.

Kelley then turns back a page in her Bible and reads this, "Praise be to the God and Father of our Lord Jesus Christ, who has blessed us in the heavenly realms with every spiritual blessing in Christ. For he chose us in him before the creation of the world to be holy and blameless in his sight" (Eph. 1:3, 4 NIV). She stops right there, and it's as if the grace and truth of Jesus have come to sit right next to her on the couch in her living room. The beauty of personally experiencing the Father's love for her in Jesus illuminates her as she meditates on the Scripture and thinks to herself:

I was far removed from God based on Eph. 2:1–3, but now for the first time, I know who I am. He chose me to be holy and blameless before Him. Before I even existed, He chose me. There's no accomplishment, there's nothing I could do, there's nothing anyone could do for me or to me (including betrayal) that could devalue this truth. There's nothing that compares to the honor of Him choosing me. This truth of being chosen by the Father before the creation of the world is better than anything you could ever gain and better than anything you could ever lose in this life. I'm freed from the stress of striving after career advancement and the betrayal of that relationship.

Then Kelley reads the next verse in her Bible, "he predestined us for adoption to sonship through Jesus Christ, in accordance with his pleasure and will" (Eph. 1:5 NIV). After meditating on this verse she realizes: *He chose me to be holy and blameless before Him, and He predestined me to be with Him through Jesus Christ. I've been adopted into His family as His daughter, and this means He's no longer a distant God. He is my Father.*

Around this time, Kelley joined a local congregation called Mission Church and was later baptized in front of the whole church. She describes the day of her baptism as the best day of her life. Filled with a joy inexpressible she felt utterly content and in need of nothing . . . not even a husband.

She prayed, "Father, I don't even need a husband, but if that's what You want for me then I'd be okay with that." The following weekend Kelley went to Amy's birthday party where she met me.

Now let's look deeper at the verse that became so real to Kelley when she realized her true identity in Christ. Eph. 1:4 states, "even as he chose us in him before the foundation of the world, that we should be holy and blameless before him." The Greek word for "chose" is *eklegó*. Let's break this word down. The Greek prefix *ek* means "out of", and *legó* means "to speak out" or "to call by name."

So, when verse 4 states, "He chose us in him" it means that before God the Father laid the foundation of the world He spoke and called us out specifically by name to select us in Christ. What kind of assurance does that give you right now? Do you ever feel like you don't amount to much before God? Do you ever say to yourself, "Man, I really blew it this time. I'm not even sure if God loves me anymore."

If I just described your day-to-day experience then I have good news for you. Our salvation in Christ was not decided on a whim, but prepared before we even existed by the Father. And that's what Kelley realized as she sat on her couch reading her Bible. In Christ, we can take great comfort in His choosing us from eternity past because this means we had nothing to do with persuading God to look on us with favor.

On the other hand, because He has already chosen us, we can do nothing to jeopardize His choosing us. He made His decision long ago before the world even existed. Our salvation is purely a result of God's sovereign grace. Wow! Our Father is so amazing! This should cause us to worship when we realize how dead we were in our sins. Thank you, Father, for choosing me in Christ! I don't deserve Your grace.

If you are not resting in God's sovereign grace through Christ, I'm asking you to repent right now and rest in the Father's love for you through Jesus Christ and all He has done for you.

Eph. 1:4 ends by instilling a profound purpose in us. For what purpose did God the Father choose us? ". . . that we should be holy and blameless before him." That is to say, God has chosen us and set us on a path to live more and more like Jesus who indeed is holy and blameless. But you know what's amazing? In God's sight, because of the finished work of Christ on our behalf, *we already are* holy and blameless, and that's why Eph. 1:1 states, "To the *saints* who are in Ephesus," (emphasis mine).

However, God is doing a thorough and complete work in us to make us holy and blameless in the way we live as well. The Greek word for "holy" means "set apart" and "distinct or different." As alluded to above, this word is the exact same word used for "saints" in Eph. 1:1. The identity of "holy one" is already spoken over us, and now we get to live in a manner consonant with our identity because the Father has chosen us in Christ. The Greek word for "blameless" means "without blemish or spot." Before the eyes of the Creator of the universe, we are spotless in Christ, and He is molding our manner of life to resemble that same image.

In the next chapter, we will explore Eph. 1:5 which speaks of our adoption to sonship. We will also meet a man who lost his earthly father at a young age and came to experience the beauty of his adoption in Christ by his heavenly Father through a profound encounter with Jesus and His grace.

7

Adoption to Sonship: Our identity in Christ

Eph. 1:5 profoundly states:

"he predestined us for adoption to sonship through Jesus Christ, in accordance with his pleasure and will" (NIV).

His name is Jos.

He grew up in a Christian home, sometimes practicing and sometimes not practicing the faith. To this day, Jos can close his eyes and vividly describe the view of God he had growing up and into young adulthood: a person far removed standing in heaven looking down with arms crossed, scowl on his face, not happy with him, and expecting him to perform better. Jos pictured God as a coach standing on the sidelines watching him fumble the ball and ready to scold him sternly and harshly. This view of God was greatly informed by how his dad raised and treated him.

During Jos' growing up years, his dad was always sick due to type I diabetes and later would be plagued by kidney disease. These chronic conditions influenced how his dad viewed God also. His dad saw his sickness as a form of punishment and judgment from God, and so he was very stern toward Jos and his brother, Daniel.

Daniel was sent away from Jos for two years to a military school for drug rehabilitation. Around this time Jos also lost his best friend, Chris, because

Chris and his family moved to another state after his parents' divorce. These two losses were emotional blows to Jos and led to a deep fear of abandonment.

But toward the end of his life his dad came to know the grace of Jesus, and this softened him a bit in how he treated Jos and Daniel. So Jos became close with his dad when he was 15 going on 16 years old.

He's now age 16 and Daniel has recently returned from his two-year stint at the military school. He has his brother back who is one of his best friends in the world and his dad who is now also one of his best friends. It's January 1st, 2001, and the family has recently returned from probably the best family Christmas trip they've ever had, but little does Jos know that this was the last Christmas he would enjoy with his dad.

On the morning of New Year's Day his dad has already missed two dialysis appointments because the clinic was shut down in Marlo, Oklahoma where they had been vacationing. Dialysis is absolutely critical for him because he has one kidney and has been on dialysis for years.

Jos and Daniel walk into their parents' room together to wake up their dad. They find the bed empty.

"Dad!" Jos calls out in a concerned voice.

He and Daniel hurry around to the other side of the bed, and the sight they see horrifies them. Their dad is lying on the floor next to the bed, blue in the face and bloated.

"Call 911!" Daniel yells.

The wait for the ambulance to come is agonizing. Both brothers are stunned and have no idea how to help their dad who is gasping and struggling to breathe. The ambulance finally arrives after a grueling eight minutes. In shock, Jos and Daniel watch the first responders load their dad onto a gurney and then drive away to the hospital.

Hours pass by as Daniel, Jos, and their mom sit at the bedside of the man they dearly love dying in an ICU room. He's connected to life support and all manner of tubes, lines, and monitors. A startling knock comes at the door. The doctor enters the room.

She addresses their mother, "I'm Dr. Patel. Due to your husband missing two dialysis appointments in a row he has had a lot of fluid build-up in his lungs and essentially drowned in his sleep."

The news comes like a punch in the face. The whole family is in shock. For the next seven days the three of them wait. The agony of these seven days would forever be imprinted in their minds.

On the night of January 8th, Jos is absolutely drained and emotionally exhausted. The inevitability of his father's death stalks him like a relentless shadow. *I've got to get out of here,* he thinks to himself. So, he leaves the hospital with plans to go hang out with a friend to get away from the pain, the grief, and the impending loss. With the medical center in his rear-view mirror Jos looks at the clock on the dashboard. It reads 8:29 PM. The traffic light at the intersection ahead glows green, so he maintains his speed to drive right on through.

In the blink of an eye a red Toyota Camry makes a left turn right as Jos is crossing the intersection. Both cars collide. The fenders, headlights, front axles, and chassis of both cars are crushed and warped in the head on collision. His vehicle is totaled due to the extensive damage. Jos stumbles out of his car to check on the other person. Within minutes first responders arrive.

Jos is dazed and confused sitting in the back of the ambulance. Miraculously, he walks away from the accident with a few scrapes and bruises but nothing requiring immediate medical attention. He gets a ride home and collapses on his bed to rest for the night.

He wakes up startled. It's about 5:30 AM. His mother is sitting on the side of his bed, tears streaming down her face. In the dim light of the early morning hour, she tells Jos the news: his dad has just passed away. He's not ready to hear this news. Is anyone ever ready? Jos unconsciously makes a decision in that moment. He decides to emotionally turn himself off.

He becomes despondent and depressed for months. Ill-equipped to handle the gravity of such loss he has no idea how to express what he's feeling to anyone at this time. So, he turns inward and almost immediately in the weeks following his dad's death he begins to numb the pain with all different types of substances and relationships with women.

One night alone in his bedroom he thinks to himself, *God, I have done what you have wanted me to do and tried to please you for so long . . . and You still do this to me. You owe me the right to sin.* Embittered toward God, he raises his hand and shakes a clenched fist in defiance at his Creator. So Jos begins what would become an eight-year period of rebellion. But Jesus never stopped pursuing and coming after Jos. The path to redemption from his destructive life-style is detailed in the next chapter.

Fast forward and Jos has now come to have a life transforming encounter with Jesus. Eight-years have passed since his dad's death. The scorching wounds he has carried these past eight-years still bleed from time to time. It's time for healing. He stands outside a beige-bricked facility staring at the glass doors. A Christian counseling conference called "Redemption Training" is being held right through those doors. He grabs the door handle, pulls, and enters the building to be greeted by a warm welcome from a volunteer sitting at a table showing Jos where to sign in for the conference.

Jos is now sitting at a white table across from a counselor named Larry for his first session. Larry asks him to tell his story. As a product of Jesus' grace, Jos spares no words and unravels his childhood, his relationship with his dad, his dad's death, and the ensuing eight-year period of rebellion. As Larry asks the right questions, the Holy Spirit reveals to Jos all of these different memories from his childhood where his dad failed him, the ways he hurt him, and the ways he misconstrued who God was by his actions.

With the help of Larry and some other counselors in subsequent sessions, they walk Jos through a process of truly grieving the loss of his dad. They take him to a place of healthy anger towards his dad and the freedom of freely admitting that anger. And then, afterwards, the counselors walk Jos through a process of forgiving his dad. They encourage him to literally speak out loud the emotions he feels towards him.

"Dad, here's where you hurt me . . . here's where you abandoned me . . . here's where you failed me. And because of Jesus, I forgive you."

In this process, Jos is even able to acknowledge his own sin against his dad, because broken relationships almost always have more than one guilty party.

He begins to express this to his dad: "Dad, I held you in the position of God and essentially made you an idol. I put expectations on you that you could never have met. And so I sinned against you when I looked for you to be God for me. No human can bear the weight of that position or responsibility."

Jesus brings healing to Jos through this redemptive process of acknowledging hurt, feeling healthy anger, totally forgiving his dad because of Jesus, and humbly confessing his own sin. Dealing with the wounds of his childhood and his dad's death also leads to a new perspective of who God is for Jos. He is his Father.

At this point in his story Jos can now proclaim, *I have a Father who loves me unconditionally apart from my actions. I have a Father who will never fail me. I have a Father who will never abandon me and will never die on me. He's with me always. And He's always pleased with me because of the perfection of Jesus given to me.*

Back then and now in the present day, the book of Ephesians was and is so powerful for Jos. I'll let him tell you in his own words:

"Specifically, chapter one talks about God's choosing and loving us. It's about how He loved us so much that He predestined us to adoption. Verse 4 is about God choosing us and then in verse 5, He predestined us to adoption *in love* through Jesus Christ. Jesus was fulfilling God the Father's purpose. He's not angry toward His children. His wrath has been fully absorbed by Jesus at the cross. And because of His love, I am a forever son of God the Father, and I will be home with Him in His presence, experiencing the fullness of joy and pleasure forever. I can be confident of this because He promised this to us in Ephesians chapter one, and He's the kind of Father whose word never fails."

I marvel at the work Jesus has done in Jos' life. He went from shaking his fist in defiance at God to proclaiming, "And because of His love, I am a forever son of God the Father . . ." Wow! Jesus is so amazing! Our Father's love is so overwhelming.

Understanding our adoption to sonship is absolutely critical to viewing all of life through the gospel lens. Eph. 1:5 is so rich and packed with so much meaning. Now let's take a deeper look at the truth that transformed Jos' view of God:

"he predestined us for adoption to sonship through Jesus Christ, in accordance with his pleasure and will" (NIV).

It's worth mentioning that verse 4 ends with the phrase "in love." So, we need to understand that God adopted His children out of His steadfast love for us. The Greek word for "predestined" in verse 5 is *proorizó* and this word literally means "pre-horizon."

Imagine you're standing on a beach looking out over the ocean. If you look as far as your eye can see, what are you able to glimpse? You should see the invisible line we call the horizon where the sky meets the water, where the heavens connect to the earth. When Eph. 1:5 states, "he predestined us for adoption," the Father is singing His delight over us.

For those in Christ, the Father is declaring: "Before I stretched out the horizon line . . . before I said to the sea, 'this far you shall go and no farther,' I had *you* in my mind. I chose *you* to be my son . . . to be my daughter."

And that's how much the Father loves you. His love is breathtaking. Receive it. Bathe in it. Soak in it. Immerse yourself in the Father's love for you through Jesus . . . right now . . . in this moment. He loves you so much.

What does verse 5 mean when it says "adoption to sonship"? This phrase introduces the profound reality of how we are to relate to God. The Greek word for "adoption" draws on the institution of Roman adoption as Paul was writing to an audience influenced by the authority and rule of the Roman Empire in the first century. What was the purpose of Roman adoption at this time?

The purpose was primarily two-fold: bestowing inheritance and passing on the family name. Notably a wealthy landowner would adopt a son to ensure his inheritance was conferred to someone he loved and trusted. So after the legal act of making an adult male his heir, the landowner could bequeath all his wealth, estate, and assets to his adopted son.

Why a son and not a daughter? To our modern ears this may sound sexist and patriarchal. But under the inspiration of the Holy Spirit, Paul tells us something profound in Eph. 1:5. The beauty of this verse is found in remembering the audience—it was written for both men *and women* Ephesian Christians. Paul applies the "adoption to sonship" to both males and females!

This reality is wonderfully inclusive and uplifting to the women of that day, who were oppressed by male dominated positions of authority. In terms of our adoption by God, we as sons *and daughters* receive a divine inheritance and so much more! We become heirs, possess anytime access to God, and experience the steadfast love and affection of our heavenly Father. First, what is our inheritance?

Eph. 1:13, 14 begins to describe our inheritance in Christ, "In him you also, when you heard the word of truth, the gospel of your salvation, and believed in him, were sealed with the promised Holy Spirit, who is the guarantee of our inheritance until we acquire possession of it, to the praise of His glory." At salvation we receive the Holy Spirit! The presence of God Himself lives inside of us. This means that the Holy Spirit is the beginning or the down payment of our inheritance. What if you lived today knowing that the Spirit of God dwells in you?

What does being "sealed with the promised Holy Spirit" mean in Eph. 1:13? In that time period, a royal seal could be a king's signet ring used to stamp and authorize a document. This action would signify the sealed item belonged to the king. So, God the Father sealing us with the Holy Spirit means that we are His possession. We belong to Him. We are not our own.

In one sense we receive an inheritance through Christ, but in another sense, we are God's inheritance or possession. The Greek wording of the passage allows for both meanings. The people of God are His treasured possession, "For you are a people holy to the Lord your God. The Lord your God has chosen you to be a people for his treasured possession, out of all the peoples who are on the face of the earth" (Deuteronomy 7:6).

What else constitutes the believer's inheritance? Our inheritance in Christ is multifaceted. Look at the following verses, "Fear not, little flock, for it is your Father's good pleasure to give you the kingdom" (Luke 12:32). This verse tells us our inheritance is the Father's kingdom, and that He has much pleasure in sharing it with us.

Not only is His kingdom our inheritance but also the promise of being glorified with Him, "For you did not receive the spirit of slavery to fall back into fear, but you have received the Spirit of adoption as sons, by whom we cry, "Abba! Father!" The Spirit himself bears witness with our spirit that we are children of God, and if children, then heirs—heirs of God and fellow heirs with Christ, provided we suffer with him in order that we may also be glorified with him" (Rom. 8:15-17).

Later in Rom. 8 we glimpse a still greater aspect of our inheritance, "He who did not spare his own Son but gave him up for us all, how will he not also with him graciously give us all things?" (Rom. 8:32). Wait a second. Did you catch that? This verse highlights the most amazing reality of our inheritance: Jesus Himself. Don't miss how this verse says "*with Him* graciously give us all things" (emphasis mine).

The most important piece of our inheritance is that we get Jesus. Everything else thrown in is superfluous, compared to having Jesus for all eternity. We were specifically designed to know Him, to love Him, and to be with Him. Listen to the verbiage Jesus Himself uses in John 14:1–3:

"Let not your hearts be troubled. Believe in God; believe also in me. In my Father's house are many rooms. If it were not so, would I have told you that I go to prepare a place for you? And if I go and prepare a place for you, I will come again and will take you to myself, that where I am you may be also."

Jesus speaks of our inheritance as being a room for us in His Father's house (e.g., His Kingdom), but the climax of the passage is where Jesus promises that

He will come to take us to Himself for Him to be where we are also. This is intimate and affectionate bridegroom language intended for a bride. We are His bride. When you think of your adoption inheritance you must think of Jesus. He is your treasure and you are His. "For where your treasure is, there will your heart be also" (Luke 12:34).

Secondly, our adoption means we have anytime access to God the Father. At the moment of Christ's death, do you remember what happened in the temple? "And Jesus uttered a loud cry and breathed His last. And the curtain of the temple was torn in two, from top to bottom" (Mark 15:37, 38). At the death of Jesus, God Himself tore the very curtain in half that once separated us from His presence. In other words, we "... who once were far off have been brought near by the blood of Christ" (Eph. 2:13).

When you realize you are His son or daughter, you realize you can come to Him at any time to tell Him anything you want. Later in Ephesians, Paul proclaims the access we have to the presence of God through Jesus, "For through him we both have our access in one Spirit to the Father" (Eph. 2:18).

This is probably the most practical aspect of our adoption. At any point in the day or night, you can speak with your Dad because of Jesus, and trust me, He is all ears to listen to what you have to say. My friend, Nick, from chapter 3, has told me that his three-year-old son, Rowan, will randomly barge right into the room, run to him, crawl up onto his lap, and tell him affectionately, "I love you, daddy." And then, immediately, he'll jump off Nick's lap and run out the door to return to playing with his toys. In the early morning, Rowan has been known to jump on Nick's bed, climb on top of him, and say, "I love you, daddy."

The first thing Rowan wants to tell his dad in the morning is that he loves him, and Nick never tires of hearing it! What if your first thought in the morning was a child-like prayer to your heavenly Father? What if you woke up tomorrow morning whispering in your heart to the Father telling Him how much you love Him? What if "I love you, Daddy" was the first prayer you prayed to start the day? We can learn more about prayer from this three-year-old than many other older, "wiser", and "more spiritual" people. Oh, that we had this kind of prayer life with our Father in heaven!

It all comes down to how you view God. Have you "received the Spirit of adoption as sons, by whom we cry 'Abba! Father!'" (Rom. 8:15)? By the way, the Aramaic word *Abba* is the equivalent of our English word "papa" or "daddy." Or do you view God as your landlord where you're just trying to spiritually pay rent to keep Him happy with you? Do you live to earn His approval and acceptance, or do you already have His complete acceptance through Jesus Christ?

What does your prayer life look like? Is it quid pro quo and transactional, or do you randomly stop in the middle of doing something and tell Him, "Daddy, I love you so much!"? Or are you incessantly weighed down by fear, anxiety, guilt, or shame? The key to transforming your view of God is to look at the third aspect of our adoption to sonship: the steadfast love and affection of our Father.

In Luke 15, Jesus tells the religious leaders (the Pharisees) a famous parable called the Prodigal Son where the younger son asks for his share of the father's inheritance prematurely. In other words, he shames his father by essentially wishing he was already dead, so he can take his father's wealth for himself. In a perplexing and astonishing act of grace, the father divides His wealth between both his sons. The elder son stays at home with the father while the younger son goes and squanders all his wealth on prostitutes and extravagant spending.

After coming to his senses, he decides he will return to his father and beg to be made as a hired hand. He knows he's no longer worthy to be called "son" after the immense shame he has brought on his father and the family name. This does not resonate with us if we do not understand that the cultural setting of the parable is a shame-honor culture. In such cultures, the goal of honoring the family name and generational heritage is paramount.

The shame the prodigal son feels is utterly debilitating, so he prepares a speech for his father, "... Father, I have sinned against heaven and before you. I am no longer worthy to be called your son. Treat me as one of your hired servants." (Luke 15:18, 19). Now let me take you to the climax of the parable: the steadfast love and affection of the father.

"And he arose and came to his father. But while he was still a long way off, his father saw him and felt compassion, and ran and embraced him and kissed him" (Luke 15:20). This verse is so rich and profound! Let's unpack it.

The father saw his son while he was "still a long way off." This means that the father was daily straining his eyes in search of his son on the horizon. His love is steadfast and enduring for his son. When he finally saw his son, he "felt compassion." The Greek word for "compassion" means to be "moved in the inward parts" and specifically refers to a person's visceral organs.

In the Bible, the inward parts connote the emotive or affectionate aspect of a person. So, this verse is telling us that there is a deep and profound affection

God the Father has for those who come to Him in repentance and faith. In the parable, the father is moved inwardly to the point that something happens. He's driven to action. What action? He runs.

An important point to make here is that patriarchs or fathers of that time wore long robes, and so they never ran . . . anywhere. Why would that be? In a shame-honor culture, it would be shameful for a man to hike up his robes to run and thereby show his bare legs. But that does not stop the father in this parable. He would rather lose face than lose his son. His compassion and affection for his son is that profound. This father is unlike any father you've ever known.

He hikes up his robes, shows his bare legs, and sprints to his son. He can't get to him fast enough. The Greek word for "run" in this verse conveys the concept of a competitive athlete sprinting with passionate yearning to reach the finish line. The father runs as fast as his legs and long flowing robe will let him. He loves his son that much.

What do you think the father should do when he gets to his son? Should he scold him with a scorching hot scowl on his face? Should he shame him the way this prodigal has already besmirched the family's good name? No, I don't think so. What does this father do? He embraces him . . . he kisses him.

In a lavish show of affection, the father wraps up his unworthy son in his loving arms. The Greek word for "embrace" in Luke 15:20 is literally "to fall upon the neck." With reckless, affectionate abandon, the father falls upon the neck of his son. He begins to kiss his son. Was this merely a peck on the cheek? Nothing could be further from the truth. The Greek word for kiss here is *kataphileó*, and this word means to kiss fervently. The Greek prefix, *kata*, intensifies the root word *phileó* which means affectionate love. The father smothers his repentant son in kisses. He showers him with fatherly affection.

Come with me for a moment. Imagine yourself in the place of the prodigal son. You are on the road back to your father's house and rehearsing the speech you will give your father to convince him to have you back as a hired hand . . . no longer as his son. The shame you feel as you tread the dusty trail back home is eating you up inside. You despise yourself for what you've done. You hate how you've brought so much shame on your father and the family name. You almost consider turning around, but something keeps you trudging forward, one step at time.

You force yourself to look up from the ground and see a figure coming toward you. He appears to be running with both hands hiking up his robe.

A cloud of dust kicks up behind him as he sprints directly for you. *It can't be,* you think to yourself. *This man looks just like my dad.* The gap between you and him narrows even more. *It is my father!* The disgrace you feel is unbearable as he approaches you. Your eyes are fixed on the ground, and shame will not allow you to look up and meet his gaze.

Suddenly, your father is embracing you. He wraps you up in his arms and squeezes you close to his chest, affectionately. You feel his heart beat thumping rapidly as his chest is pressed up against yours. He's out of breath. Tears of joy are streaming down your father's face. He begins kissing you all over your face. At first, you are shocked by this lavish show of affection. *What is happening to me right now? I don't deserve this!* Now, the tears stream down your face too. You start to tell your dad how unworthy you are. But he interrupts you and calls out to his servants, "Quickly! Bring out the best robe . . ."

Do you view God this way? "In love he predestined us for adoption to sonship through Jesus Christ, in accordance with his pleasure and will" (Eph. 1:4c, 5 NIV). The Prodigal Son parable gives us a dramatic glimpse of our Father's pleasure and will. Look at what he does next to his returned son. The son tries to give his "I'm not worthy to be called your son" speech. But the father interrupts him and has the best robe, a ring, and shoes put on his son. He then begins party planning, and a great feast is prepared for his son. The fattened calf is killed to provide the warmest welcome for him. Our God celebrates sinners who repent (see Luke 15:10).

Notice how Eph. 1:5 highlights how our "adoption to sonship" is "through Jesus Christ." Without Jesus, our adoption is impossible. Jesus is our true and better elder Brother. Do you remember how the parable of the Prodigal Son was addressed to the Pharisees (the most elite religious leaders of the day) in Luke 15?

Well, the story ends with the elder brother being ruthlessly bitter toward his father for throwing such a lavish party for his returned prodigal son. The father goes out to his elder son and tells him, ". . . Son, you are always with me, all that is mine is yours. It was fitting to celebrate and be glad, for this your brother was dead, and is alive; he was lost, and is found" (Luke 15:31, 32). And that's the end of the parable. What a cliff hanger!

We never see the Pharisees' reaction to this profoundly moving narrative. By telling them this parable, Jesus was artfully rebuking them for being bitter toward the lavish grace Jesus had on ". . . the tax collectors and sinners drawing near to hear Him" (Luke 15:1). The elder brother represents the Pharisees. But Jesus is our true and better elder Brother.

Remember what the father did when his son returned? After kissing him affectionately, the father has the finest robe, a ring, and shoes put on his son. However, all of these items, including the fattened calf, do not belong to the father anymore. They belong to the elder brother. Recall how the father divides the whole estate at the beginning of the parable between his elder and younger son. The father's celebration for his repentant son enrages the elder brother. How could his own assets be used to throw a party for the one who shamed the whole family? He's so embittered that he refuses to go into the party.

But Jesus, being our true and better elder Brother,[2] was thrilled to leave the heavenly estate of His Father to come after us prodigals. He is overjoyed to share His inheritance with us. "The Spirit himself bears witness with our spirit that we are children of God, and if children, then heirs—heirs of God and fellow heirs with Christ..." (Rom. 8:16, 17a). We are co-heirs with Christ!

And at the cross, Jesus made His inheritance available to us by giving up His own life. In Jesus, we have One who leaves the Father's estate to pursue us. In Jesus, we have One who gladly died to save us from our sins. In Jesus, we have One who took our shame upon Himself on the cross in order to clothe us with His robe of righteousness. In Jesus, we have One who gave up everything to make us co-heirs with Him. And in Jesus, the Father predestines us for adoption to sonship.

---

2. Thanks to Dr. Timothy Keller for his inspiration in understanding the "True Elder Brother" in *The Prodigal God* (Penguin Books: Random House, 2008), 82ff.

8

Redemption through His blood: Our Identity in Christ

In the last chapter, we discovered that Jos entered into an eight-year period of rebellion after his dad passed away. He felt that God owed him a season of sin. After all, for 16 years he had been like the elder son in the Prodigal Son parable. When he was young, he grasped Jesus dying to forgive sin, but he did not understand the gravity of this sacrifice. Jos lived very religiously by following the rules to keep God happy with him, or so he thought. He believed that what he did or did not do made him better or worse in the eyes of God. He thought that he was a pretty good kid up until he was 16 when his dad died. He had kept the rules pretty well by comparison to the other kids around him. He was prideful and self-righteous. He was viewing life through a broken lens.

When his dad died Jos thought to himself, *what good has being good got me?* The other facet to this was he had no idea how to handle the grief he was experiencing after the passing of his dad. So in his mind, it was time for him to experience a bit of freedom ... the kind of freedom we see in the younger of the two sons in the Prodigal Son parable. Almost immediately after his dad's death, Jos started running with a rough crowd.

He began smoking weed on a daily basis. He started stealing his mom's pain pills that were supposed to be for her neck and back pain. He was drinking regularly and doing cocaine on occasion. Essentially, Jos tried to numb the pain and misery he had bottled up after his dad's death. He began spiraling downward, and the crew he surrounded himself with made matters worse.

☙

On the Christmas eve after his dad's death, almost a year later, Jos and his crew hatch a plan to rob a drug dealer that some of them knew. They even bring some of the older gang bangers on board to carry out the robbery. The plan is to have one of them knock on the door with guns at the ready and proceed to rob the dealer of his stash and cash.

The guys sit huddled in a circle in a glibly furnished apartment. One gang member speaks up, "We need a volunteer. Who's gonna knock on the door?"

"I'll do it," Jos says.

The expression on his face is cold and angry. He's a completely different person compared to who he was a year ago.

After nightfall, the crew drives to the drug dealer's apartment. One of the guys is crouched behind the stairwell that is positioned in front of the door with pistol in hand. Jos walks up to the front door slowly and knocks three times. He moves to the side and stands with back against the wall. After twenty seconds or so, the door creaks and cracks open about three inches. It's restricted from opening any farther by a metal safety chain. The guy behind the stairwell quickly comes out of his crouched position. He fires four shots through the door. Wood fragments and splinters fly as the gunshots echo through the breezeway. Jos flees the scene.

Later that night he meets up with a couple friends in his crew involved in the shooting. They commit to each other to never say a word about this to anyone. The gang members pledge to come after anyone who becomes an informant. Jos goes home and hardly sleeps that night replaying the shooting over and over in his head.

The next morning, he turns on the local news and the headline at the bottom of the screen stuns him cold right where he stands. The headline reads: "43-year-old man dies of gunshot wounds at his local residence last night."

Jos is 16 years old at this point and in his junior year of high school. The trauma of that fatal night haunts him like a nightmare from which he's unable to wake up. He begins to skip class for weeks on end until he finally decides to drop out. Three months later, Jos joins the army. He goes through basic and combat medic training.

Before he knows it, he's on a plane to Fort Benning, Georgia to go through airborne school to become an airborne medic. After airborne school, Jos transfers right down the street to the 75th Ranger Training Detachment. He then tries his hand at becoming an Airborne Army Ranger. But after six months in the Ranger indoctrination program, Jos washes out.

The army transfers him to Holdover Company, and Jos waits to be sent to an airborne unit elsewhere. During this time, he begins drinking heavily and smoking a lot of marijuana. One morning during routine inspection, his superior discovers a stash of weed under his bunk bed. Jos is penalized, yet discharged under honorable conditions from the army. On the plane flight home, he stares blankly at the mesh material holding the flight safety pamphlet in the seat in front of him. He's ashamed and feels like an absolute failure. Once again Jos is met with the decision of whether to come back home and deal with the unsolved murder as well as the unwelcome family dynamics he doesn't want to face.

After a month of being home from Fort Benning he decides to move up to Denver to be closer to his childhood friend, Chris, and his family. Chris's mom, Lisa, has been like a second mother to Jos for all these years.

On the night he leaves his hometown to go to Denver the police pull up at his mom's house to arrest him, but Jos is already gone. As soon as he arrives in Denver, the police and district attorney contact Lisa to ask about his whereabouts. They try to convince her to persuade Jos to meet with them, so they can record his testimony about the night of the murder. Chris and Lisa side with the police and successfully persuade Jos to testify. In the present day, Jos believes he would still be running from the law if it weren't for Chris and Lisa.

Detective Hathaway now speaks with Jos on the phone to strike a deal, "We ensure you complete and total immunity in exchange for your eyewitness testimony about the night of the murder."

"Okay. I'll do it."

Jos almost cannot believe the words as they leave his mouth.

Two days later District Attorney, Jay Fisher, and Detective Simon Hathaway are on a plane to Denver. The plan is to meet Jos in a back office of the Arvada police station to record his testimony.

With heart pounding, Jos steps through the door and sees the two officials seated at a table with an empty chair across from them and a recorder set on the table. The room is small, the walls are gray and drab, and the feeling of the place is sterile. The attorney and the detective greet Jos cordially. They are not rude or interrogative, like you see on TV, but they appear to be looking forward to closing a murder case that has gone cold for four to five years.

Jos shares his eyewitness testimony as completely as he can, and D.A. Fisher slides documents of immunity across the table in front of Jos for him to sign. Within a few months Jos is back in his hometown and ready to testify before a judge and jury.

The day of the trial comes swiftly. Jos enters the courtroom. The whole experience is so surreal it feels like he's in a dream. Two bailiffs stand on either side of the entrance as Jos enters. He's wearing a gray suit and blue tie. He looks around the room to take in the whole scene. All eyes are fixed on him as he walks toward D.A. Fisher and then takes his seat next to him. The legal proceedings pass by like a blur. It's as if time is suspended in the courtroom. The preliminary statements are made by the judge and finish abruptly.

As if jarred out of a dream Jos hears his name called, "Mr. Joseph Duce, please take the stand."

Silence fills the courtroom as Jos takes his seat in the stand next to Judge Contreras. D.A. Fisher begins a brief questioning about the night of the murder. Jos' voice shakes slightly as he replays for the jury the sequence of events of that night . . . the plan, the approach, the knocks on the door, running at the sound of gunfire, and the sleepless night that ensued.

The final question D.A. Fisher asks Jos remains indelibly etched on his soul to this day.

He looks at Jos in the eye and asks, "Mr. Duce, do you believe that you deserve to go to jail for this?

After a brief pause, Jos exhales and confesses, "Yes, I do."

"No further questions, your Honor."

D.A. Fisher turns around and walks back to his seat. Judge Contreras adjourns the trial with a swing of the gavel, and the jury is released to deliberate and make their decision.

The jury doesn't take long to reach a verdict. Within 30 minutes court is reconvened.

Judge Contreras addresses the jury, "Have you reached a verdict?"

The jury spokesperson stands up and replies, "We have, your Honor."

The verdict is read aloud, and Jos sinks back into his chair in ecstatic relief. The man who pulled the trigger is convicted, and Jos walks out of the courtroom a free man, exonerated of all charges.

As dramatic as the courtroom experience is, it simply is not enough to orchestrate the complete redemption Jos needs. He proceeds to live the next few years of his life taking for granted the lavish grace he has been given. Even still, in all of his wandering, this monumental act of grace is not quickly forgotten.

After his time in court, Jos flies back to Denver and lives there for just over a year. He takes a job as a truck driver for a hardwood flooring distributor called Denver Hardwood. And during this time, he continues to live the way he wants, which involves parties, drugs, and girls.

Jos' brother, Daniel, who became a Christian soon after the death of their dad, calls at least once a month if not every two weeks. Daniel is fully aware of the prodigal path Jos has chosen. He knows how far his brother is from Christ. On these phone calls, Jos and Daniel catch up and hear about each other's lives.

At the end of every phone call Daniel's refrain is, "Hey man, if you ever wanna come home . . . you've got a place to stay."

With every phone call and every closing refrain, Jesus pursues Jos through his brother, Daniel.

This goes on for months until one morning Jos wakes up with an emptiness in his chest that rattles his core. *It's time to go home,* he thinks to himself as he sits at the edge of his bed massaging his temples trying to clear his mind of the pounding hangover. Within a week, Jos is back in his hometown in close proximity to his brother again. For the next two and a half years Jos continues to live on his own terms, but Jesus begins to soften his heart as Jos spends more time with Daniel and the Jesus followers who are his friends.

At this point, Jos is still hostile toward the message of Jesus, but Daniel discerns that Jos does enjoy engaging the gospel intellectually. Specifically, Jos loves to think and talk about the Christian faith, but if the conversation ever turns personal, he quickly distances himself. And because of this, Daniel turns Jos on to some speakers and authors that he thinks he would enjoy. So Jos begins to voraciously consume sermons and books written by Matt Chandler, Tim Keller, and John Piper. Jesus continues to soften Jos' callused heart more and more.

On the night of the eight-year anniversary of his dad's death, January 7, 2009, Jos sits comfortably on his couch in his studio apartment drinking a six pack, smoking a bowl, and listening to a John Piper sermon. Smoke fills the air as the preacher's voice echoes through the apartment. But something happens in the next moment. For one reason or another, the gospel message now echoes resoundingly in Jos' soul. He has heard the gospel a thousand times before this night, but this time Jos actually hears the gospel for the first time. He sees Jesus for who He really is . . . God in the flesh . . . who loves him and gave Himself for him.

And Jos believes.

He wakes up the next morning, and he literally is a different person. He no longer sees life through a distorted lens because Jesus has given him a completely different perspective. He now sees life through the lens of the gospel. The drugs, the sex, and the parties are dim and tasteless now compared to the radiant brilliance of Christ and the call to follow Him.

Jos actually wants to know Jesus . . . to really know Him . . . and to be close to Him. Jos sees his sin for what it truly is, and he sees the cost and the price that Jesus paid to set him free. For the first time, deep in his soul, Jos feels free. He now understands that, in Jesus, he has ". . . redemption through His blood, the forgiveness of [his] trespasses, according to the riches of His grace" (Eph. 1:7 NASB).

In reflecting on the way Christ redeemed his life, this is what Jos has to say in his own words, "I think about that scene in the courtroom . . . such a gripping vignette or picture of the gospel. I deserved punishment, but I didn't get it. Just like I received undeserved immunity from my trespass in that courtroom, I knew that I deserved to pay a penalty for my sins against God, but Jesus paid it for me. Because of His sacrifice, all of my sins (past, present, and future) are paid for and forgiven."

Before Jesus, Jos thought there were only two ways to live: you can either be righteous by obeying God's law (this was Jos' mindset up until his dad died), or you can live according your own law and be "free" (this was Jos' mindset after his dad died up until he met Jesus).

But now in Christ, Jos sees a third way to live: you can recognize that there really isn't a way for any of us to be righteous by keeping God's law and, on the other hand, you can recognize that living according to your own law is just as enslaving as trying to attain your own righteousness by God's law.

So where does that leave us? *The third way to live is to live by the grace of Jesus* . . . to realize that your righteousness is given to you through the perfect life, death, and resurrection of Jesus Christ. By His death, He purchased our freedom, so we can freely choose to love and obey Him. We now, in Christ, can truly find ultimate joy and satisfaction in Him.

So what became of Jos after Jesus took ahold of his life? Jos continued to grow in his life with Jesus. He became one of the original members of a startup church in San Antonio called Mission Church. Would it surprise you if I told you that Jos also became a pastor of this church? Jesus took a man who should either be dead or in prison, and empowered him to be a shepherd over His flock. Jesus took a military washout and transformed him into one of the hardest working men I know. Jesus took a promiscuous drug user and transformed him into a devoted husband full of integrity.

This once hardened and cold criminal is now one of the kindest, one of the warmest, and one of the most grace-filled people I have ever known. His life is truly a product of the lavish grace and redemption of Jesus. And yes, at times he still takes for granted the immensity of grace he's been shown, but because of Jesus he has been completely transformed. Jesus redeemed Jos through his blood and gave him forgiveness of his trespasses, according to the riches of His grace.

Let's now spend a few moments meditating on the riches of Eph. 1:7, 8 and what these verses mean for our daily living. The verse says: "In him we have redemption through his blood, the forgiveness of our trespasses, according to the riches of his grace, which he lavished upon us, in all wisdom and insight."

The critical word in verse 7 is "redemption." What comes to your mind when you think of redemption? The Greek word Paul uses here means to *re-purchase*. The definition of this word is "a release effected by payment of ransom."[3] This firstly implies that we are held captive and enslaved to our sin, and we are therefore indebted to a most holy and just God because we have sinned against Him. The word "redemption" in verse 7 conjures up the horrifying image of people being sold like cattle at a slave market in first century Asia Minor.

Sin is slavery. Every time we sin against God, we embrace the chains of sin. But God is rich in mercy (see Eph. 2:4). Eph. 1:7 declares that Jesus has walked into the middle of the slave market, as it were, and looked upon us with great compassion as we sit shackled by our sin with no hope or recourse of becoming free. Jesus has paid the price for our freedom from sin. He has paid the ransom. "For even the Son of Man came not to be served but to serve, and to give his life as a ransom for many" (Mark 10:45). The word "for" when it says, "a ransom *for* many", is actually better translated "a ransom *instead of*

---

3. *Greek*. (2021). Bible Hub. https://biblehub.com/greek/629.htm

or *in place of* many." Redemption is possible because Jesus substituted His life for ours, in our place.

What is the ransom price to purchase our freedom from sin? The price is the very life and blood of Jesus Christ. He gave His life as a ransom for us in our place. Eph. 1:7 states, "in Him we have redemption *through His blood*" (emphasis mine). How much does Jesus love you? He loves you more than the value of His own precious blood.

Verse 7 also defines what redemption means in the next words of the verse: redemption is "the forgiveness of our trespasses, according to the riches of His grace." What is forgiveness? This word means *to pardon or free a person from a debt that is owed*. This gives us insight into why verse 7 ends by qualifying our redemption: it's "according to the riches of His grace." If you think about the depth of all your sins for a moment, you may become overwhelmed by how greatly you are indebted to God. You and I are utterly unable to pay Him back for all that we have done against Him.

Behold the beauty of how rich the grace of Jesus is! His grace is so rich and so glorious that He's able to completely cover the cost of our debt. By the way, this includes *all* of your sin: past, present, and future. Jesus paying for the immensity of your debt underscores the immensity of His grace. And that's why Eph. 1:8 uses the word "lavish" to describe how our redemption is bestowed upon us.

God the Father unreservedly lavishes forgiveness upon us "in all wisdom and insight." The final phrase "in all wisdom and insight" indicates that our redemption was not an afterthought, but part of God's intricate plan ordained before time began. This plan is "to the praise of his glorious grace, with which he has blessed us in the Beloved" (Eph. 1:6).

How should knowing about our redemption and forgiveness through Christ shape our daily living? When you know how deeply Christ has forgiven and redeemed you, you will most certainly seek to forgive those who have wronged you. Paul exhorts the Colossians to be "bearing with one another and, if one has a complaint against another, forgiving each other; as the Lord has forgiven you, so you also must forgive" (Col. 3:13). Who do you need to forgive right now?

Another point of application is our call to radical generosity (see chapter 26). Look at how radically generous Jesus has been with us. He shed His very blood in our place to purchase our freedom from sin! How can you be radically generous to those around you in sacrificing your time, your gifting, and your money?

The rest of this book will be dedicated to exploring how we can view the various aspects of life through this gospel lens. Now, let's take a moment to recall our identity in Christ from what we have covered in chapters 6, 7, and 8.

We are chosen, we are adopted as sons and daughters, and we are redeemed in Christ. If you are in Christ, this is who you are. This is how God sees you. Let every other self-image and false identity fade away and meditate on how the most important Person in the universe sees you. He has called you to Himself. He has predestined you to adoption. He invites you to call Him "Abba, Father!" He has redeemed you from all of your sins. All of this leads us to worship Him because of His glorious grace. Consider the following illustration as you meditate on how stunning the redemptive work of Christ is for you.

Imagine yourself at a slave market right now. You sit in the dirt, shackled in chains next to your brothers and sisters. Your wrists are red and callused by the constant rub of the metal against them. Cacophonous voices call out from left and right shouting the price they are willing to pay for such and such slave. Before your very eyes, human beings are yanked around and dragged by rope or chain like animals to their new owners. The experience is nauseating.

Suddenly, a man comes into the middle of the slave market. He has an air of authority and confidence about Him, but He also appears to be extremely approachable and loving. He walks over to you. Your knees are pulled up to your chest. You're all balled up because you feel less exposed in this posture. Fear grips you.

What happens next utterly jolts you by surprise. The man now stands over you and looks into your eyes. His eyes are full of love and kindness. He kneels down before you. He reaches out and takes hold of your chains. You can feel the strength emanating from His powerful hands. With one swift and gentle movement He pulls the chains between your wrists, and they break apart like the snapping of a twig. Awe-struck you look down at the broken chains as the bonds that once shackled you fall to the ground. You alternate massaging each wrist where the chains have left imprints.

Suddenly, He reaches out His hand, gently places his fingers under your chin, and lifts up your head so that your gaze meets His. His love for you envelops and embraces you. You are now held by the presence of perfect love, and it's as if your heart starts beating for the very first time. In a single moment, you are reborn.

Time stands still as you behold the beauty of the One your soul has always longed for but never knew existed until now. He reaches out His hand and pulls you up to your feet. "Who are you?" you ask Him.

"Fear not, for I have redeemed you; I have called you by name, you are Mine." His voice is deep and unmistakably affirming.

"What is your name?" you ask Him.

And then what happens next tears your heart in half. He sits down in the dirt where you were just sitting. You do a double take as you cannot believe the sight before you.

The broken chains previously on the ground are intact and now fastened securely around His wrists. You look at your Redeemer in shock.

"I am Jesus," He tells you. "Your redemption comes at a price."

Before He can finish speaking, a crowd of men come up to Him and brusquely pull Him to His feet. One of the men spits in His face, and they lead Him away to His execution. You try to shout at them to stop, but no sound comes out of your mouth.

Instinctively, you follow at a distance. After sentencing Him to death by crucifixion, they lead your Redeemer to the top of a hill outside the city. They have Him lie down on the crossbeams and stretch out His arms. A soldier places a large iron spike on top of His left wrist, and with several swings of the hammer he drives the spike through flesh and bone into the wood. You kneel down on the ground to be eye level with Jesus.

While lying on the cross, He turns His head to look at you. His blood trickles from the entry of the nail wound down the rough wood and drips to the ground. Your eyes behold the ransom price for your redemption.

Looking at you, He whispers one last time, "Fear not, for I have redeemed you; I have called you by name, you are mine" (Isaiah 43:1).

Part 3

The Gospel Lens and Self-Talk

"Why are you cast down, O my soul,
and why are you in turmoil within me?
Hope in God ..."
(PS. 42:5).

9

Self-Talk

In future chapters, we will look at different situations in life through the lens of the gospel or through the heart of Jesus. But in this chapter, I want to explore with you how the gospel impacts your *thought* life. You see, the gospel must take deep root in your mind before it impacts your actions. This is why Paul exhorts the church in Rome, "And do not be conformed to this world, but be transformed by the renewing of your mind, so that you may prove what the will of God is, that which is good and acceptable and perfect"[4] (Rom. 12:2). As you already read in chapter one, the Greek word, *metamorphoó,* used for "transformed" in this verse, is where we get our English word *metamorphosis*.

The takeaway for us is that gospel transformation through the renewing of our minds is a *process* that takes time, like a caterpillar undergoing metamorphosis to become a beautiful butterfly. The result of our spiritual metamorphosis is being able to prove what the will of God is. Therefore, we can conclude that mind renewal *empowers* us to look at life through the gospel lens. But this begs the question: how do you renew your mind?

Specifically, I want to explore mind renewal through gospel self-talk, or what I have termed intra-soul dialogue. In her groundbreaking novel entitled *Mrs. Dalloway,* Virginia Woolf employs the use of a literary device known as stream of consciousness. In other words, she gives the reader insight into the thought life, or the stream of consciousness, of her characters to advance the narrative forward. I would like to take this idea of stream of consciousness and apply it to intra-soul dialogue.

Imagine the thoughts you have during your waking hours as a constant flowing stream meandering through a forest. Now imagine that you are floating

---

4. All Scripture used in chapter 9 are from the New American Standard Bible (NASB 1995).

on top of the water of your stream of consciousness. What intra-soul dialogue does is allow you to put your feet down on the floor of the stream and plant yourself firmly on the bedrock of the gospel. No longer are you carried along by the current of the whims of your mind and circumstance, but your thoughts become anchored in who Jesus is, in what He has done, and who you are in light of Him.

Oftentimes our thoughts oppose the gospel and originate from anti-gospel worldviews. In these moments, we need to employ intra-soul dialogue to anchor ourselves in Christ and walk upstream against the current, or one could say, 'against the spirit-of-the-age.' This is why the renewal of our minds necessitates that we "not be conformed to this world" (Rom. 12:2). A robust and intimate knowledge of Scripture is essential to this metamorphic process of intra-soul dialogue.

But what do I mean by intra-soul dialogue? Let's take a few moments to consider Ps. 42, especially verse 5:

> "Why are you in despair, O my soul?
> And *why* have you become disturbed within me?
> Hope in God, for I shall again praise Him
> For the help of His presence."

Did you notice who the psalmist is talking to here? Not another person, not to God (not yet anyways), *but to his own soul!* The psalmist finds himself in immense distress, and all of a sudden, his addressee in the middle of the psalm, and at the end in verse 11, becomes his own soul. He's engaging in intra-soul dialogue. No longer is he being carried along by the depressing thoughts of his stream of consciousness, but he is anchoring his feet to the bedrock of the living God being his only hope.

His name is Asaph, a descendant of Korah.

He is alone. He finds himself looking skyward beyond the peaks of Mount Hermon impressively sprawling before him. A cool wind cuts across his face afforded by the frosty, arid climate. With a disheartened exhale, he puts his foot on the rocky snow-covered crag before him and commences his climb. Asaph prays silently with every step. His prayers are met by an echoing silence briefly interrupted by gusts of wind. Exhaustion weighs on his emaciated, sleep-deprived body. He's not even half-way to the summit when he collapses to his knees. He winces as the rocks press into his skin.

He cannot rid his mind of the scoffers' voices, "Where is your God, Asaph? Where is your God?" His head sinks down in despair. A rumbling disquietude ravages his soul. He cannot bear the weight of his hopelessness anymore. Tears begin streaming down his chapped cheeks.

Suddenly, a profound thirst overwhelms him; not merely physical but a longing deep in his soul for an encounter with the living God.

🙢

Let's consider Ps. 42:1–6 so we can appreciate Asaph's intra-soul dialogue in context and with proper perspective.

Ps. 42:1 famously begins with these words:

"As the deer pants for the water brooks,
So my soul pants for You, O God."

This verse immediately gives us insight into what kind of state the psalmist, Asaph, finds himself. He's spiritually parched. His spiritual thirst is overwhelming. If you see a deer panting in the woods with its tongue sticking out, you know immediately something is wrong with the animal. Here the psalmist is longing for God intensely. He's in a spiritual drought. Now let's look at verse 2.

"My soul thirsts for God, for the living God;
When shall I come and appear before God?"

Verse 2 further demonstrates the spiritual wilderness in which the psalmist finds himself. The second line of verse 2 indicates a longing for intimacy with God. Some manuscripts say "*see the face of God*" as an alternative rendering of the phrase "appear before God." The psalmist is desperate for an intimate encounter with the living God, but instead he is confronted with an endless silence permeating the corridors of his soul. Now look at verse 3 for further insight into the psalmist's condition.

"My tears have been my food day and night,
While *they* say to me all day long, 'Where is your God?'"

Here in verse 3, we can perceive that Asaph's perpetual spiritual drought has inevitably led to depression. We see indicators of depression in his unceasing sorrow or "tears" accompanied by the onset of insomnia as these tears are his only sustenance both "day and night." In other words, Asaph is exceedingly sorrowful, sleepless, likely malnourished due to poor appetite, and therefore sinking into depression.

The second line of verse 3 indicates one of the exacerbating factors or sources of his depression: the people around him are speaking lies into his ear: "Where is your God?" Talk about insult to injury! The psalmist cannot catch a break. By the way, the scoffers are speaking these lies "all day long" to him. We can almost certainly infer that a spiritual battle is being waged in his mind: *should I believe the voices of these scoffers or should I hope in the living God?* Now, look at verse 4 to see how Asaph copes with his distress.

"These things I remember and I pour out my soul within me.
For I used to go along with the throng *and* lead them in procession to the house of God,
With the voice of joy and thanksgiving, a multitude keeping festival."

What's happening in the first line of verse 4? The psalmist is practicing the blessed discipline of self-reflection. He's remembering and reflecting on "these things." What "things" is he referring to? He's pondering his profound spiritual thirst for the living God. He's recalling his sleepless nights filled with tears. He's hearing the voices of the scoffers on repeat as they reverberate in his mind saying, "Where is your God?" He self-reflects on all of this and begins pouring out his soul within him. In so doing, he takes the first step towards intra-soul dialogue.

But the bulk of Ps. 42:4 unveils to us more of the exacerbating and causal factors of the psalmist's depression and spiritual drought. Here we see his *isolation* from a worshiping community. Notice the past tense of "For I used to go along with the throng." He then speaks of his leadership role in bringing the people of God into the presence of God. He remembers what his voice used to sound like when it resonated with joy and resounded with thanksgiving amidst a "multitude" of believers "keeping festival."

A brief sidebar worth mentioning here: there is definitely something to be said for in-person corporate worship. During the Covid-19 pandemic I came to a much deeper and richer appreciation of gathering with other followers of Jesus in person. Staying at home and doing online church is no substitute. Period. I definitely felt more down-hearted during those months of being disconnected from engaging with the church body in person.

God has designed us for community. This is why we are told in Heb. 10:24, 25, "and let us consider how to stimulate one another to love and good deeds, not forsaking our own assembling together, as is the habit of some, but encouraging *one another*; and all the more as you see the day drawing near."

Ps. 42:4 also reveals that the psalmist has now become isolated from the assembling together of his worshiping community. There is no stimulation to love and good deeds in his life. There is zero encouragement from other worshipers of God. There is only scoffing "all day long" (Ps. 42:3). He looks back with longing for the joy he used to have when he found himself surrounded by a multitude keeping festival. He misses the festal joy of community.

Ps. 42:1–4 is the backdrop, or the psalmist's stream of consciousness, leading up to his intra-soul dialogue in verse 5. Verse 5 is the moment where he stops floating along passively in the stream. Instead, he plunges his feet below the surface of the water and plants them down firmly, being anchored to the bedrock of his living God. In the following chapter, we will consider this verse in greater detail.

10

Intra-Soul Dialogue: Going Deeper

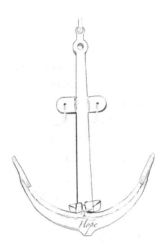

"Why are you in despair, O my soul?
And *why* have you become disturbed within me?
Hope in God, for I shall again praise Him
For the help of His presence"[5] (Ps. 42:5).

The psalmist does three things here in verse 5 with his intra-soul dialogue that especially need to be highlighted.

1. He interrogates his soul
2. He reorients his hope
3. He anchors himself in God's salvation

He Interrogates his Soul

The first two lines of Ps. 42:5 include two "why" questions. The first question is about the psalmist's despair: "why are you in despair, O my soul?" The Hebrew word for "despair" here literally means "sunk down." This corroborates the conclusion we drew earlier that this man is depressed. His countenance has fallen. The Swahili translation of depression, a "drop of heart," adds a pictorial insight.

---

5. All Scripture used in chapter 10 are from the New American Standard Bible (NASB 1995).

The second "why" question is: "*why* have you become disturbed within me?" The Hebrew word for "disturbed" here can also be translated as "disquieted" or to be made "boisterous" or to be in "uproar." There is a deep and profound restlessness in his soul. But what is the point of interrogating your own soul about things you already know intimately?

The point is that soul interrogation takes the intra-soul dialoguer deeper into self-reflection and self-knowledge. When you question your soul this way you take the upper hand so to speak. You sort of back your troubled soul into a corner and grab it by the shirt collar.[6] You are no longer a passive victim of your circumstances or choices, but you take an active role in your thought life. This is when we investigate our own condition and take it seriously. These 'why' questions help us face the gravity of our condition. They take us to the heart of our problem and alert us to the depth of our need.

On the one hand, there is something soothing and calming about asking your soul why you have the condition you do. Ironically, these 'why' questions serve to diminish the ferocity of our condition because on the other side of these questions is better understanding of the condition's cause and therefore an implied hope for a solution or cure. On the other hand, we may conclude the condition we are in is hopeless. And the answer to these 'why' questions may frighten us even more. This is what leads us to reorient our hope.

He Reorients his Hope

In the third line of Ps. 42:5 the psalmist takes an authoritative tone and tells his soul to "hope in God, for I shall again praise Him." He reorients his hope. Up to now the psalmist's stream of consciousness has revealed nothing but spiritual drought, despair, scoffing, isolation, and longing for what used to be. We need some hope. We need some good news. At this very point in Ps. 42 the psalmist is anchoring himself to the bedrock of hoping in the one he so desperately thirsts for. He does not ask, but commands his soul to hope in God.

As New Testament believers we can do the same, but with all the more clarity. We can reorient our soul's hope and firmly place it in the person and work of Jesus Christ. As the writer of Hebrews assures us, "This hope we have as an anchor of the soul, a *hope* both sure and steadfast and one which enters

---

6. I am grateful to Dr. Timothy Keller and his sermon entitled Finding God for helping me understand soul interrogation.

within the veil, where Jesus has entered as a forerunner for us, having become a high priest forever according to the order of Melchizedek" (Heb. 6:19, 20).

At this point in our intra-soul dialogue, we are turning away from all the false hopes we have pursued, and we are reorienting our soul to hope in the person and work of Jesus. Consider the metaphor of Jesus being the anchor of your soul. An anchor ensures a ship will not be tossed here and there by the whims of the winds and waves. An anchor ensures rock solid security and buoyancy amidst the turbulence of life. This is Jesus for us. He is "both sure and steadfast." He has entered within the veil as our great high priest to represent us, who are utterly sinful, before the Holy One of heaven and earth.

Jesus as our high priest has made atonement for us. He is the priest and the atoning sacrifice all at once. He is the forerunner for us. He goes where our sins will not allow us to go. He has made atonement for our sins at the cross and torn the veil to give us access into the very presence of God. He is our only hope. And the unassailable promise of Heb. 6:20 is that He is our "high priest *forever*" (emphasis mine). The hope of Jesus will never fade because He holds his priesthood permanently.

"He always lives to make intercession for [us]" (Heb. 7:25). Think about that for a moment. If you are "in Christ," you have Jesus, your high priest, speaking a better word of intercession on your behalf before God the Father *right now*. ". . . and He who searches the hearts knows what the mind of the Spirit is, because He intercedes for the saints according to *the will of* God" (Rom. 8:27). Wow, what a Savior!

What does your soul tend to hope in? Is it your job or your performance? Then practice intra-soul dialogue and tell your soul to hope in Jesus and His finished atoning work for you. Is it human approval? Then tell your soul to hope in Jesus and His forever, ongoing priestly advocacy and affirmation of you. Is it money or financial security? Then tell your soul to hope in Jesus and "the unfathomable riches of Christ" that are yours in Him (Eph. 3:8). Is it your obedience to God? Then tell your soul to hope in Jesus and His perfect obedience to God the Father on your behalf (see Matt. 5:17).

In other words, "fix your hope completely on the grace to be brought to you at the revelation of Jesus Christ" (1 Peter 1:13b). We have to continually and daily preach the gospel to our souls because, if we're honest with ourselves, our hope is not completely in Jesus . . . it's only partially in Him. Therefore, we must practice reorienting our hope to be placed in Jesus completely.

What accompanies such reorientation of hope? Ps. 42:5 says, "Hope in God, for I shall again praise Him." Hope in the living God is accompanied by praise of the living God. This is what we were made for! Notice the confidence of the psalmist here in this line, "for I *shall* again praise Him" (emphasis mine). We know from verses 1–4 that he's in a spiritual drought and is depressed, but with the plunging of his feet below the surface of his stream of consciousness through intra-soul dialogue, the psalmist is grounded in a rock-solid confidence that he *will* again praise his God. That's the beauty of fixing your hope completely on Jesus Christ. *He* anchors your soul: "This hope we have as an anchor of the soul, a *hope* both sure and steadfast . . ." (Heb. 6:19). *He* gives you confidence to praise God, which is the very purpose of your soul.

So, we've seen intra-soul dialogue involves interrogating our souls and reorienting our hope. Ps. 42:5 lastly reveals the foundation of our hope and praising of God.

He Anchors Himself in God's Salvation

In Ps. 42:5 Asaph says he ". . . shall again praise Him *for* the help of His presence." The Hebrew word for "help" in this line can literally be translated as "the saving acts of." In other words, we can tell our souls to hope in God so that we may praise Him all because of the saving acts of His presence.

Step back and consider what this means from an Old Testament perspective. The greatest saving act of God that the people of Israel witnessed was when He powerfully delivered them out of slavery in Egypt through ten plagues and the dividing of the Red Sea. This is a picture of salvation. The presence of God was with them to accomplish their salvation, to deliver them out of slavery into freedom.

For us as New Testament believers, the presence of God has literally come to dwell with us through the person of Jesus Christ. "And the Word became flesh, and dwelt among us, and we saw His glory, glory as of the only begotten from the Father, full of grace and truth" (John 1:14).

And Jesus has delivered us out of slavery from sin through the greatest saving act of God ever known when He bled and died on the cross, ". . . that through death He might render powerless him who had the power of death, that is, the devil, and might free those who through fear of death were subject to slavery all their lives." (Heb. 2:14, 15).

Jesus brilliantly describes His saving acts in John 8:34–36. "...'Truly, truly, I to say, everyone who commits sin is the slave of sin. The slave does not remain in the house forever; the son does remain forever. So, if the Son makes you free, you will be free indeed.'"

Ps. 42:5 tells us the importance of anchoring your soul in the saving acts of God's presence when no presence of God can be felt . . . when spiritual drought is all your soul knows . . . when the only thing you feel is a profound thirst for the living God.

Now, it's important to know that intra-soul dialogue is not the end but simply a means to the end. The end or the purpose of intra-soul dialogue is to connect your soul with the living God, to lead you into the green pastures of intimacy with Him, and to plunge you head first into the constantly cascading waterfall of His refreshing presence.

Notice what happens in the very next verse, Ps. 42:6:

"O my God, my soul is in despair within me;
Therefore I remember You from the land of the Jordan
And the peaks of Hermon, from Mount Mizar."

Did you see the change that occurs from verse 5 to 6? Instead of the psalmist addressing his soul, he now addresses God in heartfelt prayer. *This is the goal of intra-soul dialogue: to springboard you into the presence of God.* In verse 5, he questions his own soul about his despair, but in verse 6 he passionately expresses his despair *to* God.

Do you see the fervent longing for intimacy with God in verse 6? "Therefore I remember *You* from the land of the Jordan and the peaks of Hermon, from Mount Mizar" (emphasis mine). The phrase "I remember You from" in this prayer connotes a palpable feeling of isolation and distance from God in these different geographical locations, which are far from the temple in Jerusalem (in case you are wondering, it's about a 3-hour flight or 7.5-hour train ride from Mt. Hermon to Jerusalem!).

What method does the psalmist give us for handling spiritual drought and despair? Psalm 42 begins with prayer in verse 1, followed by self-reflection in verses 2–4, interrupted by intra-soul dialogue in verse 5, returning back to prayer in verse 6, and lastly the psalm concludes with intra-soul dialogue down in verse 11. This is a biblical example of how we can deal with our sin, the circumstances around us, and the suffering of life.

I would like to conclude this chapter by taking you to one more psalm that employs the use of intra-soul dialogue to help you see that such a discipline can be more broadly applied to your life, not just during times of spiritual drought and despair. Lastly, look with me briefly at Ps. 103:1–5.

"Bless the LORD, O my soul,
And all that is within me, *bless* His holy name.
Bless the LORD, O my soul,
And forget none of His benefits;
Who pardons all your iniquities,
Who heals all your diseases;
Who redeems your life from the pit,
Who crowns you with lovingkindness and compassion;
Who satisfies your years with good things,
So that your youth is renewed like the eagle."

Are you thinking only about yourself today and wrapped up in self-absorption? Then use intra-soul dialogue and tell your soul to bless the Lord with all that is within you. "Bless the LORD, O my soul, and all that is within me, *bless* His holy name." But how can our self-centered souls be enticed into praising our holy God with all that we are? Let Ps. 103:2 provide our Lord's guidance . . . it tells our soul to "forget none of His benefits."

But your soul may respond, "What are His benefits? I feel nothing but bitterness, guilt, and shame today." Then remind your soul of Ps. 103:3—O my soul, this holy God is the One "who pardons all your iniquities." The Apostle Paul drills the beauty of this glorious benefit down even deeper for us New Testament believers when he reminds us of the following:

"When you were dead in your transgressions and the uncircumcision
of your flesh, He made you alive together with Him, having forgiven
us all our transgressions, having canceled out the certificate of debt
consisting of decrees against us, which was hostile to us; and He has
taken it out of the way, having nailed it to the cross" (Col. 2:13, 14).

Did you catch how Col. 2:13 proclaims the astounding truth that He has "forgiven us *all* our transgressions" (emphasis mine)? That is to say, all your sins (past, present, and future) are completely atoned for by the work of Jesus

Christ on the cross. If you are in Christ, you *are* forgiven. You *are* exonerated. You *are* acquitted. You *are* justified (declared righteous before God). All your sins have been utterly erased and expunged by Christ's blood. Does your soul know this today? Are you beginning to sense the warm embrace of Jesus on your soul through this breathtaking truth?

Now, not only does He pardon all our iniquities, but Ps. 103 promises healing as well. Are you sick today? Is your body riddled with pain and disease? Then tell your soul about the Healer of "all your diseases" (Ps. 103:3).

But your soul may respond, "I feel nothing but irreparable brokenness. I feel as though I am stuck in a pit of despair." Then tell your soul about the One "who redeems your life from the pit, who crowns you with lovingkindness and compassion" (Ps. 103:4).

But your soul may respond, "I feel dissatisfied right now. Nothing in this world seems to truly satisfy or fill me. I feel old, weak, and tired." Then tell your soul about the One "who satisfies your years with good things, *so that* your youth is renewed like the eagle" (Ps. 103:5).

Do you notice how intra-soul dialogue reminds our souls of the gospel? This discipline of gospel self-talk is how we can preach Jesus to our own souls. Intra-soul dialogue reminds us of who Jesus is and what He has done. Intra-soul dialogue re-instills into us our new identity in light of who He is, what He has done, and what He continues to do for us right now. Ps. 103:1–5 is ultimately true because of who Jesus is and what He has done to accomplish salvation for us.

Our souls can bless the LORD with all that is within us because Jesus was condemned in our place on the cross.

Jesus "pardons all your iniquities" (Ps. 103:3).

Our souls can bless the LORD with all that is within us because Jesus "was pierced through for our transgressions, He was crushed for our iniquities; The chastening for our well-being *fell* upon Him, And by His scourging we are healed" (Is. 53:5).

Jesus "heals all your diseases" (Ps. 103:3).

Our souls can bless the LORD with all that is within us because Jesus was broken and cast down into a pit of despair for our redemption when He cried out on the cross, "My God, My God, why have you forsaken Me?" (Matt. 27:46).

Jesus "redeems your life from the pit" (Ps. 103:4).

Our souls can bless the LORD with all that is within us because Jesus was crowned with a crown of thorns.

Jesus is the One "who crowns [us] with lovingkindness and compassion" (Ps. 103:4).

Our souls can bless the LORD with all that is within us because Jesus ". . . was oppressed and He was afflicted, Yet He did not open His mouth; Like a lamb that is led to slaughter, And like a sheep that is silent before its shearers, So He did not open His mouth" (Isa.53:7). He was oppressed and afflicted so we could be satisfied.

Jesus is the One "who satisfies your years with good things, *So that* your youth is renewed like the eagle" (Ps. 103:5).

Jesus was condemned. We receive pardon. Jesus was scourged. We receive healing. Jesus was cast down into the pit, so He could redeem our life from the pit. Jesus was crowned with thorns. We are crowned with lovingkindness and compassion. Jesus was oppressed and afflicted. We are satisfied with good things and renewed like the eagle.

O my soul, do you realize who Jesus is and what He has done for you? O my soul, do you realize who you are because of Jesus? O my soul, Jesus has pardoned you, He has healed you, He has redeemed you, He has crowned you, He has satisfied you, and He has renewed you.

"Bless the LORD, O my soul,
And all that is within me, *bless* His holy name."

Part 4

The Gospel Lens
and Sexuality

*"but whoever drinks of the
water that I will give him will
never be thirsty again . . ."*
(JOHN 4:14).

11

Pornography Addiction

His name is Joseph.

You have already met him briefly in chapter 2. The following is a true account of his encounter with Jesus in the midst of pornography addiction.

Joseph grew up as the youngest of five children in a small Pennsylvania town. His first introduction to pornography was at age 11. He had a friend whose father had Playboy magazines stashed away in the attic, and they used to secretly go and gander at those. In his initial encounters with porn, he would feel the thrill of excitement intrinsic to that which is forbidden, but at the same time these feelings would be mixed with shame. He began to feel the burden of a guilty conscience surrounding his use of porn.

Two years later, his parents started going through a divorce. At the age of about 13, he was still forming his identity. He didn't know who he was, even though he had grown up in church and had a great childhood. His parents' divorce sent shockwaves through his formless identity, as he longed for love and support from his home environment. But now that environment was being torn in two. Even though his parents told him they loved him, Joseph still felt the need to search elsewhere to feel accepted, valued, secure, known, and loved. With porn, there was this sense of being in control and accepted in a fleeting sort of way. Additionally, the transient pleasurable feelings afforded by porn helped him to temporarily forget about his emotional sadness regarding the divorce. Thus began Joseph's introduction to pornography.

Around age 11 to 13, he recalls growing spiritually and sensing the presence of God in his life. He remembers vividly how he used to skip Sunday service at their small church in Pennsylvania and go to the library by himself to pray.

He now sits in a secluded corner of the library. The silence engulfing him is peaceful. This quiet place has become to him a sanctuary, a much-needed respite from the conflict at home. To his right sits a small book case and several chairs fill the space. He sits there praying for about thirty minutes straight, offering up petitions to God. His petitions include things like food for the hungry and world peace and different circumstances in his life. As he prays, he has a palpable sense of God's nearness. This connection with the Lord would sustain him during these difficult times in his childhood.

∂ఄ

Once his parents divorced, he moved in with his grandmother rather than split time between mom and dad. This afforded significant periods of alone time where Joseph was left to his own devices. Porn became an emotional pick-me-up for him during this period. Watching porn and then masturbating to have a sexual release started to become a vicious cycle of temporary emotional lifting, followed by a swift crash characterized by profound shame. For he knew from the Bible that sexual gratification is only reserved for marriage.

The pattern of addiction began to build up to the point where if he didn't use porn and masturbate, he would feel incomplete. He would not be able to fall asleep at night unless he looked at porn. In the quiet solace of his room the pornographic images became seared into his mind and the consequential shame felt unbearable. He quickly realized the addiction ensnared him, holding him captive and powerless without hope of deliverance. At this point, Joseph believed the lie that he would not be okay, or have a sense of security, unless he used porn and had a sexual release.

But the real issue was not about sexuality. The real issue was much deeper. Joseph's porn addiction was merely a symptom and a coping mechanism for a deeper, unresolved problem and pain. This deeper problem was a lack of identity in Christ, a false belief that his sense of security could be found outside the arms of his Savior. The solution, he thought at the time, was just to stop looking at porn and prevent the addiction. But this method proved ineffectual.

A double life ensued. Although he was very active in his church, Joseph began to have promiscuous dating relationships in high school. His deeper personal problems were manifested in these relationships with girls. Even though he thought his porn addiction was merely a personal issue between him and God, this problem began to have an insidious ripple effect. He started viewing women as objects for sexual gratification rather than sisters in Christ and unique women created in God's image. The beautiful purpose of sex within the covenant of marriage became extremely distorted in Joseph's life at this time.

His unbelief or false premise was this: if he had his sexual desire fulfilled, he would have a sense of security and would be someone worth intimately knowing. He began to see physical and sexual gratification as true intimacy. But this is false. Pornography gives a person a sense of false intimacy. The false intimacy that porn gives to the user is based on a fantasy that has only a physical component or, in other words, a physiological response. There's no real knowledge of another person. It's totally about an image of a person being there to serve the physical and sexual appetite of the porn user.

Rather, true and real *intimacy* can be broken down into four words: in-to-me-see. This means that intimacy comes from a deep and abiding knowledge of who someone is and being relationally close to that person in light of having such deep knowledge. This knowing of the other person creates an intimate relationship with physical, emotional, spiritual, and sexual components. The lives of two people knowing one another this way become profoundly and mysteriously intertwined, the intermingling of souls. This type of relationship is based on covenant love and is reserved for marriage. This love does not ebb and flow like the ocean's tide, but remains perennially firm, solid, and unmoving.

The illusion of intimacy that porn seductively offers could not be further from true intimacy. So, Joseph found himself intensely seeking this counterfeit intimacy and in turn bearing the consequential shame. Every time he would falter and use porn or go beyond appropriate limits with his girlfriends in high school, the resultant shame was like wearing a 100-pound weighted vest while climbing a mountain.

All through high school, from ages 14–19, he had a constant conflict between who he portrayed himself to be in public and who he was when he was all alone. Although he was leading worship at Bible study and active at his youth group, he became a different person in the solitude of his bedroom at night. On the one hand, was sociable and outgoing Joseph, while on the other was the Joseph hounded by a lingering sense of insecurity that could only be temporarily held at bay by his use of porn. He constantly struggled with the dualistic nature of his existence, and he could never seem to achieve victory over his addiction. He became an intractable sexual version of Dr. Jekyll and Mr. Hyde.

Encountering Jesus

The following summer after graduating high school, Joseph had the opportunity of being a children's group leader at a historic Methodist campground in Massachusetts. The place is renowned for being founded amidst the Great Awakening when circuit preachers would come and preach during weekly revivals.

And so, Joseph would teach a Bible story and a craft for the kids in the community who were around 8 to 12 years old. But in the midst of this, his porn addiction came to a head when some neighbors moved in next door to him at the campground. His neighbor's wife was very attractive, and he began to fantasize about her.

During the inception of this lust, Joseph concurrently began an online Bible study called "The Way of Purity" from the website *settingcaptivesfree.com*. As he began reading the Scriptures and working through the online lessons, Jesus began doing spiritual surgery on Joseph's heart and mind. He realized through this study that his intimacy with God, similar to when he was younger and praying in the library, had essentially become non-existent in his life.

Without even knowing it, Joseph had entered into a spiritual drought. His soul was parched. He knows now that Jesus was actively pursuing and protecting him the whole time leading up to this point, but his relationship and responsiveness to God were not there. He had plenty of Biblical knowledge but no thriving relationship with Jesus.

Although the study was 32 lessons long, it only took the first four lessons for Joseph to experience a very significant encounter with Jesus. The first thing that shocked him as he began was the reality of his fantasizing over his neighbor's wife, and he was quickly reminded of the Ten Commandments when God specifically says, ". . . you shall not covet your neighbor's wife"[7] (Ex. 20:17b).

So, Joseph began to experience the gravity of his own sinfulness and depravity. Coveting his neighbor's wife, fantasizing about sleeping with her, and then thinking about ways to pull this off became a shocking conviction to him. He didn't realize until this point just how deep the roots of his addiction had grown and what his sin had done to him. Imperceptibly and perniciously, Joseph's sin had grown deeper and deeper. And now the reality of his sin was being laid bare before him.

---

7. All Scripture used in chapter 11 are from the New American Standard Bible (NASB 1995).

As he peered into different Bible passages during the first four lessons, he thought he was reading the Scriptures. But he soon realized the Scriptures were actually reading him. Like a mirror, the Bible reflected back to Joseph his true nature and the depths of his sin. Jesus revealed to him the reality of his empty pursuits in pornography and how the addiction was destroying his relationship with God.

The Bible study also impacted him profoundly by revealing to him what his true motivations were for quitting his addiction and, in contrast, the study also showed him what his motivations should have been. The study revealed that humanity is created to be motivated by God's glory:

"For My own sake, for My own sake, I will act; For how can My name be profaned? And I will not give My glory to another" (Isa. 48:11).

The first lesson in the study taught Joseph that God undergirds blessings in our lives to lead to His glory. His blessings on us are consistent with things that will glorify Him.

But Joseph's motivation for quitting his porn addiction was, at its core, self-centered and self-focused. His motivation was always, "If someone finds out about this, I'll be finished . . . or this porn addiction needs to stop so I don't lose my job." So, he had always endeavored to just try harder each time he fell back into his addiction.

At the end of the day, Joseph's original motivation to stop using porn was all about him . . . his reputation . . . all about not wanting people to think he had any problems. His mantra had always been: "My life is my own, and it's what I make of it." Ironically, this mindset is the precise reason why he could never escape his porn addiction. The first lesson taught him that God doesn't promise His blessing on us for our glory, but for His alone. He began to understand that life is not about seeking one's own glory and reputation, but rather life is all about Jesus and bringing Him honor and glory.

The next two lessons were about Jeremiah 2 and John 4, respectively.

The Jeremiah passage was the nail, so to speak, Jesus hammered down to pierce Joseph's sin. This flooded a light onto the emptiness caused by his sin. This passage contains deep gospel truths where God convicts Israel of the following:

"For My people have committed two evils: They have forsaken Me, the fountain of living waters, to hew for themselves cisterns, broken cisterns that can hold no water" (Jer. 2:13).

The concept of building for ourselves broken cisterns that can hold no water illustrates humanity's brokenness in how we dig a hole we keep coming back to because it gives us a small surge of happiness. This analogy spoke profoundly to Joseph regarding his porn addiction.

The next lesson was about John 4 where Jesus encounters a Samaritan woman. At the time, Joseph did not realize how pivotal this chapter is in John's gospel.

∾

Her name is Photine. The blazing sun beats down on her ragged and torn dress. Sweat drips down her face as she heaves her water pot over her shoulder. Dust kicks up behind her as she briefly stumbles and catches herself. At last, she finally reaches her destination, Jacob's well. She sets her water pot down and sits on a nearby rock to rest her wearied body. Being breathless, she takes several deep breaths to recover. And suddenly, a man is standing not more than 10 feet away from her. He makes eye contact with her, and she immediately averts her gaze because she realizes He's a Jewish man.

"Give Me a drink," (John 4:7) the man requests of her. His tone is not sharp. He just seems exhausted from His journey.

"How is it that You, being a Jew, ask me for a drink since I am a Samaritan woman?" (John 4:9).

The man responds to her, "If you knew the gift of God, and who it is who says to you, 'Give Me a drink,' you would have asked Him, and He would have given you living water" (John 4:10).

Photine looks at the man intently for the first time now. She briefly scans Him up and down.

She furrows her brow and replies, "Sir, You have nothing to draw with and the well is deep; where then do You get that living water? You are not greater than our father Jacob, are You, who gave us the well, and drank of it himself and his sons and his cattle?" (John 4:11, 12)

The man looks at her before He responds. There's a gentle but strong compassion in His eyes. Photine begins to realize she may have just underestimated this man.

He answers her, "Everyone who drinks of this water will thirst again; but whoever drinks of the water that I will give him shall never thirst; but the water that I will give him will become in him a well of water springing up to eternal life" (John 4:13, 14).

Photine considers the man's words closely. They seem absurd to her. *Living water to never thirst again*, she thinks to herself. But what if He's telling the truth?

She responds, "Sir, give me this water, so I will not be thirsty nor come all the way here to draw" (John 4:16).

The man's reply seems to abruptly change the subject, but at the same time the subject of the conversation does not change whatsoever.

The man says to her, "Go, call your husband and come here."

"I have no husband."

"You have correctly said, 'I have no husband'; for you have had five husbands, and the one whom you now have is not your husband; this you have said truly" (John 4:16–18).

His words are not harsh or abrasive. He states the above information as plain facts about her life. There's a compelling tone of truthful kindness embedded within the man's words.

Photine is completely caught off guard by this statement. She thinks to herself, *how does He know all of that?* Comprehension begins to dawn on her like sunbeams peeking out over the horizon.

"Sir, I perceive that You are a prophet" (John 4:19).

She feels uncomfortably disarmed in front of this man whom she has just met. So, she decides to change the subject altogether. She decides to talk theology with him. They go back and forth for the next several moments regarding some finer points of difference between Jewish and Samaritan beliefs.

The man concludes their theological discussion by stating, "God is spirit, and those who worship Him must worship in spirit and truth" (John 4:24).

Photine seizes her opportunity at this moment. With desperate longing in her voice she says, "I know that Messiah is coming (He who is called Christ); when that One comes, He will declare all things to us" (John 4:25).

The man looks at Photine with a gaze that seems to pierce directly into her soul. He then declares, "I who speak to you am *He*" (John 4:26).

🙢

It's a Friday night. The month is late August. The first hints of autumn have already begun wisping through the air as leaves fall outside Joseph's one-room apartment. But he finds himself alone. He begins to feel a heightened sense of inadequacy, and a strong impulse comes over him to turn on his computer and look at porn.

Instead, he makes a split-second decision to do his Bible study on purity. While sitting on his bed, Joseph begins reading on his computer the biblical account of Jesus encountering the Samaritan woman (Photine) at the well in John 4. The study lesson includes a review of the previous one about Jeremiah 2 regarding the people of God forsaking the fountain of living water. The study then asks Joseph to be on the lookout for how the Jeremiah 2 passage relates to Jesus encountering the woman at the well in John 4.

Joseph suddenly finds himself engrossed in the interaction between Jesus and the Samaritan woman. The Word of God comes alive to him in that moment. It's as if the words are leaping off the page at him. He begins seeing the parallels between the broken cisterns in Jeremiah 2 and his porn addiction. He perceives how these parallels relate to Photine's idolatry of romantic relationships with men when Jesus skillfully and perceptively tells her to go call her husband in John 4:16.

Joseph understands how Photine's thirst was never quenched and how she would always have to return to the well because of this thirst. But Jesus was not speaking to her of physical water.

So, Joseph is reading this dialogue on his computer, the instrument he has used countless times to look at porn, masturbate, and fantasize over other people's daughters for his own pleasure. And suddenly the 60-watt single light bulb in his room seems to give off a deeper warmth and a brighter light. To Joseph in this moment, the room seems to become inundated with a fog of light.

He feels in the midst of this bright fog the touch of God on his inner person, not just his mind or his emotions, but in his very essence. Jesus comes and touches his mind and emotions and his very sense of who he is. It's as if the outstretched fingers of Christ are reaching out and tapping on Joseph's soul.

And he sees who Jesus truly is in this moment. Joseph feels as though he is like the Samaritan woman encountering Jesus for the very first time. The veil over his soul is lifted, and he then comprehends that Jesus has come to smash all his broken cisterns. Jesus has come to be, for Joseph, the living water we were all created to drink. There in his room, he understands that Jesus came to free him from the idols of his sin and brokenness, his profound emptiness.

Through the Scripture, Joseph senses Jesus speaking to his spirit, "Every time you use pornography you become self-centered and broken and afraid to be found out for who you really are. I died for that and there's no reason for you to drink this empty water anymore."

The Lord begins rearranging the desires of Joseph's heart and brings to him an understanding of who he truly is in Christ. It's as if the full weight of God and His love for him in Jesus breaks through and envelops him as he sits on his bed with his laptop open in front of him.

Jesus comes and reveals Himself to Joseph in the midst of his idolatry, brokenness, sexual perversion, self-loathing, emptiness, and feelings of worthlessness. Jesus unveils to him, in this moment, His offer of living water. This offer is purely based on Christ's desire to redeem and love him. Jesus does not rescind His offer even though He intimately knows how Joseph has been perpetually denying God His rightful place in his life through his addiction to pornography.

The gospel dawns on him like a sunrise; this good news of Jesus having and being the living water for him even though he has continually sought soul-satisfaction from other wells.

In this moment, Jesus freely offers Himself to Joseph. He says yes. His soul drinks the living water of Christ.

Joseph instantly feels an unexplainable physical and internal peace he has never experienced before. He weeps with joy, folds up his computer, and falls backward into his bed. He falls asleep in total peace.

He wakes up the next morning a new person. The insecurities and pain that have driven him for years are replaced, not just taken away. They have been replaced with a hunger for Jesus and an inexpressible joy over the gift he has in Jesus. He walks out the front door of his apartment and breathes in deeply the slightly cool, crisp air of the pre-autumnal morning. He looks out over the Grove campgrounds and thinks about the experience he had with Jesus last night. A wide smile breaks out over his face as he considers the gift he has in Christ.

This gift is like a never-ending source of treasure, a never-ending well from which to draw living water. He realizes how Jesus used this verse about living water to totally transform him. Now, he wants to know Jesus and share Him with others.

His motivations are different as well. He is motivated to spread the fame of Jesus for His glory. To this day, Joseph remains the most eager evangelist for Jesus that I have ever known this side of heaven. The taste of Christ's living water is so delightful to him that he cannot restrain himself from telling nearly everyone he meets about Jesus.

The above experience happened to Joseph when he was 19 years old, about 15 years ago as of this writing. Even to this very day, he has no desire for pornography. Jesus delivered him from this addiction and gave him victory. All the glory belongs to Jesus for this victory. The reason Joseph has victory is because Jesus came into his life and healed the very root of his problem and his behavior. The solution for other people is to let Jesus come in and touch the root of the pain and the addiction.

Jesus doesn't just want to keep you from pornography or drinking too much or lying habitually—He wants you to be restored to your source of life—your true identity in Christ. And then all of the outside behaviors will become transformed after Jesus transforms your inner person. How can we view our sexuality from the lens of the gospel? We must look to Jesus, and only when we look to Jesus will our sexuality become complete and healthy and holy.

Jesus must become your living water. He is the only well we can draw from to quench our thirsty souls. What well are you drawing from?

Photine tries to digest the words she has just heard, "I who speak to you am *He*." She can't believe her ears. In a moment, the man before her becomes much more than a prophet who is supernaturally perceptive of her broken romantic life. Realization dawns on her thirsty soul. This man, called Jesus, is the Messiah she has always been waiting for.

"So the woman left her waterpot, and went into the city and said to the men, 'Come see a man who told me all the things that I *have* done; this is not the Christ, is it?' They went out of the city, and were coming to Him" (John 4:28, 29).

The Samaritan woman received the living water of Jesus that day and her life was forever changed. She saw her life through the lens of the gospel. Her life became infused with a new purpose: to tell everyone about Jesus. He is the living water. He has the living water.

Jesus lovingly exposed her sin and brokenness so He could make her whole again. Beautifully laid bare before the Author of life, she found freedom from her shameful past. No longer would she have to hide in shame at the noon hour to draw water. The Messiah had freed her from shame and became for her the only man who could truly satisfy her thirsty soul.

Her response is appropriate as she declares, "Come, see a man who told me all the things that I *have* done" (John 4:29).

And so, I urge you: Come, see this man who knows all you have ever done. He still graciously offers you His living water. Will you drink from Him?

12

Same-Sex Attraction

His name is Ryan.

He grew up in a small town as an only child to young parents. His family's faith background had traditionally been Catholic, but through a series of events Ryan and his mom began attending a Baptist church when he was 7 years-old. It was at this church that he heard the gospel clearly for the first time and realized his need for a Savior. So, he trusted in Jesus for salvation and was baptized at 9 years-old. To Ryan, following Christ was the most logical course of action to take. And so, he began his relationship with Jesus.

Fast forward to late middle school. Ryan continued to grow in his love for Jesus while still attending the Baptist church. He was active in his youth group and increased in his knowledge of God and the Scriptures. He was having a very typical pre-teen American church, youth group experience. It was during this time that Ryan began spending time with one of the boys who lived down the street from him. He began to notice feelings of physical attraction for this boy. And so, Ryan's same-sex attraction presented itself at this time.

But before these feelings became explicitly sexual, there were other more subtle ways in which the stage of pre-pubescence revealed how he could naturally be emotionally drawn or intrigued by certain kinds of men for one reason or another. He just wanted to be close to these men and be noticed by them. He longed for a sort of non-sexual intimacy with certain men. But of course, at this age in late middle school he would not have been able to articulate any of these feelings or desires.

When Ryan reached his early teens and started having sexual feelings, he didn't realize that the Bible even had anything to say about homosexuality.

He had a rudimentary understanding of the subject on a cultural level from television shows where guys would be into other guys, and he knew the word for this was "gay."

His feelings were unchosen. He wasn't completely clueless, but nevertheless his same-sex attractions made him anxious and confused. He knew that in the world's eyes he would be considered gay. He didn't understand why or how this was happening to him. He only knew that it *was* happening.

And every year, these feelings grew stronger and more apparent.

⁂

It's the summer after eighth grade for Ryan. The excitement of spending the night away from home for a full week, flutters inside him. He's going to summer youth camp! For the next several days, he enjoys a typical church camp format: fun activities during the day, Bible studies, and an engaging message in the evening. Every night they would have a campfire gathering time, not around an actual campfire, but you get the picture.

On the third night, Ryan's youth pastor Carl calls for the attention of the youth group. Fireflies light up the night air. It's a mildly warm Texas evening. The campers stand gathered around, exhausted from the day's athletics and games. Carl gives about a 15-minute sermon. Offhandedly, he mentions the topic of homosexuality.

At this, Ryan perks up even more. He fixes his gaze on Carl. *What will he say about this issue? I've never heard anyone talk about it before in church.* And suddenly, he receives the shocking news. Carl references the biblical view of homosexuality as being sinful. Ryan grapples with this news. He doesn't hear another word of the sermon that night.

Fear and confusion grip him in this moment. He's still trying to understand his same-sex attraction. But one thing he knows for certain—he did not choose to have this attraction. He has no control over it. The words just spoken by Carl become a heavy burden on Ryan's chest. He's frightened. He's frightened because his attraction to other guys is not something he can switch off like a light and be done with it.

Wow, I never knew God had a stance on this. Where do I go from here?

This would become the question that would hound him for years to come.

⁂

After returning home from camp Ryan began a journey. He decided that he would try to partition these feelings off from the rest of himself and shut them away . . . wall them off and ignore their existence. And then he would get on with the rest of his life.

He would continue to pursue God, be an active member of his youth group, and perform well academically to work towards college. Ryan resolved to tell no one about his same-sex attraction. He secretly just hoped that it would go away on its own. This struggle was not something he felt comfortable sharing with anyone else. He had a confident suspicion that he would be flat-out condemned for having such a struggle. If he told his parents, would they still love him? And so, he kept this whole thing in the dark. No one needed to know, or so he thought at the time.

Ryan's struggle at this time was much deeper than a sexual struggle. His feelings were not merely about physical attraction to other guys. Yes, of course, this is the most apparent aspect of same-sex attraction, or any attraction for that matter. But the sexual attraction to other guys was just the tip of the iceberg for Ryan. This is the part a person feels the strongest, but there's so much more to it. Under the surface, there were longings and attractions that were not sexual in nature but were something else altogether. Behind the sexual urges were emotional longings for intimacy and connection with other guys in a non-sexual way.

And whenever Ryan experienced a moment of connection with another guy on an emotional level and felt truly accepted, appreciated, and loved he felt as though a deep emptiness within him was being filled. This was and continues to be just as strong of an element as the sexual attractions themselves.

Fast forward now to Ryan's late teenage years. He embarked on a period of learning and intellectual exploration where he began dismantling the wall that had partitioned off his same-sex attraction from the rest of his life. He realized at this point that he could not ignore its reality any longer. He had to deal with it. This was essential.

He didn't know how to articulate any of this at the time, but Jesus graciously took the first step for Ryan in this process. He put him in the path of a man named Neil Turner who was a visiting speaker at an event for Ryan's youth group.

One summer during late high school, his church put on a youth revival, and Ryan decided to have a hand in organizing the event. The organizing committee had to choose the guest speaker. Some of the youth had previously encountered this guy named Neil Turner at a different event, and they said they really liked him. So, the committee elected to have Neil come and speak at the revival. During the event, Ryan also helped with vocals during worship and became the emcee to announce Neil each night of the revival.

Neil observed Ryan throughout the event as he carried out his different organizing and leadership roles.

It's the last night of the revival. Neil has just finished delivering a very engaging and edgy message. Ryan looks out across the youth group and sees that the message has resonated strongly amongst his peers. The excitement of the afterglow rings through the air of the youth gym turned sanctuary where the revival has been taking place these last four evenings. And then something happens that completely catches Ryan off guard.

Neil approaches him when no one else is around. The background music plays softly overhead through the sound system.

He lowers his voice slightly and then point blankly tells Ryan, "I know what you're going through. I know what you're struggling with, Ryan. And I want you to know that God sees you, and it's possible for you to change. I know many people who have. If you want, I can connect you with a friend of mine named Pierce Hawkins who has a similar testimony to tell you."

Now, the interesting thing about this exchange was that Ryan never felt shame regarding his same-sex attraction being exposed by Neil. He thought it was very odd that he was able to tell so easily. He had never told a soul about this struggle, and here Neil was exposing the truth and confronting him very forthrightly. To this day, how Neil knew remains a mystery, but Ryan knows that Jesus was at work in all of this.

This conversation started him down a path. The rumor that change was possible oriented Ryan's mindset to the mode of, "Okay this can be fixed if I do the right things and follow the right process."

Hope filled his soul. *Other Christians deal with this and get freedom from it. Apparently, that's possible*, he thought to himself. He had hope for the first time that he could be rid of this thing.

Ryan had a little more correspondence with Neil, but mostly communication about his same-sex attraction switched over to Pierce. He would talk on the phone with him periodically, about once a month. Now this was before cell phones existed, and Pierce would call Ryan on his home phone. There was a great fear that his mom or dad would answer the phone leading to Ryan being outed. But this never happened. Ryan still kept his secret locked up between him and Neil and Pierce.

Pierce would ask questions like, "What are you experiencing and what kind of guys are you attracted to? When do the attractions come on? What do you do in response?" And then he would counsel Ryan to take his struggle to the Lord. But more than anything, Pierce was a friend to him and someone to talk to about this deep struggle. This went on for the next year or so until Pierce and Neil began trying to convince Ryan to share his struggle with someone more locally. Ryan was highly resistant to this recommendation. But finally, they persuaded him to share this with his youth pastor, Carl. Ryan couldn't muster up enough courage to do this himself, so Neil asked Ryan if it would be okay if he broke the news to Carl. Ryan agreed.

When the outing was done, Ryan began walking through his struggle with his youth pastor. Now, Carl never shamed Ryan for having such a struggle, but both of them didn't really know where to go from there. Even still, having someone close by who knew his secret was helpful. They went through a book called *Desires in Conflict* by Joe Dallas. As you might imagine, the book speaks of how to deal with the reality of your flesh when its urges are contrary to God's will and how to integrate this conflict with your desire to love and obey God.

This book was helpful for Ryan because it equipped him to develop a framework for thinking about his same-sex attraction. He was now learning how to process his struggle in a way that reintegrated this part of himself with the rest of himself. The partitioning wall within him came tumbling down as he realized this struggle had to be a part of his walk with Jesus, by necessity.

∙⋏∙

Ryan graduated from high school and left home to attend college at Texas A&M University. He was thrilled to go off to college because he knew he could immerse himself in a thriving Christian community there. He was excited to make progress in the fight against his same-sex attraction, but more generally the prospect of making new friends, having independence, and getting out of his small town seemed especially appealing to him.

When he got to A&M, he found a church and quickly joined the Baptist Student Ministry (BSM) on campus because he grew up Baptist, and this group seemed like a logical choice. Unlike his youth group experience, this was the first time he was surrounded by numerous peers who loved Jesus and wanted to follow Him.

And so, he thought in the back of his mind, *I'm going to be surrounded by Christ followers and make great progress against my same-sex attraction.*

This did not happen.

Although Ryan had great Christian community and growth in Christ in other ways, this did not ensure any lessening of his same-sex attraction. In fact, his attractions became even more entrenched. He discovered porn at this point and found himself becoming even more entangled in his struggle. It became the thorn in the flesh of which he could not rid himself.

At the same time, he still very much retained the mindset that changing his sexual orientation was possible. Alone in his room one night after losing another battle with pornography, discouragement descended upon him. He thought, *if I can just pursue God with diligence and sincerity . . . if I can just pursue holiness this would all go away.* He clung to the hope that he could change his desires and preferences. But over time, with defeat following defeat in this arena Ryan began to experience a deep abiding shame and disillusionment.

Okay, Lord, I'm trying to do all the right things, and I'm growing in Christ in other ways. But this struggle is not changing or going away.

So, because he was giving into porn and growing tired of policing his thoughts and taking every thought captive to obey Christ, he was overcome with this shame and felt like he was sabotaging himself. *I can't sustain the degree of self-control required to overcome this thing. If I was really a good Christian and pursuing Christ the right way, I would win this fight.*

During this season of life, Ryan found himself putting excessive emphasis on changing his sexual orientation and trying to make his attractions go away. But this mindset proved to be detrimental and harmful to him. He found himself steeped in a somewhat legalistic Christian culture that stressed over-coming homosexuality to become straight. This created a crushing pressure and resultant shame when he wasn't able to live up to the church's ideal way of life.

The Christian community around Ryan wanted to address his struggle from a purely spiritual perspective and counseled him to dedicate himself more fully to the spiritual disciplines of prayer and Bible study and discipleship. His church figured this would cure him of his attractions, but this unidimensional approach proved ineffectual for Ryan. This approach could never fulfill his sexual desires and completely ignored the deeper longings he had for non-sexual intimacy and emotional connection with other men in the church.

He quickly realized that many Christians did not comprehend the deeply complex and multidimensional aspects of his same-sex attraction. His problem was and continues to be not *merely* spiritual and sexual. On the other hand, from a secular point of view, his attractional pattern was and is not *merely* biological either. Ryan found himself grappling with a multifaceted problem that was spiritual, emotional, sexual, psychosocial, and biological in nature. And his church, although well-meaning, was being reductionistic and failed to see the greater depth of the issue at hand.

So, Ryan felt that he had to integrate these aspects himself. He could see very clearly how the church and his Christian community could integrate these aspects quite easily to meet these needs, but there was no one thinking about this struggle in an integrative way at his specific church. This was until his pastor read a book called *Loving Homosexuals as Jesus Would* by Chad Thompson. In this book, Thompson demonstrates a deeper understanding of same-sex attraction and begins integrating the different components that Ryan so desperately wanted his church to integrate. But you don't have to look further than the Bible to see how amazing Jesus is at integrating His approach to redeem the whole person:

> "Jesus was going throughout all Galilee, teaching in their synagogues and proclaiming the gospel of the kingdom, and healing every kind of disease and every kind of sickness among the people" (Matt. 4:23).[8]

Did you notice what Jesus does so skillfully in this text? He taught in the synagogues to address the needs of the *mind*. He proclaimed the gospel to address the needs of the *soul*. And He healed every kind of disease to address the needs of the *body*. Our Lord made us and knows that we need His holistic redemption (mind, soul, and body). We, likewise, need to address the whole person when seeking to meet the needs of others. And through this multi-dimensional approach, we can bring them to the Savior who will holistically redeem them.

Ryan had two friends named Ted and Bill he knew from the BSM. They were upperclassmen and were the first true older brother figures he had in his life. For this reason, his brotherhood with them was super nourishing to his

---

8. All Scripture used in chapter 12 are from the New American Standard Bible (NASB 1995).

soul on a deep level. He wanted desperately to tell them about his struggle, but coming out would be a big deal because he hadn't told many people yet, and the culture surrounding him was staunchly conservative.

He decided he would break the news to them at the BSM, so he scheduled a time to meet them there.

Ryan now looks at the front door of the BSM. Angst and pure nerves pulsate within him. With heart thumping rapidly in his chest, he grabs the door handle and pulls. He notices his hand slightly shakes as a he reaches for the handle. Upon entering he goes down the hall and turns left to climb the stairs to the upstairs lounge where students routinely meet and hang out. Several brown couches, a coffee table, and chairs are arranged in the center of the room. Nervously, Ryan takes a seat opposite to where Ted and Bill are seated on the couch.

Ryan begins talking with them and the flow of his conversation is circular, not at all to the point. While trying to delay the coming out moment further, the truth leaps out of his mouth.

"Guys, I'm gay," he blurts out. He quickly adds, "But I don't really wanna be. And I don't feel like God made me this way."

Nerves overtake Ryan at this point, so he doesn't give them time to respond. He stands up abruptly from his chair.

"I think I'm going to go throw up and I'd like to leave now."

And with that, Ryan quickly speed-walks out of the room and takes the steps two at a time to expedite his escape back to his dorm room. His bottled-up adrenaline and nervous energy propel him rapidly away from Ted and Bill.

Back at the lounge, they look at each other thunderstruck by what has just occurred.

"Should we go after him? I think we should," Ted suggests.

"No, let's give him some space and time to decompress," Bill advises.

All three of them were able to meet up eventually and talk more about Ryan's situation. They were very compassionate toward him. This response helped him quite a bit. It was nice to have Christian brothers who knew about his struggle, even if they weren't well-equipped to help him fight it.

Along with these two friends, the director of the BSM was also aware of Ryan's same-sex attraction. The director connected Ryan with a guy involved in an ex-gay ministry based out of Houston.

Ryan began to get involved in different ex-gay ministries at this time. He eventually started attending a group in Arlington. The camaraderie at the support group was helpful for Ryan to see that there were indeed other people walking through the same issue as him. It was nice to be connected with other believers who knew what he was feeling and going through. Changing to straight was talked about in the ex-gay ministry, but the main focus was on discipleship in following Jesus.

However, there were certain needs Ryan yearned to have met that could simply not be fulfilled by his comrades in arms at the ex-gay ministries. The intimate, non-sexual connection with straight guys that he longed for was not to be found in these support groups. The groups were filled with other brothers and sisters like him, all fighting against same-sex attraction.

During this time, Ryan would look at certain men in his church and long for friendship with them and to be noticed by them. He would go to his ex-gay group in Arlington, sit in a circle with the other strugglers, and listen to their problems all the while thinking to himself, *I wish the men in my church back home would see me and know me and walk alongside me in this struggle.* This remained a deep heartfelt need and desire. So, the ex-gay camaraderie was helpful to a certain extent but not entirely what he needed.

He quickly realized that he was ill-equipped to know how to convey his ongoing experience with other Christian brothers and sisters in a way that would help them understand the reality and complexity of his struggle. He feared being misunderstood. He feared his struggle would be misinterpreted and then be sorted into a pre-conceived category that is typical for more common temptations in the church. In other words, Ryan's church didn't know or understand people with same-sex attraction, and consequently, his needs would go unmet and meaningful help was not offered.

To make matters worse, Ryan did not have the nuance of vocabulary needed to aptly express his struggle in a way that his church listener could understand and then offer help accordingly. And we as the church listener need to slow down in our hectic schedules, take time to listen carefully, and then ask follow-up questions as needed to discern what redemptive help can be offered in the love of Jesus.

Compounding his lack of ability to express himself, Ryan also felt, and to some extent continues to feel, deep shame surrounding being candid about the needs a same-sex attracted celibate person has. This remains a huge obstacle for him as he feels his emotional, physical, and spiritual needs are being starved. In other words, the person struggling with same-sex attraction may not connect well with the typical discipleship, community, and accountability group models offered at churches because they have different needs.

But how can we look at this difficult situation through the lens of the gospel?

The Concept of Redemptive Experiences

Let's look at a real-life scenario where Ryan experienced shame, and then let's reimagine the scenario through the concept of redemptive experiences.

Near the end of college, a friend asked Ryan to be a groomsman at his wedding, and this of course included an invitation to his bachelor party. Ryan had a good relationship with the groom but was unfamiliar with the other groomsmen, who were your stereotypical dudes and bros. Ryan felt like a bit of an alien around the others.

At one point in the weekend, the guys decided to play a pickup football game in the backyard of the house where they were all staying. Ryan could simply not go there. He's never been very athletic, and to join in the game would have been an embarrassment to him.

He now sits on the edge of the patio watching the other groomsman hoot and holler as they vigorously play the pickup football game together. It's all sweat and competition. They seem to be having a blast running up and down the yard trying to advance the ball to the makeshift end-zone.

What appears to be a boisterous time of joy for the other men is deeply shaming for Ryan. He sits there watching them play and pat each other on the back. He forces a smile, but it's far from genuine. He shamefully looks down at the green grass in front of him. This becomes a moment of deep disconnection for him. He cannot join them. He's not able to perform or participate. A feeling of being left out grips him.

It's important to note here that a lot of straight people encounter situations where they feel left out and feel they cannot perform amongst their peers. But this can happen for guys struggling with same-sex attraction *in conjunction* with a deep sense of deficit in connection and attachment to other men. Moreover, episodes like the one just described are not everyone's experience who struggles with same-sex attraction.

But the reality remains that such disconnection and shame may very well be the experience of some. This reality is like the valley of Achor (literally "valley of Trouble") mentioned in Hosea 2. Nonetheless, the concept of redemptive experiences takes a "valley of Achor" moment and turns it into "a door of hope."

Look at Hosea 2:14, 15:

> "Therefore, behold, I will allure her,
> Bring her into the wilderness
> And speak kindly to her.
> Then I will give her her vineyards from there,
> And the valley of Achor as a door of hope.
> And she will sing there as in the days of her youth,
> As in the day when she came up from the land of Egypt."

In context, this verse refers to the people of Israel being pursued or "allure[d]" by the Lord after they have willfully committed spiritual adultery against Him. God is pictured here as the tender Husband, and Israel is His unfaithful wife. He loves her too much to see His bride forsake Him and "follow her lovers, so that she forgot Me" (Hosea 2:13). Our God is so awesome that He pursues His people relentlessly. He will woo her and "speak kindly to her" (verse 14). And "the valley of Achor" will become "as a door of hope" (verse 15).

This is exactly what is meant by the concept of redemptive experiences. Allow me to explain.

Let's reimagine the scene where Ryan is sitting on the patio sidelines watching the other groomsman emotionally connect over a pickup game of football. Now, what if one of the groomsmen, or the groom himself, came out of the game and sacrificed his desire to compete just to be a brother to Ryan at this moment? What if he knew Ryan well enough that he could discern the fake smile plastered on his face? What if he noticed that Ryan felt left out and intuited that this was a moment of deep shame and disconnection for him? What if he walked on over and sat down next to Ryan on the patio and opened a door of hope through a redemptive experience of true brotherhood?

The very moment of Ryan's shame could become the occasion for a Christ-centered brother to address the issue at hand and engage with him in a restorative godly way.

The door of hope can only be opened if the needs of our same-sex attracted brothers and sisters are known to us. *But first*, we must see through the gospel lens that Jesus Himself is the door of hope (see John 10:7 & Acts 14:27).

Jesus is the only door or entrance we must walk through to experience true redemption from shame. We must remember how Jesus came to us, allured us when we were in our wilderness of sin, and covered all of our shame with His own precious blood through His death on the cross. Brother or sister in Christ, do you remember that *all* your sin has been atoned for and *all* your shame has been covered *all* because of *Jesus*?

We can then be empowered to see the needs of our struggling brothers and sisters through the eyes and heart of Christ. This will tenderize our hearts, lift our gaze off ourselves, and galvanize us into action to come alongside the shamed and hurting. Then, and only then, may we be able to palpably extend the love and compassion of Jesus Christ in our brother or sister's moment of need.

Ryan's Present-Day Situation

To this very day, Ryan still struggles with same-sex attraction. The temptation is strong to give up this fight. Every time he witnesses a gay couple enjoying an emotional connection with one another he feels a magnetic pull and longing in his heart for just such a connection. But it is Ryan's conviction that same-sex romantic relationships are not God's design for His people, according to Scripture. He has decided to live a celibate life and not indulge his sexual desires. He believes this is what Jesus wants for him, and he trusts that Jesus knows better than he does regarding what's best for him. He believes this will bring God the most glory.

Ryan wants to be with Jesus when he dies, and if this is the narrow path God has laid out for him to tread then it will all be worth it. Jesus is worth it. Intimacy with Jesus is far better than any same-sex romantic relationship he could have.

Ryan wants to live a life of faithfulness to his Lord and Savior. He is able to view his situation through the lens of the gospel every time he sees and believes that Jesus is better. Jesus is worth every moment of his struggle against same-sex attraction.

The most powerful thing that helps Ryan stay in this frame of mind is the body of Christ, the church. Ryan is most safeguarded when he is deeply embedded in his church community. When she, the church, is at her best she is helpful, loving, caring, biblically truthful, and able to offer compassionate accountability.

James 2:15–17 indirectly speaks to this.

"If a brother or sister is without clothing and in need of daily food, and one of you says to them, 'Go in peace, be warmed and be filled,' and yet you do not give them what is necessary for their body, what use is that? Even so, faith, if it has no works, is dead, being by itself."

The pertinent question the church today must answer is this: if our brothers or sisters struggling with same-sex attraction are poorly clothed with intimacy, how can we as the church clothe them with Christ's affectionate embrace of brotherly love and compassion?

Today as a man trying to remain faithful to Christ and live in the church, the greatest hardship for Ryan is helping other followers of Jesus to understand the seriousness and uniqueness of living with same-sex attraction and fighting against it. What we are talking about here is Ryan's struggle to find and develop a deep brotherhood. This issue is best addressed within the context of true siblinghood in the church. Ryan needs brothers in the church who are willing to go deep with him, who aren't freaked out by the needs he has, and who are willing to meet him in this space of struggle, and walk alongside him to care for him as he moves forward. Paul speaks of this kind of brotherhood in Rom. 12:10, 11:

"Be devoted to one another in brotherly love; give preference to one another in honor; not lagging behind in diligence, fervent in spirit, serving the Lord;"

Up to this point, we have spoken primarily of addressing same-sex attraction in the church from the horizontal perspective of "brotherly love," but notice how Rom. 12:11 ends with the vertically oriented phrase, "serving the Lord." We should take note that the horizontal and vertical aspects of Christian living are deeply interdependent and interconnected.

In other words, Ryan's relationship with Jesus and enjoyment of Him is optimally enhanced and strengthened if he has deep Christ-centered brotherhood and community in his life. The converse is also true. Ryan's relationships with other brothers and sisters in the church are so much richer and deeper if he is seeking Jesus and enjoying Him consistently. Now, what do we mean by seeking Jesus and enjoying Him consistently?

The Vertical Aspect for Ryan

Jesus has spoken Ps. 34:8 very tenderly over Ryan during these years of struggle with same-sex attraction. The verse says this:

> "O taste and see that the Lord is good; How blessed is the man who takes refuge in Him!"

Tasting and seeing? Clearly, the psalmist is employing poetic language to urge his fellow worshipers to engage with God on a sensory level. But this is not mere poetry to Ryan. Jesus has mercifully given Ryan's soul insight into the pure enjoyment offered to us in the goodness of God. The Lord is so good, and His presence is so sweet to Ryan. And this is why Ps. 16:11 also resonates so profoundly with him:

> "You will make known to me the path of life; In Your presence is fullness of joy; In Your right hand there are pleasures forever."

The fullness of joy in the Lord's presence? Pleasures in His right hand forever? For many people, these realities remain very abstract throughout their Christian lives, but for Ryan, the enjoyment of God's sweet presence became very concrete early on in his relationship with Jesus.

In his teenage years and into college, he recognized very clearly, he had deeper longings for male intimacy, but he had no means or knowledge of how to access such intimacy. He understands now that these longings are the very roots of his same-sex attraction. So, as he was discipled in the Scriptures, he was mercifully introduced to the truth that *Jesus* was the answer to his deepest desires. The offer of living water Jesus makes to the Samaritan woman in John 4 plucked a string that reverberated and resonated in Ryan's soul. His response was, "Okay Jesus, You say that You are the living water—and that if I drink of You I won't thirst anymore—I truly need Your living water because I have these unanswered yearnings." And Jesus has been faithful to give His living water to Ryan time and time again.

Ryan has the power to say no to his flesh when he cultivates a deep satisfaction in Christ. As John Piper has famously coined, "God is most glorified in us when we are most satisfied in Him."[9] No Christian can persevere through this kind of struggle without being satisfied by the living water only Jesus offers to us.

෴

I would like to conclude this chapter by sharing with you a personal testimony of my own to illustrate how this struggle impacts people differently. Ryan's story echoes similarities of many other people who have same-sex attraction. But it's important to note that every story is unique, and the issues Ryan faces may look different than another person who has the same exact struggle. In other words, the roots and effects of same-sex attraction impact people in many different ways. This is probably because this issue is so multifaceted. As has been reiterated throughout Ryan's narrative, this struggle is not merely sexual in nature.

Therefore, I would like to give you one more brief narrative before closing this chapter so you can see the similarities and differences between the story I'm about to tell you and the one you have just read.

My Story

My name is Jonathan.

I grew up in a loving Christian home. My mom and dad showered me with love and affirmation. I look back on my childhood and I'm so thankful to the Lord for how He blessed me with such a rich upbringing filled with the encouragement and love of Jesus Christ.

Jesus captured my heart at a young age. I told my dad on numerous occasions that I wanted to be saved, but my dad's reply was always, "Son, you first have to tell me what it means to be lost?" In other words, my dad pointed out to me that before I could have Jesus as my Savior, I needed to understand the reality of my sin against God. I needed to understand my lostness and need for a Savior.

---

9. Piper, J. (2008, November 5). God is Most Glorified. Desiringgod.Org. https://www .desiringgod.org/interviews/how-is-the-statement-god-is-most-glorified-in-us-when-we-are -most-satisfied-in-him-true-for-those-who-wont-be-saved

When I was 8 years old, on July 23, 1998, I remember explaining to my dad that I needed Jesus to save me from sins, and so he took me through several passages in Scripture to cement the fact of my need for Jesus as Lord and Savior. I believed the Scriptures, and Jesus came into my life that night and forgave me of all my sins. And though I would doubt the authenticity of this conversion later, I am fully convinced that Jesus became the Hero of my story that night.[10] Afterward, I remember running through the halls of our 2nd-floor apartment just bursting with joy and elation for the salvation I had just received through Christ. Jesus is so, so good! I remember beaming with joy and telling my dad, "Dad, this is the greatest day of my life!"

Fast forward with me now to 11th grade, my junior year of high school. Suddenly, I began to have these thoughts and feelings that scared me.

I began to have same-sex attraction.

Whenever I would have an impure thought about another guy, the thought would weigh on my soul, and I could not help but feel trapped inside my own body. I was thinking to myself, *I don't want to keep having these thoughts, what should I do?* So, I tried suppressing these sexual thoughts and found my attempts to be utterly futile. Like a relentless bird that kept landing on the same branch, these thoughts continued flitting into my mind. I feared that they would build a nest one day and stay for good.

I had to do something. I had to tell someone.

At age 16, I now stand in my bedroom with a cell phone in hand. For the past hour or so I have been feeling angst weigh upon my soul over a sexual thought I had recently about another guy. I look out through the window over the balcony where I can see the waters of Lake Windcrest move rhythmically with the impulses of the wind.

I have to do this. I have to tell him. I walk a few nervous steps into my room, my bed alongside me. I look down at my phone and press the favorites icon. I scroll to the contact entitled "Dad." With a trembling finger, I press his name and the dialing sound begins ringing. My arm trembles slightly as I hold the phone up to my ear. *I've got to tell him. I'll go crazy about this if I don't.*

He answers on the third ring.

"Hey, son! How you doing?"

---

10. Vanderstelt J. (2017), *Gospel Fluency, Crossway,* p.157. A special thanks to Jeff for seeing Acts 17:28 as Jesus being the hero of our stories, as used in other pages of this book.

"I'm okay, Pops. I just need to tell you about a lustful thought I've been having recently."

I get straight to the point. No preamble. I question how long my courage will last. *I've got to tell him. I've got to tell him.*

"Who's the girl?" my dad asks directly but lightheartedly.

"Actually, it's about a guy."

There's a pause. A pause that feels like an eternity to me. I can feel the tension building as the pause tarries on. In actuality, this pause is only for a brief moment. The lighthearted air of the conversation on his side of the phone has dissolved. *How is this man who raised me, my dad, going to respond to his son having homosexual thoughts? What will he say?*

I do not recall his exact response at this moment. However, I do remember feeling a huge weight on my soul evaporating as I stood in my room talking with my dad that day on the phone. This is because I never felt judged or shamed or condemned during this phone call, or during the numerous conversations that would follow as a result.

My dad loved me even more relentlessly than the relentless pestering nature of my same-sex attraction. From that moment forward, I often went to my dad to unburden my soul of the feelings and thoughts I continued to have throughout high school and into college. Every time I went to him, his counsel was the same.

He would say, "So what was your response when you had that thought? Did you use this struggle as a springboard to take you into the presence of Jesus?"

His focus was *never*, "Jonathan, you better not turn out gay. You better become straight." He never even told me that I had to change my attraction. His focus was always encouraging me to use my same-sex attraction as a means to bring me into the presence of God. He would often say, "Have you turned it over to the Lord? Have you brought these thoughts to the feet of Jesus?"

And I'm eternally grateful for this counsel I received from my dad. Jesus is so good!

He didn't know how to articulate this at the time, but my dad, in essence, was saying Jesus is better. The heart of Jesus is for the same-sex attracted struggler to come into His presence . . . to come to Him and find rest for his or her soul. Jesus makes this promise burn indelibly bright as a beacon of hope in Matt. 11:28, 29.

"Come to Me, all who are weary and heavy-laden, and I will give you rest. Take My yoke upon you and learn from Me, for I am gentle and humble in heart, and YOU WILL FIND REST FOR YOUR SOULS."

In his book, *Gentle and Lowly*, Dane Ortlund beautifully pens the following about the above verses.

"But all Christian toil flows from fellowship with a living Christ whose transcending, defining reality is: gentle and lowly. He astounds and sustains us with his endless kindness. Only as we walk ever deeper into this tender kindness can we live the Christian life as the New Testament calls us to."[11]

My dad and I had numerous conversations after this regarding my same-sex attraction. But what he probably didn't realize at the time was how much he embodied for me the very heart of Christ . . . the gentleness and lowliness of Jesus . . . the accessibility and approachability of Christ. If Jesus had not given me the dad I have, I'm not sure where I would have ended up.

Did my struggle with same-sex attraction go away the first time (or the hundredth time) I took it to Jesus in prayer? A thousand times no. Definitely not. But every time I came to Christ and laid these thoughts at His feet, my angst over them would abate. Jesus has been so, so gentle and kind to me. He has proven how gentle and lowly His heart is toward me time and time again.

The verses I clung to during this period of great struggle were 2 Cor. 12:7–9:

"Because of the surpassing greatness of the revelations, for this reason, to keep me from exalting myself, there was given me a thorn in the flesh, a messenger of Satan to torment me—to keep me from exalting myself! Concerning this I implored the Lord three times that it might leave me. And He has said to me, 'My grace is sufficient for you, for power is perfected in weakness.' Most gladly, therefore, I will rather boast about my weaknesses, so that the power of Christ may dwell in me."

My same-sex attraction was a continual thorn in my side, but every time I came to Jesus with my struggle His gentle and lowly heart was there for me. Now, I'm not saying I had some amazing spiritual experience every time I prayed, but I know that He was there for me every time. And I found the

---

11. Ortlund D., 2022, *Gentle and Lowly: The Heart of Christ for the Sinners and Sufferers* (Wheaton, IL: Crossway), p.22.

evidence for this in 2 Cor. 12:9 where Jesus told me in red letters, as He did to the Apostle Paul, "My grace is sufficient for you, for power is perfected in weakness."

What is so striking about this verse is that Jesus makes no promise to Paul, or any of the rest of us, that He will remove our thorns in the flesh. This may seem oddly perplexing to many, but how else would we be encouraged to continually come to Him for His power to be perfected in our weakness? This is the "Christian toil" Ortlund refers to as referenced above.

But I want you to know that Jesus is faithful and extremely gracious. He has been so gracious to me. My desires and thoughts *did* change over time. I would say my 5-to-6-year struggle with same-sex attraction faded away around my senior year of college. I cannot explain how or exactly when, but it did. Jesus is the Hero of my story, and He still would be the Hero if I were to have this struggle for the rest of my life. He has blessed me with a beautiful wife who loves Him, along with three children (you've already read in chapter 6 about the night I met my wife, Kelley).

Now, I want to make this abundantly clear though: everyone's experience with same-sex attraction is vastly diverse, and I want to stress that changing your sexual orientation is not the ultimate goal. Jesus is the ultimate goal. Intimacy with Him is better than being heterosexual! He is eternally better than anything we can strive for in this life.

As you can see, Ryan and I have very different narratives to share. His same-sex attraction did not fade but persists to this day. He continues to honor Christ by leading a celibate life devoted to Jesus. As brothers who have borne the weight of this struggle, Ryan and I both realize that Jesus is far more beautiful, and intimacy with Him is far better than anything offered on this earth.

Gospel Takeaways

The church has a vital role to play in bringing the gentle and lowly heart of Christ to bear on those who have same-sex attraction. This is what it means to view same-sex attraction through the gospel lens. Let us move forward with our eyes wide open to the needs around us. Let us put on the gentle and lowly heart of Christ as we foster a culture of compassionate accountability and warm acceptance for the struggling and broken in and outside of our churches.

I want to close this chapter with a challenge: the next time you're in church and you see someone sitting alone and perhaps disconnected from the rest of the body, I want to encourage you to walk over to that person, and sit next to him or her and initiate conversation. Listen well to them and let them know the love and heart of Jesus. We cannot let those on the outside looking in fall through the cracks.

But first, we must receive the warm acceptance of Jesus in our own lives. Can you feel the gentle and lowly heart of Christ beating for you? He is better. He is more beautiful. His grace is sufficient for you.

Part 5

The Gospel Lens
and Marriage / Family

*"This mystery is profound,
and I am saying that it refers to
Christ and the church"*
(EPH. 5:32).

13
Marriage

Let's continue building on our solid gospel foundation and our identity in Christ. How can we look at marriage through the gospel lens, or through the heart of Jesus? This perspective will help us realize that marriage is not about us. It's all about Jesus.

I pray that you will see through these next chapters that something much greater than your personal happiness and fulfillment is at stake in your marriage. Your witness of the very gospel message is at stake. According to Scripture, marriage is to be a real-life embodiment and display of the gospel of Jesus Christ to a dying and broken world.

In other words, if you're married, your marriage is to be a living and breathing gospel presentation. What does that mean? We will look at several different married couples and their stories to understand this. We will also interweave these narratives into a closer look at Eph. 5:25–33 to peer through the gospel lens at marriage.

Her name is Amanda.

Amanda grew up in a single-parent home. Her mom was a teen mother whose partner left shortly after Amanda's birth. Amanda also has a brother and a sister. Her mom married another man when Amanda was 12, but then got divorced five years later. Being the middle child, it was hard growing up in this environment. One of the hardest things she experienced was longing for her dad to be present, but he never was.

The final bell of the day rings throughout the halls of her elementary school. All day Amanda, at seven years old, has been thinking that her dad would come home. So she grabs her backpack from her cubby in the back of the classroom and sprints home with nervous excitement filling her. She thinks to herself, *oh I hope daddy comes home today*! But he never does. She sits there, gazing longingly for her dad as the hours pass by . . . as the sun goes down . . . as the room darkens to melancholic shades of blues and grays and blacks. As the sunlight fades from view, so do Amanda's hopes for her father's return and loving embrace.

His name is Jordan.

He grew up as an only child in a stable home with two loving parents who are still married to this day. Jordan received devoted attention, time, and resources from his mom and dad. But as far as having a personal relationship with God, Jordan knew little more than simply attending church on Sundays.

At age 18, Jordan's parents insist that he be baptized before going off to college. He does so, but not by choice. He packs up and heads to Texas A&M where he becomes involved in several different Christian organizations and meets several people devoted to following Jesus. But his involvement with these Christians is superficial. The faith he does have is solitary, and he has no true accountability to other followers of Christ at this point.

Jordan begins dating a girl, and this becomes a sinful relationship not honoring to God. He starts to feel conviction about the sinful life he is living, and Jesus begins drawing Jordan to Himself through this conviction. On the other hand, the girl he's dating drifts further from any vibrant faith, and the controversial topics of the day serve only to confuse and distract her from any pursuit of God. The differences in faith trajectory for the two of them culminate in a painful breakup.

The sunset casts a fading golden glow over the Texas A&M campus, and the sky glimmers like paint strokes in shades of gold and purple overhead as Jordan kneels in the middle of a grassy green field. A light breeze blows against his face. He's broken and yet freed at the same time. The life he has lived up to this point has been all about him . . . what he wants . . . what he thinks would be best for him.

In the quiet of the brokenness, Jordan understands that his identity has not been found in Jesus all along. Inexplicably, Jesus reveals Himself to Jordan, and sweet clarity comes upon him as he realizes that Christ must have first place in everything. He surrenders his life to Jesus anew in the holy solitude of this moment. One relationship has just been shattered for Jordan so another can become truly whole.

☙

The father Amanda always longed for never came. She never knew a constant, loving father. The male attention she lacked in her absent father turned her attention to pursuing romance. She began a relationship with a guy that became abusive and sinful. The shame she felt from this relationship was unbearable. She believed in God but her boyfriend at the time did not. During this time, Amanda became a first-grade teacher.

At age 25, she now sits in her empty classroom talking with her boyfriend on the phone. They are discussing what Amanda should do about a difficult situation with one of her fellow teachers.

"Yeah, I don't know what to do about this. I wonder what God would want me to do," Amanda muses in a pensive tone.

At the mention of "God," her boyfriend starts chuckling on the other line.

"I don't think God has anything to do with this," he replies condescendingly.

An awkward pause follows. In the next moment, something breaks through in Amanda's spirit. A wave of conviction crashes over her. She knows beyond any doubt what God is calling her to do. She must end this poisonous relationship.

And so, right then and there on the phone, and by the grace of Jesus, Amanda musters up enough courage to utter the words, "I'm sorry. I can't be with you anymore. We can no longer be together."

This last sentence comes out with a force and finality indicative of Amanda's intention to never get back with him again.

"What? Are you serious? You're breaking up with me because of God. You're pathetic," he insults scornfully.

"That's right. It's because of God. We're done. Goodbye." And Amanda hangs up.

Suddenly a weight is lifted off her chest, and she feels as though she is breathing fresh air for the first time. She puts her phone down on her desk with a trembling hand. A smile lights up her face. She whispers, "Thank you, Jesus."

☙

After college Jordan moved to San Antonio just southeast of his hometown, Boerne. He was supposed to go abroad to China for a position as an English teacher, but this ended up falling through. Instead, he took up entrepreneurial endeavors and began a day job as a financial analyst. He also started attending Mission Church at the recommendation of a staff member from a previous church he had attended. He was in a place where he was ready to pursue Jesus in a community of believers.

Amanda, having broken up with her abusive ex-boyfriend, was also ready to start seeking Jesus with other followers of Christ. She began attending a small group called Vertical, which met at Mike and Kathryn's house.

Amanda walks through the door and makes her way to the kitchen to set out the chips and salsa she's brought. The house is abuzz with about twenty people, all in their twenties and thirties. Amanda begins socializing with another girl there near the appetizers. She finds out her name is Alyssa. A handsome dark-skinned guy, who appears to be in his mid-twenties, approaches Amanda and Alyssa. He confidently introduces himself to the both of them with a firm handshake.

"Hi, I'm Jordan."

After introductions, the three of them begin conversing. At first, Amanda finds herself intimidated by Jordan's outgoing and confident personality. Another friend of hers, named Amy, comes up to her from the dining room and energetically greets her. Amy whisks Amanda away to leave Jordan and Alyssa to continue talking. A few weeks later, Jordan and Alyssa begin dating, but this relationship does not last.

After going through his breakup with Alyssa, Jordan continues to see Amanda at church and Vertical. Come July, Jordan ends up inviting Amanda to his birthday party. While at the party, Amanda catches Jordan looking her way, and she has a sneaking suspicion that he's interested in her. The two of them have only one encounter with each other at this party. Amanda tells Jordan of her upcoming mission trip to Greece to serve refugees.

A couple of days later, Amanda receives a text out of the blue from Jordan telling her that he wants to donate toward her trip. He offers to go to lunch with her "to hear more about the trip." He ends up paying for Amanda's meal as well, and still to this day Jordan denies that this was their first date.

Providentially, nothing immediately comes from this one-on-one lunch. Looking back, Amanda sees this as a blessing because she had asked the Lord to keep her from any distractions leading up to and in going to Greece. After the trip, she returns to San Antonio full of a passion to communicate the gospel of Jesus to the lost. This passion for the lost does not squelch the question forming in her mind: what would become of this guy named Jordan who seems interested in her?

Amanda ascends the staircase leading to the second floor of a restaurant called Bar Louie to find a large table packed with friends, many from Vertical, for Kathryn's birthday dinner. I am also seated at this packed table, but Jordan, my roommate at the time, could not make it. Amanda sits next to me, and the conversation is casual. Our friend, Amy, sits across from us and begins telling of her online dating woes.

Amy offhandedly comments, "Yeah, I can't tell if this guy is interested or not. He keeps sending these mixed messages. It's very frustrating. You know what . . . he just needs to poop or get off the pot."

Amanda chuckles at this and shrewdly responds, "Amy, I know exactly what you mean."

The not-so-hidden message is easily deciphered.

When I get home that night, I relay the whole interaction to Jordan, "Bro, I think she's telling *you* to poop or get off the pot."

And so, Jordan takes action.

Amanda sits with her friends, eating late-night tacos, at Datapoint Taqueria when she suddenly feels a buzz in her purse. She takes her phone out and sees that Jordan is calling her. Nervous excitement rushes through her.

"Sorry, I gotta take this call," she says while getting up, and then she walks outside.

Amanda asks, "Hey, Jordan, what's going on?"

He asks her out on the phone, and the date is set for a pizza joint downtown called The Esquire. One date leads to another, and the rest is history.

Amanda remembers in her college years desiring marriage and knowing what she wanted in a husband. She feels that the Lord blessed her with exactly what she wanted. She was enslaved in such a sinful past, but the Lord has not treated her as her sins deserve. Jordan is a glimpse of her dreams coming true. You can see through the above narrative that Jesus brought them together. Jordan sees Amanda to the bottom of her soul and knows the entirety of her past and loves her even still. This is a picture of Jesus knowing the entirety of our past and loving us even still.

Their marriage, though far from having arrived, is a picture of the gospel: Amanda, abandoned by her father, ashamed and enslaved by her past, was transformed by the steadfast and faithful love of Jesus. He took her shame upon Himself at the cross . . . Jesus bore the bondage of her sin when He was nailed to the cross. This same Jesus took hold of Amanda's life and set her free from slavery to sin by His saving grace. He then granted her a real-life embodiment of the love of Christ in her husband, Jordan.

Jordan, lost in his selfishness and caught up in the wounds of a shattered relationship, was restored and made whole again by the power of Christ. Jesus freed him from fear of commitment and led him to intentionally pursue Amanda with the same steadfast love with which Jesus first pursued him when he was broken.

The points below depict how Jordan and Amanda viewed marriage before surrendering to Christ, and the following set of points depict how Jordan and Amanda now see marriage through the gospel lens.

Jordan's view of marriage:

- What can I get out of this relationship?
- How can my wife serve me?
- Am I being personally fulfilled by this relationship?
- Does she meet all the requirements I have for marriage?

Amanda's view of marriage:

- How can I receive the male attention I never received from my father?
- Am I being personally fulfilled by this relationship?

The gospel lens for viewing marriage:

- How can I serve Amanda?
- How can I facilitate the love of Jesus into her life?
- How can I give myself up for her?
- How can I wash Amanda with the word?
- How can I nourish and cherish her as my own body?
- How can I lead Amanda into greater holiness?
- How can I build Christ's kingdom with her?

- How can I serve Jordan?
- How can I submit to Jordan's Christ-honoring leadership?
- How can I help Jordan grow in holiness?
- How can I build Christ's kingdom with Jordan?
- How can I create a home where our marriage flourishes?

Where did Jordan and Amanda get the above gospel view of marriage? To find out let's take a deeper look at Eph. 5:22–33, the classic biblical text on marriage. We will divide these verses up into three questions:

1. What is the nature of biblical submission in marriage? (verses 22–24)
2. What is the nature of sacrificial love in marriage? (verses 25–29)
3. What is the relationship between Christ and the church? (verses 30–33)

First, what is the nature of biblical submission in marriage? Eph. 5:22–24 states:

> "Wives, submit to your own husbands, as to the Lord. For the husband is the head of the wife even as Christ is the head of the church, his body, and is himself its Savior. Now as the church submits to Christ, so also wives should submit in everything to their husbands."

What is biblical submission according to this text? This term has been brutally misapplied to the great detriment of many marriages over the history of the world. Consider the following exchange between a husband and wife.

Marissa and Carson have been married for seven years. They have two children, ages three and five. Marissa stands near the sink, and Carson stands on the other side of the kitchen near the pantry. They have been arguing for the past thirty minutes on whether to homeschool their children or put them in public school in light of the recent Covid-19 pandemic and anti-biblical worldviews espoused by the government regarding education.

Marissa has been arguing that it would be much safer for the children to be homeschooled, and Carson has been staunchly asserting that they need public school for socialization and peer-to-peer interaction. Both of them raise their respective points and keep their cool until Carson loses his temper.

He raises his voice, and declares with finality, "Our children are going to public school. Marissa, you need to submit to what I say. It's in the Bible."

Marissa glares back at her husband.

"You did not just pull the "submission" card on me." And she storms out of the room seething with anger and frustration at her husband.

What went wrong in the above exchange? It all comes down to Carson's misinterpretation and misapplication of biblical submission. The key to interpreting and applying these verses on submission is careful consideration of the

complete context of Ephesians 5. In other words, what are the verses before
the ones about wives submitting to husbands? To get a more holistic view of
biblical submission we need to back up to Eph. 5:18–21,

> "And do not get drunk with wine, for that is debauchery, but be filled
> with the Spirit, addressing one another in psalms and hymns and spir-
> itual songs, singing and making melody to the Lord with your heart,
> giving thanks always and for everything to God the Father in the name
> of our Lord Jesus Christ, submitting to one another out of reverence
> for Christ."

This is the famous text on being filled with the Holy Spirit. This reality
honestly deserves a whole chapter to itself, but for now, I want to briefly
point out three results of being filled with the Spirit. The three results or
fruits of being filled with the Spirit are a joyful heart singing to the Lord, a
comprehensive thankfulness to God the Father in Christ, and thirdly, (and
most pertinent to our discussion) submission to one another in reverence
for Christ.

Notice how these results are contrasted to drunkenness in Eph. 5:18, "do
not get drunk . . . but be filled with the Spirit . . ." If you've ever been drunk
then you know that such a state leads to an impaired sense of reality where
the alcohol controls your actions. On the other hand, a person being filled
with the Spirit leads to a heightened sense of reality and to the Holy Spirit
taking control of your actions. The contrast could not be starker, like an image
juxtaposed to its photo negative on the same table.

"Do not get drunk . . ." Drunkenness leads to "debauchery," and this word
in Greek means "wastefulness" or literally "without saving." The picture con-
veyed by this word, debauchery, is a man dying of thirst in the desert holding
a container of ice-cold water which suddenly slips out of his hand, and the
life-saving contents are poured out into the sand.

Conversely, a believer who becomes filled with the Spirit experiences such
fullness of joy that a melody overflows from the heart to the Lord, gratitude
for all things is given to God, and humble submission to others is no longer
duty but choice.

This is the context of the controversial passage on wives submitting to
husbands. Take note that Eph. 5:21 tells us the result of being filled with the
Holy Spirit is "submitting to one another out of reverence for Christ." Please

don't miss Eph. 5:21! This verse is not gender-specific but all-inclusive of *both* males and females, both *husbands* and wives!

We need to step back here and marvel at how earth-shattering this command to submit to one another would have been for a first-century audience. Remember, the book of Ephesians was written to both male and female Christians in Ephesus; a male-dominated culture where a woman's testimony was not even admissible in court. Here Paul, under the influence of the Holy Spirit, is saying that a man can biblically submit to a woman.

Dare I say that a husband will submit to his wife when he is filled with the Spirit? Yes! Why should he do this? This verse tells us we are to submit to one another *out of fear of Christ*. This fear or reverence for Christ is positive, not negative. There is a wholesome fear we are to have of Christ because of His supreme position as our Lord and King.

Furthermore, the Greek text does not use the word "submit" in Eph. 5:22 when Paul says, "Wives submit to your own husbands . . ." Rather the Greek text simply says, "wives to the own husbands as to the Lord."[12] Thus, verse 22 is a carryover from verse 21 where believers are called to *mutually submit to one another*. The truth of mutual submission is brought to bear specifically on wives relating to their husbands in verse 22. Why would that be? Much to the vexation of modern western culture, there are indeed unique and distinct differences between males and females. There is also something unique to how each gender is impacted by the original curse of sin.

In Gen. 3:16 God speaks to Eve about the curse she will receive because of sin, "To the woman he said, 'I will surely multiply your pain in childbearing; in pain you shall bring forth children. Your desire shall be contrary to your husband, but he shall rule over you.'" What is the significance of the woman's desire being contrary to her husband? What does that mean? This means that, because of sin's curse, the wife will naturally set herself against her husband's will at some point in the marriage. She will inevitably oppose the leadership of her husband and assert her control in the marriage due to the curse of sin.

God clearly states, however, at the end of the curse, "but he shall rule over you." This means that the husband is called to the position of leadership in the marriage as Christ is the head of the church. This leadership, as we will see later, is not domineering but is self-giving and sacrificial. Look at Eph. 5:23, "For the husband is the head of the wife even as Christ is the head of the church,

---

12. *Ephesians 5:22.* (2021). Bible Hub. https://biblehub.com/interlinear/ephesians/5-22.htm.

his body, and is himself its Savior." The husband is to look to how Christ leads His body, the church, to inform him on how he should lead his wife.

What does true leadership look like in the home for the husband? The husband is to be the first to apologize and admit when he has done something to hurt his wife. He is not to wait for his wife to initiate the hard conversation when any schism in the marriage arises. As husbands, we are to quickly and thoroughly repair any damage that has been done in the marriage. This begins with the husband leading in confessing where he has fallen short of loving his wife like Christ has loved the church. As Christ has done for the church, husbands are to pursue their wives even if such pursuit is costly. Admitting that you are in the wrong first is difficult, but it's also critical to true leadership.

True leadership also means having the humility to let her lead in the areas she's strong at or gifted in. I am not skilled in organization or planning, but my wife, Kelley, certainly is. I would be foolish not to ask her to lead out in these areas. Letting your wife lead where she is more capable than you is not a sign of weakness but strength and wisdom. On the other hand, when a husband knows he is being called by God to lead his family in a certain direction, his wife is to see that he loves her so much that submission to his leadership is not only wise but also life-giving for her.

Now there is a caveat to wives submitting to husbands. The ending of Eph. 5:22 insinuates this caveat, but a parallel passage on marital submission in Col. 3:18 explicitly states it. The ending of Eph. 5:22 is "wives submit to husbands *as to the Lord*" (emphasis mine). This means that a wife is to submit to her husband as she would submit to Christ, but if a husband is leading his wife in a way contrary to Christ (or the Scriptures) then she has no business submitting to him. And this is exactly what Col. 3:18 states directly, "Wives, submit to your husbands, *as is fitting in the Lord*" (emphasis mine).

The command to submit only applies when the husband is leading his wife "as is fitting in the Lord." Accordingly, everyone's first and only "submit" *command* is to God, "Submit yourselves therefore to God" (James 4:7a). This is important to consider when interpreting and applying Eph. 5:24, "Now as the church submits to Christ, so also wives should submit in everything to their husbands."

Now, remember, the purpose of marriage is for both husband and wife to beautifully display the gospel message of how Christ loves the church and how the church submits to Christ. The curse in Gen. 3:16 brought upon Eve, and therefore all women, creates dynamic opposition to God's original design and purpose for marriage.

With this curse in mind, it makes sense for Paul to specifically address wives submitting to husbands immediately after calling for mutual submission in Eph. 5:21. And this is precisely why viewing this passage in relation to the greater context of being filled with the Spirit is so important.

If both husband and wife are not continually seeking to be filled with the Holy Spirit, there will be no divine resource or power for biblical submission on the wife's part or Christ-centered leadership on the husband's part. Without any doubt, marriage is an uphill battle because of the curse of sin. So, we need divine intervention to fulfill God's design for marriage.

As Eph. 5:18 directs us, we need to be filled with the Holy Spirit to win the uphill battle of marriage. The Greek verb tense used for "be filled" suggests not a one-time filling but a continual present action. We need the ongoing filling of the Spirit in our lives for our marriages to truly thrive. How do we do this? A parallel passage in Colossians 3 is quite helpful.

"Let the word of Christ dwell in you richly, teaching and admonishing one another in all wisdom, singing psalms and hymns and spiritual songs, with thankfulness in your hearts to God" (Col. 3:16). Notice how the results of the word of Christ dwelling richly within you are essentially identical to being filled with the Spirit in Ephesians 5. Even the command for wives to submit to their husbands "as is fitting in the Lord" comes two verses later (Col. 3:18). These similarities are not coincidental! The Holy Spirit has woven a beautifully interconnected biblical tapestry in Ephesians 5 and Colossians 3.

This means that letting "the word of Christ dwell in you richly" is how the Holy Spirit's presence is facilitated in our lives. The word of Christ dwelling in you richly indicates a thought life saturated with Scripture. The more you meditate over and over on the words of Scripture the more Jesus will become real to you and the more the Holy Spirit will fill you. I have tasted this first-hand in meditating on Eph. 2:1–10. His presence is so sweet! The Spirit has overflowed my being with a joy so inexpressible that tears of praise have streamed down my face in such times.

Now, not only does Paul call for being filled with the Spirit in Ephesians 5, but he also takes us to the heart of the gospel to empower us in marriage: the sacrificial love of Christ and the church's submission to Christ.

What does this look like in real life? Practically speaking, when you and your spouse disagree, more energy needs to focus on if the point of disagreement and the responses given to one another are fitting in the Lord. Are you arguing based on a personal preference or based on a biblical precept? How is your tone? Are you approaching your spouse in humility, empowered by the Holy Spirit?

The answers to these questions will determine the conclusion of the argument. Let's return to the disagreement about homeschool versus public school between Marissa and Carson. How could this disagreement be handled through the lens of the gospel?

At the point when Carson loses his temper and pulls the "submission" card on Marissa, I would argue that he is not sacrificially loving his wife as Christ loves the church. He's taking a domineering posture towards his wife rather than being filled with the Spirit in humility. Paul tells the church in Corinth that "love is patient and kind; love does not envy or boast; it is not arrogant or rude. It does not insist on its own way; it is not irritable or resentful; . . . Love bears all things, believes all things, hopes all things, endures all things" (1 Cor. 13:4, 5, 7).

Carson's response to his wife is clearly not in line with Scripture. He is not emulating the role of Christ in the marriage. His tone and response invariably put walls up between him and his wife. This leads Marissa into anger and resentment toward her husband. She naturally will not want to submit to her husband when he is not loving her the way Christ loves the church.

Alternatively, Carson could have acknowledged and affirmed the points his wife was making and then calmly provided his point of view. She could then honor him by reflecting what he has said and then lovingly counter with her concern for the safety of the children. The question both spouses need to ask is: "What is fitting in the Lord?"

In this case, I would contend that Marissa has strong biblical evidence supporting her view. This is an opportunity for Carson to lead out in humble servant leadership. He could respond with something like, "Honey, let me hear your perspective again to see how it lines up with Scripture." Next, both husband and wife can open the Bible and read God's perspective on children receiving Christ-centered education and discipleship. And then they can pray together.

Taking time to pray with your spouse is so critical. When we pray together with our spouse, we are inviting Jesus to be the center of our marriage. When we pray together the enemy is not allowed a foothold in our marriage. When we pray together, we are humbling ourselves before the all-knowing and all-powerful Lord of the universe to seek His help and guidance. We will be peering through the gospel lens if we stop and pray in the middle of our disagreements.

In regards to a wife's submission and a husband's sacrificial love in marriage, a divine cycle can be seen. The divine cycle is this: the more Carson sacrificially loves Marissa, the more she will want to submit to his leadership in marriage. And the more Marissa lovingly submits to Carson's leadership, the more he will want to love her sacrificially. This divine cycle will only make sense when you look at marriage through the gospel lens. What do I mean by this? Consider the following example of how the gospel lens can empower us to submit to the leadership of Christ.

Carson fell captive to the ruthless predator of pornography when he was 12 years old. Ever since then he has struggled on and off with his porn addiction to the great detriment of his marriage. What if the next time Carson was tempted to look at porn, he stopped to pray about the sacrificial love and grace of Jesus Christ?

What if he first prayed, "Jesus, You are amazing, I praise You for the fact You died for what I am about to do."[13]

Do you think Carson's desire for porn would still be knocking on the door at this point? The love of Jesus will not only melt your heart, but His love for you will also melt your desire for sin. Gazing upon the glories of Christ and His sacrificial love for us will empower us to submit to Him.

So shall it be with wives and husbands.

Husbands will be empowered to love their wives sacrificially, and wives will joyfully submit to a man who more closely resembles her loving Savior. Now we come to the critically important question: "what does it mean for husbands to love their wives as Christ loved the church?"

---

13. Vanderstelt J., *Gospel Fluency—Part 1*, https://www.youtube.com/watch?v=-vtTkahgcSo, 09/07/2013.

14

Husbands, Love Your Wives

"Husbands, love your wives, as Christ loved the church and gave himself up for her, that he might sanctify her, having cleansed her by the washing of water with the word, so that he might present the church to himself in splendor, without spot or wrinkle or any such thing, that she might be holy and without blemish. In the same way, husbands should love their wives as their own bodies. He who loves his wife loves himself. For no one ever hated his own flesh, but nourishes and cherishes it, just as Christ does the church," (Eph. 5:25–29).

How did Christ love the Church? Verse 25 tells us, that He "gave Himself up for her ..." (NASB). The Greek word for "love" in the command for husbands to love their wives is *agapē*. This word conveys a sacrificial, action-oriented love from the will based on choice, but by no means is devoid of affection or emotion. *Agapē* is the highest form of love and characterizes the sacrificial love of Christ for us.

The supreme example of Christ's love for us is Jesus giving Himself up for us. Paul is essentially saying here in Eph. 5:25, "Husbands, look at how Christ has loved us by giving Himself up for us. Now go and do the same in how you love your wife." Practically speaking, husbands need to continually ask themselves, "Okay, in this situation with my wife, am I loving her the same way Christ loved the church and gave Himself up for her?" This question is a game-changer and if asked consistently will change a husband's perspective on marriage and the very lens he peers through to view his wife.

If a husband is to carry out this command to love his wife this way, then a couple of things need to happen first. He must be emptied of himself through the gospel daily. The good news of Jesus frees a man from domineering, self-seeking practices and readies him for servant-leadership. "For even the Son of Man came not to be served but to serve, and to give his life as a ransom for many" (Mark 10:45). The infinitely holy, glorious, and almighty God came not to be served but *to serve!* He gave His life as a ransom, in our place, to redeem us from slavery to sin. Jesus, in His magnificent grace, frees us from serving ourselves so we can serve others.

If husbands are servant-leaders, then what does that look like practically? Husbands must become black belts in understanding the needs, cares, and wants of their wives. For example, if Marissa functions better in a home free of clutter and disorganization, then Carson needs to sacrifice his time to arrange the house in an orderly fashion and ensure everything is put away in its proper place regularly. If Marissa does not like to be rushed when getting ready, then he needs to create more margins in the family schedule to allow for a greater time buffer.

When Marissa gets home, he can have the thermostat set at the temperature she prefers rather than his preference. He can offer to get her something to drink if she easily forgets to stay hydrated during the day. He can make sure the dishwasher is emptied for her. He can do the laundry and fold the clothes for her if she finds such tasks exhausting. Maybe she prefers to be served by Carson spending one-on-one quality time with her, or perhaps she feels loved by encouraging text messages or hand-written notes. Or she may feel loved by spontaneous gifts given to her outside of holidays and birthdays.

Whatever the case, Carson needs to spend time asking Marissa intentional questions to better understand how he can best love and serve her. Some wives are not an open book. A sacrificial husband will become an excellent detective in discerning his wife's needs, preferences, and desires. In short, Carson has to become an expert on all things Marissa. Sacrificial love is found in the details of life.

Meditate with me for a moment on the phrase "gave Himself" in Eph. 5:25. This signifies the self-giving nature of Christ's love for us. He gave Himself up for us. There is an utter abandonment of His preferences and safety exemplified for us in this phrase. Husbands, in every situation with our wives we are to consider her needs and her wants before we think of our own. We must give and give and give of ourselves until there is nothing left to give. This is what Christ did.

He gave and gave and gave of Himself until His blood ran down the cross unto death. Husbands, is this realistic for us to do practically every day? Such sacrificial love is impossible. And, again, we are brought back to Eph. 5:18, "... be filled with the Spirit ..." The only way to sacrificially love our wives as Christ has done is by the power of the Holy Spirit.

Paul details more specifics on how this love can be shown in Eph. 5:26. The verse says that Jesus gave Himself up for the church to "sanctify her, having cleansed her by the washing of water with the word." What does this verse mean?

Let's first look at the word "sanctify." This word in Greek means "to make holy, to set apart." This gives us specific insight into the purpose of marriage. A husband is to love his wife in such a way that she becomes more holy because this is what Christ has already done for the church as the Author and Perfecter of our faith (see Heb. 12:2).

It's helpful to be mindful of the end goal of marriage throughout every day of your marriage. Where are both spouses headed? They are headed to stand before the throne of God where they will be counted as holy and blameless because they are covered in the blood of Christ. But before they get there, they are to sanctify one another. This gospel mindset towards marriage is selfless rather than self-seeking. This mindset is unconditional rather than transactional.

How does a husband practically sanctify his wife or make her more holy? Look at the next part of Eph. 5:26, "... having cleansed her by the washing of water with the word." Cleansing and washing signify the removal of filth ... the filth of sin. Ultimately, this is what Christ has already done for His bride at the cross, and such washing of sin is symbolized by water baptism.

A believer is showing outwardly the inward washing Jesus has already done of the heart as he or she is completely immersed in the water at baptism. Jesus has washed away all of His bride's sins! Believers in Christ have been entirely bathed in the blood of Jesus, the Lamb of God (see John 1:29). This is the gospel. Thank you, Jesus!

This phenomenal picture of washing and cleansing is applied to marriage. Notice how Paul, by the inspiration of the Holy Spirit, continually looks at marriage through the lens of the gospel. As Christ has washed us in *the word*, so should husbands wash their wives in *the word*. The Greek word used here for "word" is not *logos*, as in John 1:1, but is actually *rhéma*. Although these Greek words are similar, *rhéma* specifically refers to the "spoken word."

Now, what does this mean practically for husbands? Certainly, this will involve husbands speaking the truths of Scripture over their wives. My sister told me about her husband, Joseph, playing the book of Psalms audio Bible the other night, and she felt this simple act served to bathe her in the spoken words of Scripture.

Now I need to add a caveat here about washing your wife with the word. There's a certain finesse needed in bathing one's wife in Scripture. It's very important that the wife does not feel like the pupil and the husband is the teacher. I have made this mistake in my marriage. Preaching a sermon to your wife does not accurately capture the meaning of washing her with the spoken word or *rhéma*.

Instead, it may be more helpful for the husband to come alongside his wife as a fellow learner to explore the truth of God's word together. Both husband and wife are fellow travel companions as they journey towards growth in holiness together until they both stand before Christ without blemish or wrinkle or any such thing. Practically, Kelley and I have previously studied Genesis together and going deeper into the text as fellow learners was enriching for both of us.

Engaging in daily and frequent gospel conversations with your spouse is critical to bathing one another with the word of God. It's helpful to ask questions like: how does the good news of Jesus and His finished work speak into this situation? Or how can we see Jesus at work in our marriage and family right now? When you're watching a movie or show with your spouse and family, you can point out what elements are contrary to the gospel and what parts highlight a longing and need that only Jesus can fulfill.

I would also like to broaden the scope of a husband washing his wife with the word. If a husband is to sanctify his wife with the spoken word of God, then he will also consistently speak to her in an uplifting manner to build her up in Christ. Look at Eph. 4:29 (NASB):

"Let no unwholesome word proceed from your mouth, but only such
a word as is good for edification according to the need of the moment,
so that it will give grace to those who hear."

This is extremely practical and critical for marriage. We need edifying words when conflicts arise, tensions are high, and constant proximity with one another can lead to harshness and outbursts of anger. We need edifying words when finances are tight, children are ill, and date nights are sparse. Spouses, are you speaking to one another to build one another up or to prove your point? Husbands, are your words giving your wife grace or does she feel condemnation coming from you instead?

What is the purpose for washing with the word? Eph. 5:27 gives us the answer. Jesus washed His bride with the word, "so that he might present the church to himself in splendor, without spot or wrinkle or any such thing, that she would be holy and without blemish." Again, we are brought back to the overarching purpose of marriage. Paul tells us that glory and holiness is the destination of the bride.

I clearly remember the moment when my wife turned the corner and began walking down the aisle toward me. From my vantage point, she was "in all her glory, having no spot or wrinkle or any such thing (Eph. 5:27)." At the marriage altar, enraptured by my wife's splendor, I received a foretaste of where she is headed eternally. And now I get to live with her, alongside her in such a way that she will be prepared for that eternal glory. But what does this look like practically? Look at the next verse (Eph. 5:28).

"In the same way husbands should love their wives as their own bodies. He who loves his wife loves himself." The opening words to verse 28 are "in the same way." Men, Christ must be our perpetual example in how we love our wives. Our marriages are living, breathing displays of the gospel message itself. In marriage, a husband and wife are bound together so intimately and their lives are interwoven through so many threads, strands, and facets that they essentially become one body and one tapestry.

Wait a minute. This is how Jesus is with us, His bride! Stop for a moment with me and stand in awe of our union with Christ. Our union with Jesus means that if He loves us, He is loving Himself. If you are in Christ, your life is unassailably bound to His. You are interwoven with Jesus through so many threads, strands, and facets that you are now part of Christ's body. What are the threads that inextricably bind us to Jesus?

They are the threads of His love . . . His faithfulness unyielding, His obedience without relenting, His sacrifice beyond measure, His forgiveness transforming, His grace transcending, His power resurrecting, His beauty beyond bearing, His truth without compromise, His discipline unshakeable, His Word irrefutable, His promises unbreakable, His intercession never-ending, His advocacy heart-melting, His Spirit ever empowering.

And the threads are limitless. And these same threads are what motivate you and empower you to remain as one flesh with your spouse no matter what. The purpose of Jesus is now ours, and what happens to us invariably happens to Him. And what happens to your spouse invariably happens to you.

A picture of this is found in the movie, *Pacific Rim*, where two pilots are side by side and have to become synchronized in mind and memory so they can effectively operate a machine powerful enough to prevent global extinction. In the movie, both pilots will inevitably suffer the same defeat or the same victory. This is exactly how marriage is. The husband's gain is also the wife's gain. The wife's loss is also her husband's loss. So, when a husband loves his wife, he loves himself because she is indelibly part of his being and he is part of hers. "My beloved is mine, and I am his" (Song of Solomon 2:16). Now, what happens if the husband and wife are not living as if they are one flesh?

His name is Ian. Her name is Isabel.

Ian grew up as an only child in a single-mother household. He was showered with affection throughout childhood from his mother and never overtly craved the fatherly attention he had missed out on. Now as an adult, Ian is a very driven and hardworking criminal defense attorney. His only friend and confidant is his wife, Isabel.

Isabel, on the other hand, grew up in a very loving two-parent household of five brothers and sisters. Isabel's family comes from Latin American roots, and so the eight family members are very close. Familial bonding time is a high priority for Isabel, and this priority has inevitably carried over into her marriage. Specifically, Isabel is especially close to her brother, Manny, who is just one year older than her.

Isabel and Ian have been married for five years now, and though they love each other dearly, there have been some bumps along the way. Unresolved issues continue to gnaw at the very fabric and harmony of their marriage. It began with the setting of their wedding date. Isabel confided to her brother, Manny, after Ian had proposed to her that they were going back and forth on when to set the date for the big day. Manny and his wife were planning on moving to Kansas in November, and he pressed Isabel to push for setting the date in October so no conflict would arise between the big move and the wedding of his beloved sister.

Ian graciously went along with the earlier wedding date, but this would soon cause him unavoidable stress because the earlier date would be in the middle of a politically charged, high-profile murder case. Inevitably, he had to spend long hours at the office preparing for the case instead of helping his fiancée with the last-minute details of the wedding, honeymoon, and moving preparation (they planned to move into Isabel's apartment after the honeymoon). Ian had decided to forgive Manny's insistence on the earlier date, but he still had a sneaking suspicion that Isabel was more concerned with her brother's wishes than his.

Another bump in the marriage came when Isabel's family had planned a two-week-long trip to New Zealand during Spring Break. Isabel wanted to go, but when she brought the trip up to Ian, he told her that his work would not allow so many consecutive days off.

"I've got a national law conference the week of Spring Break too," Ian added. Deflated by this response Isabel pushed him on it.

"Babe, can't you have your partner, Louis, cover for you and forgo the conference . . . this is a trip of a lifetime."

Ian stands firm and asserts, "Isabel, it's just not feasible."

The finality of this last statement punctures and releases the last bit of hope for the trip Isabel has as she stares out the car window sulkily. Perturbed by his wife not honoring the importance of his career, and suspecting Isabel has yet again prioritized her family over him, Ian does not say another word for the remainder of the car ride home.

Ian's suspicions are further confirmed when he and Isabel take a trip out to her parent's house in Ashville, North Caroline during Thanksgiving of the following year. Manny and his family are there as well. At one point during the holiday, Isabel goes off with her nieces for about two hours, leaving Ian alone on the couch to stare at the smoldering fireplace.

Later that night Ian confronts Isabel about the incident. "Why did you leave me alone in the living room for so long while you went off with Ally and Amy?"

"Well, I thought you were enjoying yourself by the fire," Isabel counters innocently. Moments pass as both husband and wife stare up at the ceiling lying side by side in bed. The silence is tense.

"Why am I starting to feel like an extra in the movie of your life, Isabel?"

"You are not an extra, Ian. You're my husband."

"Well, why do you seem to keep prioritizing your family over me, if I'm not an extra?

"Why do I feel like you're cross-examining me right now?" Isabel responds in frustration.

Ian snaps back, "I'm not a prosecutor! I don't cross-examine witnesses or anything like that if that's what you think."

"Well, I'm sure you've seen your clients being cross-examined loads of times. Anyways, when have I prioritized my family over you," she asks.

"Okay, let's see . . ." Ian begins revving up and flicking up each finger consecutively as he gives instance after instance of Isabel prioritizing her family over him.

"How about changing our wedding date to before your brother and his family moved to Kansas? How about 'the trip of a lifetime' we missed because of my work? You've never called any of the trips we've been on together a 'trip of a lifetime.' How about today when you left me alone on the couch for two hours?"

Something breaks in Isabel as the indicting record of grievances sinks deep into her conscience. Tears begin to stream down her face. Ian sees this happening and reaches out his hand to grasp hers. Ian's tone softens towards Isabel.

"Look, if we're going to do this, we have to prioritize our marriage over every other relationship. I don't feel like you've truly left your family to become part of the one you and I are starting. I've been wrong in holding onto these feelings of jealousy."

"No, you're right," Isabel says through tears of contrition. "I'm glad you feel jealous because that feeling is probably motivated by a desire to have me as your own instead of me enmeshed with my family. But I also feel that you need to prioritize me over your career."

"That's fair. I could see why you would feel that way," Ian concedes.

In a moment of resolve, Ian decides to do something he realizes he should have done long ago: "I'm going to commit to prioritizing you and our marriage over my career and anything else. Will you pray with me and commit to prioritizing our marriage? We're supposed to be one flesh. Right now, I don't feel like we are living as one flesh."

"You go first." Isabel says reluctantly.

Ian prays, "Father, I realize that I have prioritized my career over my wife instead of sacrificially loving her the way Jesus does. I'm sorry I have not prioritized being one flesh with her the way I should. Please, Father, help me by Your Spirit to love her as I do my own body in Jesus' name amen."

There's a pause and Isabel chokes up, "Jesus, I'm so sorry I've put my family over my own husband. Help me to put Ian over any other earthly relationship and for us to be one together as husband and wife in Your name, Lord Jesus. Amen."

&

Now how does such oneness inform the husband's treatment of his wife? "For no one ever hated his own flesh, but nourishes and cherishes it, just as Christ does the church, because we are members of his body" (Eph. 5:29, 30). How does a husband nourish his wife? The word, nourish, in Greek means to bring about growth. Recently, my front lawn was scorched by the stifling heat of a south Texas summer and had turned a lifeless faded yellow color. In reviving the lawn, I learned something about the conditions needed for the growth and nourishment of grass. First, I had to rake out the dead grass to prepare the soil.

Next, I sowed new grass seeds with fertilizer. Then, I scattered compost over the seed to prevent water from washing the seed away. Lastly, I watered the specific area that had died. I did this for two weeks straight every day. In the first few days, I was a bit discouraged. Growth did not occur as fast as I expected. But after about two weeks I began to see tiny blades coming out of the soil.

There's a certain satisfaction to seeing the fruits of your labor burst through the soil, no matter how small these fruits may be. In about a month these tiny blades turned into grass. What a picture of growth in marriage! Conditions need to be just right for a wife to feel nourished by her husband and the husband by his wife. If we begin laying down faithful seeds of prayer for our spouse, we will get to watch God cause the growth.

What are the specific conditions needed for growth in marriage? Each spouse needs his or her emotional, physical, and spiritual cups filled daily, and these areas need tending to for the growth and flourishing of both spouses in the marriage. But before the appropriate conditions are set for growth in these areas, there's one foundational aspect that needs to be addressed: each spouse's identity.

Husbands will also do well to remember what Jesus quoted to Satan when tempted in the wilderness, "But he answered, 'It is written, 'Man shall not live by bread alone, but by every word that comes from of the mouth of God.'"

(Matt. 4:4). When Satan came to Jesus to tempt Him to turn a stone into bread, he first questioned His identity. He said, "If you are the Son of God," (Matt. 4:3). Jesus immediately responded with Scripture, for in the Scriptures we find our true identity. In the Scriptures, we find food for the soul. In the Scriptures, we find the Bread of Life . . . our Lord Jesus.

This is why Peter calls us to have such an intense craving and hunger for God's word, "Like newborn infants, long for the pure spiritual milk, that by it you may grow up into salvation—if indeed you have tasted that the Lord is good." (1 Peter 2:2, 3). We must be daily rooted and grounded in Scripture to such an extent that when we see our spouse's identity being shaken, we can nourish her with the word of God and let her see herself through the gospel lens. Husbands and wives, there will be times when your spouse's identity will be questioned and shaken to the core. These are times for nourishment of his or her true identity in Christ: "For no one ever hated his own flesh, but nourishes and cherishes it . . ."

Her name is Kate.

Constantly gnawed by anxiety and stress, she finds herself utterly exhausted at the end of each work day. She is an orthopedic surgeon at a level-one trauma hospital in Austin, Texas. It's Monday, and she has scrubbed in for a routine elective cervical spine surgery. She has performed this operation hundreds if not thousands of times. Seventeen minutes into the surgery, Kate, with a scalpel in hand makes a longitudinal cut for the anterior cervical discectomy and fusion (ACDF). The next moment changes her life. The blade suddenly slips and nicks a vital artery in the neck called the common carotid artery. A look of horror spreads over Kate's face.

"No! No!" she shouts with a quivering voice.

The surgical team frantically initiates a sequence of lifesaving efforts as the patient begins losing blood rapidly. The emergency response team is activated due to the patient's plummeting blood pressure. Kate steps back from the operating table. Amidst the whirlwind of activity, time seems to stand still. To Kate's horror, the patient tragically passes away within minutes.

Hours later, Kate is sitting in her office replaying the scene over and over in her mind. She buries her face in her hands as the tears stream down her face. Her colleague, Dr. Harris, knocks on the door and then quietly enters the room. He sits down next to Kate and puts a hand on her shoulder to comfort her.

"I'm so sorry this happened, Kate. I've also lost a patient on the table because of a slip. If you need to talk or anything I'm here." Kate remains silent. Moments pass. Dr. Harris leaves the room.

On the drive home, Kate calls her husband, Rick.

He answers on the third ring, "Hey, babe, how you doin'?"

"Rick I . . . I lost a patient today on the operating table. My hand slipped during the surgery."

Rick pauses for a moment and then responds, "Oh baby, I'm so sorry this happened. Can I come see you right now or are you on your way home?"

"I'm headed home now. I'll be there in about ten minutes."

"Okay, I'll head home right now as well. Gosh, that's so tragic. How are you holding up right now?"

"I'm devastated. I just notified the patient's wife. Rick, I can't stop thinking about her uncontrollable gasps and sobs after I told her he passed away. Because of me, she's . . . she's a widow and their children are fatherless. I don't know if I'll ever be able to operate again." Kate chokes up as she says these last words.

"Oh Kate, I love you so much. I can't imagine what you're feeling right now. I want you to know that whatever you decide to do, I'll support your decision."

"I'm almost home. We can talk more in person." Kate hangs up.

She arrives home before her husband. When Rick walks through the door he strides quickly across the room and wraps Kate up in a warm embrace. He holds her for a few minutes as she silently cries on his shoulder.

"I don't know how I'm going to get over this, Rick. I entered this profession to heal people, but today I'm responsible for a man's death. I don't think I can do this anymore. I feel like I don't know who I am anymore."

Rick waits a minute, and then he asks, "Can I pray for you, babe." Kate moves her chin up and down on Rick's shoulder nodding.

Rick prays, "Father in heaven, You know exactly what Kate's going through right now, way better than I do. I know You feel her pain and all the emotions she has right now. Father, because of Jesus and His work on the cross, Kate is first and foremost Your daughter before she's a surgeon and even before she's my wife. I thank You that You have chosen her to be Your daughter before You laid the foundation of the world. I thank You that You have redeemed her and have forgiven her of all her sins through the blood of Christ. Please, Father, I ask that You would comfort her and bring healing to her right now. And I also ask that You bring healing and comfort to the grieving family right now in Your holy name, Jesus Christ. Amen."

Kate whispers, "Thank you. I needed to hear that right now."

✿

What was Rick doing right there? He was nourishing his wife by reminding her of her true identity in Christ when her identity as a surgeon was being shaken. Most situations are not as dramatic as Kate's. Not only are husbands called to nourish their wives with the gospel in identity-shaking situations but also in the everyday mundane routine. This could take the form of a thirty-second prayer over one another before parting ways in the morning to go to work. The husband's joy is to nourish his wife with the seeds of the gospel every day. This calling is not limited to the husband by the way. Wives, your husband needs to be nourished daily with the gospel and his identity in Christ as well.

The second important word in Eph. 5:29 is "cherishes." The husband is to cherish his wife as he does his own body. The word "cherish" literally means "to keep warm." The picture here is of a wife shivering in the cold and her husband coming and wrapping her up with a warm blanket. The implication is whatever a husband seeks to do for the benefit and well-being of his own body he is also to do for his wife. This not only involves the husband proactively meeting the physical needs of his wife, but cherishing also means keeping her warm emotionally, spiritually, and psychologically. There is a holistic cherishing to be done in marriage because this is what Christ does for the church, as the last part of verse 29 states.

What does nourishing and cherishing look like practically in marriage? Husbands, I want to encourage you to ask yourself continually throughout your marriage: "At this moment, am I nourishing and cherishing my wife the way I would my own body?" Remember, you two are one flesh. Practically, the next time you go to the fridge, or the pantry, or to the store ask your wife if you can get something for her as well. What about emotionally? You can cherish your wife emotionally by asking the Holy Spirit to give you insight into her emotional state.

As husbands, sometimes we can be quite clueless if we are not paying attention to the emotional needs of our wives. After seeing your wife go through any type of experience (could be her day at work or a recent argument you had together) you can ask her how she *feels* about what has happened. Listen closely when she says something like, "I just feel really ____ about that." Instead of providing advice on how to fix her emotional state ask her more questions about what led her to feel this way. After taking the time to genuinely listen, praying over her will go much farther than counseling her. In your prayer over her, you will be renewing and warming her soul with Christ's love.

You can also nourish and cherish her emotionally by offering to take care of the kids for an afternoon so she can relax and do what fills her up and provides emotional nourishment for her. We are to nourish and cherish our wives physically, emotionally, and spiritually; in other words, holistically.

As stated previously in chapter 12, we can see how holistic Jesus was in His earthly ministry, "And he went throughout all Galilee, teaching in their synagogues and proclaiming the gospel of the kingdom, and healing every kind of disease and every affliction among the people" (Matt. 4:23). Again, recall how Jesus taught in the synagogues (engaging the mind), He proclaimed the gospel (engaging the spiritual), and He healed every kind of disease (engaging the physical). Our Savior is wonderfully holistic in how He cherishes His bride, the church. And so shall it be with husbands and wives.

The next verses in Ephesians 5 answer our last question: "What is the relationship between Christ and the church?"

15

Christ and the Church

"For no one ever hated his own flesh, but nourishes and cherishes it, just as Christ does the church, because we are members of his body. 'Therefore a man shall leave his father and mother and hold fast to his wife, and the two shall become one flesh.' This mystery is profound, and I am saying that it refers to Christ and the church. However, let each one of you love his wife as himself, and let the wife see that she respects her husband" (Eph. 5:29–33).

Let's begin this chapter by examining Eph. 5:33 first: Paul ends this classic marriage text by telling each husband to love his wife as himself and the wife to respect her husband. This first command makes sense given what has already been said. The husband is to recognize that he is one flesh with his wife, and therefore when he loves his wife, he is indeed loving himself. But I would like to spend a few moments on the second command, the wife is to "respect" her husband.

The word for "respect" in Greek deserves special attention because the Greek definition will not sit well with modern readers. It's the word *phobeó*, and this means "to fear" (it's where we get our English word "phobia"). Why would Paul conclude the classic marriage passage by telling wives to fear their husbands? I personally do not want my wife to fear me, but this appears to be the calling of Scripture. How can this tension be resolved?

1 Peter 3:1–6 provides some clarity. In these verses, Peter gives instructions for believing wives to win their unbelieving husbands to Christ by being respectful (literally "fear" in 1 Peter 3:2) to them in conduct, but verse 6 ends

by saying this to the believing wife, "if you do what is right without being frightened by any fear." Verse 6 insinuates that a believing wife may have reason to fear her unbelieving husband in the male-dominated society of the first century (to which 1 Peter was written), but the timeless words of Scripture tell her not to be frightened.

In other words, such a wife who is respecting her unbelieving husband in a Christ-honoring way has nothing to fear according to Scripture. There seems to be a nuance in the Greek language here suggesting that wives will not be afraid of their husbands but at the same time will have a healthy respect (or literally "fear") of them in their conduct. This distinction helps one understand why the translators render *phobeó/phobos* in Eph. 5:33 and 1 Peter 3:2 as "respect" / "respectful" instead of using the word "fear."

Still, if there is any continuing abusive sin with an unbelieving husband (or even a "believing" husband) and a fearful home situation ensues, safety for self and the children is paramount. This issue is also addressed in chapter 17, "What does the Bible say? The Gospel Lens and Divorce / Remarriage."

The rest of this chapter will focus on Christ's relationship to the church. I hope you will see the emphasis is on how amazing our glorious Savior is. Will you look at Jesus with me and behold His wondrous love for you?

The above verse from Eph. 5:31 is a quote from Gen. 2:24 where God calls the man to leave his father and mother and hold fast to his wife. The word for 'hold fast' in Greek means "to glue together." Some translations will use the word "cleave," "join," or "unite." The next verse in the passage (Eph. 5:32) states this "leaving and cleaving" call is a profound mystery that refers to Christ and the church. What is this mystery here and why is it so profound?

Herein rests the profound mystery: Jesus Christ has left His Father to come to earth to ultimately hold fast to His wife . . . to be joined with her . . . to be united to His bride, the church. He has left His throne and emptied Himself of His heavenly majesty to come after His bride. This is the greatest love story of all time! Jesus left his Father so He could come here and be ostracized by his own earthly family, rejected, spat upon, mocked, beaten, and unjustly condemned to death . . . the death that you and I fully deserve.

Yet out of His death came the resurrection and not only of His own physical body. The church, called the body of Christ in Scripture, was also born because of Jesus' death, resurrection, and ascension. The ascension of Jesus triggered the coming of the Holy Spirit, and when He came on the day of Pentecost, the church, the bride of Jesus, also came into existence.

And now Jesus, as our patient and faithful Bridegroom, longs for the day when He will finally be united to us ("the two shall become one flesh"). I'm not exactly sure what this profound mystery will look like, but I do know this—the relationship between Christ and the church means that we, His bride, will forever experience the perfect, unmitigated, heart-melting, and boundless love of Jesus Christ in the fullest measure for all eternity.

This love is the lens through which all Christians should look at their spouses. This love is the basis for all our marriage relationships. This love of Christ is the unassailable foundation that will never be shaken no matter how thunderous the storms of this life may become. No matter how much you dislike your spouse at times, this love will be the glue that keeps the both of you united as one flesh. Now, how does Jesus practically love the church?

His name is Jairus.

A deluge of anxiety floods his whole being. Nervous sweat trickles down his forehead as his face is buffeted by grains of sand from intermittent gusts of wind by the seashore amidst the stifling heat of first-century Palestine. He has heard stories about a man called Jesus. He has read the prophesies foretelling a coming Messiah. *Could this be the One?* he asks himself. *Does He have the power to heal my dying daughter?*

Jairus approaches a crowd gathered around a man about a stone's throw from the shoreline. *It's Him! It has to be Him!* he thinks to himself as hope surges inside him like a swelling wave. Jairus begins to run. His sandals sink frustratingly into the sand as he sprints as fast as can towards the crowd surrounding Jesus. Undeterred, Jairus threads his way through the throng of people until at last, he is face to face with Jesus.

Dust kicks up as he falls down at the feet of Jesus. Jairus looks up at Jesus and pleads with a quivering voice, ". . . My little daughter is at the point of death. Come and lay your hands on her, so that she may be well and live" (Mark 5:23). Jesus reaches His hand down to Jairus, pulls him to his feet, and begins walking with him.

Jesus, Jairus, and the growing multitude begin the journey toward the moribund daughter. The crowd presses all around and against the two men. *We are not going to make it in time with this huge crowd slowing us down!* Jairus anxiously thinks to himself. But he does not dare tell this to Jesus. And then Jairus' worst fears are realized. Jesus stops walking, and the caravan comes to a standstill. Jesus begins looking all-around at the crowd of people surrounding Him.

He turns completely around and shouts above the noise of the multitude, "Who was it that touched me?" (Luke 8:45a).

Everyone becomes quiet, and all eyes are fixed on Jesus.

Peter replies, "Master, the people surround you and are pressing in on you (Luke 8:45b)."

But Jesus responds, "Someone touched me, for I perceive that power has gone out of me" (Luke 8:46).

A moment or two passes and Jesus resolutely does not take another step forward. An awkward silence persists, and the only thing heard is the distant squawk of a seagull. And then the silence is broken. A woman bursts through the inner circle of the crowd and falls at Jesus' feet, trembling. The locals of the region see her and immediately take a step back from her, repulsed by her presence. They know who she is. They know about her hemorrhage of twelve years. According to Levitical law, she is unclean, and the crowd's very proximity to her puts them all at risk of becoming unclean as well.

The woman speaks loud enough for the crowd to hear every word, "Please, Sir, I have heard of Your power. I thought to myself, 'If I just touch His garments, I will get well.' I have suffered for these twelve years now, and no doctor has been able to cure me. I have been an outcast for so long."

With eyes full of compassion, Jesus looks at her, pulls her up to her feet, places a hand on her shoulder, and declares in the presence of the multitude, "Daughter, your faith has made you well; go in peace" (Luke 8:48).

How do we see the love of Jesus for His bride practically displayed in the above account? Jesus shows love to the woman physically, then socially, and lastly spiritually. What a picture of marriage! We are to look out for our spouse's physical, social, and spiritual well-being. Notice how Jesus first heals her physically upon her touching the hem of His garment. Wow! What power Jesus has! She approached Him thinking about the stories she had heard about Him, and now she was taking action.

What a picture of how we, as His bride, should respond to Jesus. The woman first heard about Jesus, then she came up to Jesus, and then she touched Jesus. She *heard*, she *came*, and she *touched*. Jesus, as our Bridegroom is inviting us to hear about Him, come to Him, and touch Him. And when we touch Jesus, He heals us. He restores us. What do I mean by touching Jesus? Touching Jesus means you bring your affliction to Him and call upon Him for restoration. It can be as simple as this: "Jesus, heal my marriage! Show me how to love my spouse like You love me. Jesus, please restore my family!"

This woman's problem was internal, but the horrific effects of her affliction pervaded her whole life. Mark 5:26 tells us she had spent all she had in search of a cure but had only become worse. What a picture of attempting salvation by good works! All human effort to achieve true wholeness is futile and only makes matters worse. Not only was she experiencing ongoing and worsening physical suffering, but her illness had financially bankrupted her as well.

When she comes to Jesus and touches Him, we can appreciate the kind of desperation she is experiencing. Her desperation led her to reach out and touch Jesus, "And immediately the flow of her blood dried up, and she felt in her body that she was healed of her disease" (Mark 5:29). The Greek word for "disease" used here literally means "scourge," which was the whip used for torture or flagellation in the first century.

When the woman touched His garment, the power of Jesus went out from Him to hold back the scourging whip of affliction that had ravaged her entire life. And you know what? Jesus does not let her healing go unnoticed but turns her healing into an opportunity for a testimony, so that all may know of her healing and His power to heal. This leads us to the second facet of this woman's healing: her social restoration.

How does Jesus restore her socially? The last thing this woman appears to have wanted is to be noticed by the multitude. Luke's account tells us, "And when the woman saw that she was not hidden, she came trembling, and falling down before him declared in the presence of all the people why she had touched him . . ." (Luke 8:47). She most likely wanted to escape public notice because of her status as a social outcast.

The Levitical law tells us this about such a woman with abnormal bleeding, "If a woman has a discharge of blood many days, not at the time of her menstrual impurity, or if she has a discharge beyond the time of her impurity, all the days of her discharge she shall continue in uncleanness . . ." (Leviticus 15:25).

The passage in Leviticus 15 goes on to enumerate all the specifications of her uncleanness. Any bed or chair which the woman contacts shall be considered unclean and anyone who touches these objects shall also be considered unclean and will have to wash his clothes and bathe and also be considered unclean until evening (see Lev. 15:26, 27).

What is truly remarkable about Jesus is that when *He* is touched by this woman, He does not become unclean, but instead *she becomes clean*. He's so amazing! But the Levitical law also gives us insight into just how repulsed the Jews in the crowd would have been at the mere sight of their proximity to this "unclean" woman.

So, the woman obviously wanted a clandestine healing, but Jesus will have none of it. His plans for her are so much better because His restoration is holistic and not one-dimensional. Jesus created this woman, and He knows her brokenness is not merely physical but is also social.

Notice how brilliantly Jesus stops the whole crowd, no doubt at the exasperation of Jairus, to point out to everyone that this woman is now clean and can be restored to the community. "And when the woman saw that she was not hidden, she came trembling, and falling down before him declared in the presence of all the people why she had touched him, and how she had been immediately healed" (Luke 8:47). Luke, the beloved physician, specifically details how this woman was able to give her testimony to the whole crowd to demonstrate in the presence of everyone the immediacy of Jesus' profound work of healing and her resulting cleanness.

It's important to remember that this event is taking place in a shame-honor culture. The woman, who has known nothing but shame in her community for 12 long years, is now honored in the presence of all. Jesus has powerfully and skillfully removed the shame of her affliction and has now clothed her with honor. She is no longer an unclean outcast, but she is a healed and cleansed daughter of the Most High God. Jesus calls her "daughter" in Luke 8:48, and this brings us to the third facet of this woman's healing: her spiritual restoration.

Jesus calls the woman "daughter." Immediately, this clues us in on Jesus' identity as well. He alone has the authority to bring this woman into the family of God and call her daughter. What allowed her to secure such a status before Jesus?

It was her faith in Jesus.

He tells her, "Daughter, your faith has made you well; go in peace" (Luke 8:48). The word "faith" here in this verse is the Greek word that means faith, trust, or confidence. Scripture shows us that this kind of faith or trust is always given to us by God as a gift and does not come from any innate ability in ourselves (see Eph. 2:8, 9).

Her faith in Jesus leads to her being made well. Interestingly enough, the phrase "made you well" in Luke 8:48 is a translation of the Greek word that can also be translated as "to save." Jesus, therefore, is indicating that the woman has experienced salvation because of her faith in Him. According to Lev. 15:30, the priest must make atonement for the woman who is unclean because of her bleeding: "And the priest shall use one for a sin offering and the other for a burnt offering. And the priest shall make atonement for her before the Lord for her unclean discharge."

When Jesus tells the woman she has been healed because of her faith in Luke 8:48, He is assuming the role of a priest in pronouncing her clean and addressing her as "daughter." It's as if her impure discharge is atoned for by the spoken word of Jesus in the presence of all the people. But how can Jesus do so?

He can because He is the Priest to end all priests, and at the cross, He became the atoning sacrifice to end all sacrifices. And what is the result of His declaration of her spiritual healing? At the end of Luke 8:48, Jesus tells her to "go in peace." The woman now has "peace" which in Greek means "wholeness." Jesus has not only restored her physically and socially, but He has also saved her and given her wholeness.

What can we conclude about the love of Jesus from the account of the woman's healing? We can conclude that Jesus loves His bride by using His power to heal her physically, socially, and spiritually.

Now how do we apply this to looking at marriage through the gospel lens? We most definitely can and should follow the example of Christ in loving our spouses the way He loved this woman (holistically).

But stopping there is a common pitfall we must not fall into. If you *only* see Jesus as your example, you will inevitably be crushed by the weight of striving to imitate His perfection. There is a better way. It is the gospel. Jesus did not *only* come to be our example. He ultimately came to be our Savior. So let me apply this concept to the account of the woman being healed of her hemorrhage.

You must first see yourself in the woman. We all have the internal hemorrhage of sin that needs healing. We all have experienced shame because of our uncleanness before a holy God. We all have experienced alienation from others because of our sinful nature. We all have, at one point or another, felt like the outcast. We all have experienced spiritual bankruptcy from our futile human efforts of searching for a cure to remedy our disease of sin. We all have experienced the scourging whip of affliction beating us down. Do you see yourself in the woman yet?

And secondly, we must come to Jesus, reach out, and touch His garment in faith. We must call upon His name and experience His power coming upon us to staunch our hemorrhage of sin. Meditate with me for a moment on the honor Christ has bestowed on you because He has removed your shame and taken it on Himself at the cross. He was subjected to a cosmic level of public shaming, so you could forever be honored as a son or daughter of the Most High.

He has atoned for the impure discharge of your sin and clothed you with His righteousness. Now you can come before the Father free from all condemnation and accusation of sin. You stand before Him holy and blameless in Christ. Can you see Jesus telling you, "Daughter (or son) your faith has made you well; go in peace"?

When you see yourself in the woman you will be both humbled and honored by Jesus. When you see yourself in the woman you will become aware of your desperate need for Him. And when you reach out to Jesus, His love for you will overwhelm you. Then, and only then, will you be empowered to love your spouse in the same way that you have been loved by Jesus.

Then, and only then, will you live out Col. 3:12–15, "Put on then, as God's chosen ones, holy and beloved, compassionate hearts, kindness, humility, meekness, and patience, bearing with one another and, if anyone has a complaint against another, forgiving each other; as the Lord has forgiven you, so you also must forgive. And above all these put on love, which binds everything together in perfect harmony."

Husbands, you will then love your wives as Christ loved the church and gave Himself up for her. Wives, you will then be able to joyfully respect and submit to your husband, as to the Lord.

Both spouses will no longer see marriage as a means of personal fulfillment and achievement of happiness. But instead, they will see marriage, primarily, as an intimate opportunity to facilitate the love of Jesus into one another's lives to grow in holiness together as a beautiful display of the gospel message itself.

You will then see, and be empowered by, the mystery of a Man leaving His Father to be joined to His bride, to become one flesh with her. "This mystery is profound; and I am saying that it refers to Christ and the church" (Eph. 5:32).

16

Divorce / Remarriage

His name is Matt.

He was born into a Christian family but was raised in a legalistic church environment. The church culture around him boiled down to this: if you do what's right, you'll be blessed, and at the end of your life God will grant you eternal life. Inevitably, this mindset and theology led to shame-motivated living for Matt. He knew he did not live up to the standard of always being good, and so a sense of nagging shame would plague him for his failure of never being good enough.

Matt's parents also bore the weight of this shame during their time at this legalistic church. When they heard the message of being consigned to hell for not meeting the expected standard, they stopped going to church altogether. At the time, Matt was in sixth grade.

Fast forward now to Matt entering adulthood in his twenties. He moved to Corpus Christi, Texas. Although he identified as a Christian and was baptized into the above-mentioned legalistic environment, Jesus remained on the periphery of Matt's life. He never found a church home.

He remembered being taught in church that sex was only to be reserved for marriage, and so there in Corpus, he entered into his first marriage with Amy. He had originally met her in high school, but they reconnected in college at Texas A&M Corpus Christi. Although Amy was as sweet as can be, Matt would describe his marriage with her as very duty-bound instead of the mutual enjoyment of soul-mates. Over time, Matt felt as though they became strangers to one another.

❧

It's 10 PM. Matt has just spent his whole day teaching and coaching at Corpus Christi High School where he works. He tosses his workbag off to the side where it slides to rest in the corner nook in the kitchen. He takes his shoes off and goes to his bedroom. After showering and performing the nightly routine he jumps into bed exhausted. He looks over with longing to the side of the bed where his wife ordinarily sleeps. Her side of the bed is vacant. She's away for another stint to pour herself out serving children with special needs at group homes as part of her daily occupation. It's more than an occupation for her, though. Her work is her passion.

Likewise, there are days when the reverse happens. Amy would sometimes come home to an empty bed because Matt would be spending long hours and late game nights owing to his coaching position at the high school. With the subtlety of time, a pernicious distance settles into Matt's heart and the woman he married becomes more like a roommate to him, present or absent.

Date nights disappear. Exclusive time together vanishes. And all that is left for Amy and Matt are family get-togethers and attendance at the Methodist church on Sundays. But the truth of the matter remains that no vital relationship with Christ binds them together as husband and wife during this time.

Matt now lays awake and alone in his bed staring up at the ceiling. All the lights are turned off. It's the end of a long day of teaching and coaching. Negative thoughts begin to course through his mind like an imperceptible current of electricity. These whispering thoughts begin subtly and then grow louder. They instigate a mental campaign to influence his desires and emotions.

This marriage isn't working. I want out. We're just not meant to be. I could be happier with someone else.

All the while Matt and Amy grow further and further apart.

And then the day comes when Matt meets Rachel. She recently began working as an administrative assistant in the front office of the high school where Matt teaches and coaches. They bump into each other one day when Matt goes to make copies for his economics class. He's drawn to how attractive Rachel is, but what piques his curiosity about her is the numerous interests they share in common. Matt begins making excuses to drop by the front office to strike up conversations with her day after day, and then after a few weeks, Rachel makes the first move. She asks Matt out to the movies to see the film *Big Fish*. Matt agrees to go with her.

But what Matt doesn't realize at this moment is the Man with holes in His hands standing right behind him with arms open wide beckoning his repentance.

"All that the Father gives Me will come to Me, and the one who comes to Me I will certainly not cast out" (John 6:37 NASB).

A brief sidebar: the literal Greek text of the above verse uses a double negative when Jesus says "certainly not" in the phrase "certainly not cast out." The use of a double negative in Greek serves as an intensifier to magnify what is being negated. This verse emphasizes the supreme and lavish grace of Jesus on all who would come to Him in faith and repentance. Never, not ever, will Jesus cast out the person coming to Him. He's that gracious. He's that compassionate.

After the movie, Matt and Rachel go to a bar. After the bar, they go to Jim's Diner and stay out until one in the morning. During this extramarital encounter, Matt begins to experience an emotional connection with Rachel. He parts from her with a kiss on the cheek.

He goes back to his house that night and sleeps on the couch. He lays awake replaying in his mind the date he's just gone on. The forbidden nature of the encounter brings a thrill to him, but he also has to suppress a slight pang of guilt lingering deep in his soul. His longing for more of the emotional connection he has with Rachel outweighs his guilt. This longing drives him to his next course of action.

The following morning, he wakes up and walks over to his wife as she's getting ready for work.

"Amy, I want to get a divorce."

No knock-down, drag-out argument ensues.

Over the next couple of months, Matt and Amy go through an amicable divorce, which is finalized by April 2004.

During the initiation of the divorce process, Matt stays at Rachel's house. They begin a full relationship with one another. At this time, Matt is viewing his relationship with Rachel as adulterous because his divorce from Amy is not yet finalized. He sinks into the mindset afforded by his legalistic church upbringing. In the rare moments when he stops to consider the Lord amidst his relationship with Rachel, he thinks to himself, "God is going to get me one day for doing this." This mindset embeds in Matt deep feelings of shame and insecurity that would haunt him for years.

But what Matt doesn't realize through all of this is the Man with holes in His hands standing right behind him with arms open wide. Jesus is right there beckoning his repentance.

⁀

Three months later, Matt and Rachel move away to Alabama. After two years, they get married. And the blessings begin to flow into their life like a deluge. Matt is admitted into one of the top law schools in the country when the odds seem utterly impossible. He graduates number five in his class. Also, during this time, Rachel obtains her Ph.D. in Sports Communication. And two years later they move back to Texas and have their first child, a baby boy named Henry.

Matt lays awake one night with his wife next to him and their newborn in the pack-in-play near the bedside. He considers all the achievements and blessings over the past four years. A smile forms on his face. And then out of nowhere, another thought seeps into his mind. His smile begins to fade. The legalistic mindset so deeply ingrained in him since childhood rears its ugly head. The shame of his past affair and divorce overshadows him now. His joy is robbed from him at this moment and a deep abiding restlessness settles over his soul.

But what Matt doesn't realize is the Man with holes in His hands standing right at his bedside with arms open wide, beckoning Matt to come to Him.

⁀

Four years pass and they have another child, a girl this time, named Lizzy. As the family grows, Matt and Rachel decide to start a business together. With the added stresses of raising two children and running a family business, a great strain is placed on their marriage during this time. The stresses of being co-owners together and having responsibility for about 400 kids through their business prove to be too much for them; not to mention the responsibility of raising two children of their own. And then the real problems would begin for Matt and Rachel.

On Memorial Day of 2015, Matt walks into his bedroom and looks down to discover evidence of an affair that has been going on for two years. He stares at the evidence before him and suddenly becomes completely numb to his surroundings. Like a computer whose internal cooling fan has been whirring loudly and then suddenly turns off, Matt shuts down. He shuts down emotionally. He shuts down mentally. He shuts down spiritually. This goes on for the next hour or so, and then his numbness is replaced with deep abiding anger and bitterness.

He realizes he's at a crossroads. A decision has to be made. *Do I stand in this with her and confront her about the affair or do I leave?* He chooses the former. That night he enters the bedroom where Rachel is folding clothes and begins his interrogation.

"Rachel, I saw the evidence. You've been cheating on me."

She pauses and looks up. She says nothing.

Suddenly, Matt cannot restrain himself any longer and a barrage of questions erupts from his mouth. Questions like, "When did this start? How could you? Did you not think I would find out?" One after the other and Rachel begins explaining her side of the story, but Matt is blinded by bitterness and anger. And suddenly both spouses have tears streaming down their faces.

"Rachel, we have to rebuild our relationship. Let's go to counseling."

She agrees.

Their counselor, Kasey, now sits across from Matt and Rachel, a beautiful mahogany table situated between them. Both spouses share their different sides of the story. Matt owns that it was his fault for being emotionally aloof from Rachel. During the second counseling session, he acknowledges the part he played in disconnecting from his wife.

"If I'm honest, I let the business relationship I have with Rachel consume our marriage relationship. I was pouring in conflict and withholding love rather than detaching from the business and pouring love into Rachel like I should have. At the end of the day, we have come to be business partners rather than marriage partners. It makes sense why Rachel turned elsewhere for love and affirmation because she received none from me," Matt admits.

The conclusion Kasey draws after several consecutive sessions with them is that Matt needs to make changes regarding his admission about emotionally detaching from his wife, and likewise, Rachel needs to put up guardrails regarding her use of social media and the danger such technology poses to their marriage. Both Matt and Rachel agree to these so-called rules of engagement and try to begin again . . . a fresh start.

Over the next months, they take trips to the beach and go on a family vacation to Disney World. Matt and Rachel start working and focusing on their marriage. But at the end of the day, a swarm of lingering doubts and questions regarding inconsistencies in their previous season of marriage pesters Matt's mind, like the buzzing of a busy beehive. In addition to these doubts, the social media guard rails established in therapy begin to come down at this point. Consequently, Matt and Rachel embark on a rollercoaster cycle of highs and lows in their marriage.

Matt's insecurities become magnified and begin pouring into their relationship. Rachel decides to leave Matt. Matt comes home one day and walks through the laundry room into the kitchen. He goes to the living room. No one is there. He calls out to see if anyone is home. No response. After searching the upstairs and downstairs the reality dawns on him: his wife has taken the children and gone.

After hiring an attorney and following his advice, Matt is able to pick up his children at daycare four days later.

Matt begins spiraling downward into depression and despair. He stands on the scale a week later and realizes that he's rapidly losing weight. Food becomes tasteless. Sleep becomes evasive. He lays awake at night for hours on end. The darkness in his bedroom seems darker, heavier now. He feels as though he's walking down an endless tunnel of darkness without a singular hope of light at the end. He is overwhelmed by the fact that he has done something terribly wrong, and this is his penance for the affair he had during his first marriage.

But what Matt doesn't realize at this moment is the Man with holes in His hands standing right beside him with arms open wide.

As if on cue, the next day at work Matt shares briefly what he's going through with one of his co-workers named Susan. Now, Susan loves Jesus. She is married to a man named David who also loves Jesus, and he also happens to be a licensed professional counselor (LPC) as well as a Board-Certified Professional Christian Counselor (you'll meet David again in chapter 22).

"Matt, tell you what. Why don't you reach out to my husband, David, and see if he can be of any help to you during this difficult time."

"Done. I'll do it. Shoot me his contact info."

Two days later, Matt is pulling into the Oak Hills Church parking lot. He's nervous. But he's also desperately broken. He walks into the church and finds that he's lost without any direction of where to go.

He stops a random person in the hallway and asks, "Can you give me directions to the prayer chapel?"

The stranger cordially responds affirmatively and points him in the right direction. Matt stumbles upon a sign at the bottom of a staircase indicating the direction of the prayer chapel.

He climbs the stairs leading up to the prayer room. He enters the room and immediately notices the peaceful silence greeting him and ushering him in. He looks up and sees a wooden cross as the centerpiece of the room. He walks in slowly and looks down observing chairs and then a padded kneeler before him. He kneels.

He looks straight up to see a steeple overhead. Stone white walls surround him and two windows afford the luminescence of natural light to fill the room. There, in this place of refuge, Matt kneels and prays to Jesus. It's the first time in all his life that he can remember kneeling and surrendering to Jesus. In his surrender, he goes to Him in prayer.

"Lord, if you just get me through this, I'll give my kids to you and they are yours forever. Oh, God please take care of my kids through all this mess."

Matt knows that this is exactly what Jesus has done to this day. He has taken care of his children.

After meeting with Jesus in his moment of surrender, Matt heads to see David at his counseling office. David greets Matt warmly at the front entrance and shows Matt to his office. They make their way to the office and sit down opposite one another. Matt finds him to be very approachable, warm, and kind. He feels very quickly that this is someone he can trust with the mess he's made of his life and relationships. Matt shares the experience he just had with Jesus in the prayer chapel, and David can tell by the joy on his face that his friend has just encountered Jesus. He then pours out his soul to him. Every hurt and every dysfunctional detail is met with the love of Christ and a nonjudgmental countenance.

A counseling and discipleship relationship is born that day.

Three weeks pass. Matt now sits on his living room couch with his iPad on his lap scrolling through family photos. He smiles at the memories he's had with his kids. And suddenly something unexpected happens. The iCloud Matt still shares with Rachel abruptly begins uploading a host of photos and screenshots that undeniably point to his wife having moved on to another man. Matt's eyes open wide and shock hits him like a sucker punch. The evidence before him quickly thrusts him out of his depression. Instead, he's left with a profound brokenness.

He does not respond to this brokenness in a godly way. He thinks to himself, *I'm done. That's it.* He picks up the phone and calls his attorney.

"What can I do for you, Matt."

Matt's response is quick and concise, void of doubt, "I want to divorce my wife."

That night he begins visiting dating sites. An insatiable desire to move on to someone else overwhelms his soul. Within the next several days he's already going on dates. His brokenness overcomes him during this time.

During the divorce process, every emotion of brokenness becomes amplified in Matt. Shame, insecurity, imposter syndrome, loneliness, envy, and lust hound and consume him. Matt quickly realizes that each of these emotions had previously been masked by his depression over another failed marriage. And now that the depression has been lifted, Matt is left to his own devices with all of these charged emotions of brokenness. Driven by these emotions, Matt is led to quickly pursue another relationship.

But what Matt doesn't realize at this moment is the Man with holes in His hands standing right behind him with arms open wide.

What about what happened in the prayer room? Where is Matt's heart of surrender to the Lord? At this time, Christ is in Matt's story, but Matt is not in Christ's story. Jesus is not the center of Matt's life. Matt's focus remains on himself rather than on Jesus. He has a relationship with Jesus at this point, as opposed to merely identifying with Christ, but Jesus has not become Lord over his romantic life and pursuits. So, Matt begins dating women and earnestly searching for someone to fill the massive void in his soul; the void that only Jesus can truly fill and satisfy.

Matt is missing the soul-quenching truth claim Jesus declares in John 6:35, "I am the bread of life; whoever comes to me shall not hunger, and whoever believes in me shall never thirst."

Matt previously learned from his time with David about his "discipline of darkness" (as coined by Oswald Chambers in his devotional, *My Utmost for His Highest*).[14] And now, Matt sees and feels that his world has plunged him in the same direction.

And so, Matt meets Monica.

The first six weeks of their relationship are fast, fun, free, and exciting. But lurking under the thrill of the new relationship is Matt's desperate longing to

---

14. Chambers O. (1935), *My Utmost for His Highest* (Dodd, Mead, & Co.), Feb. 14th.

repair the brokenness incurred by his second marriage. He thirsts for love and affirmation. So, he looks to Monica to fulfill these desires in him.

In the initial phase of the relationship, a visionary image embeds itself deep in Matt's mind. The image depicts a lasting cohesive family unit being formed through the blending of Matt and Monica's children from previous partners. Matt desperately longs to make this vision become his future reality. He firmly attaches himself to this image to heal the brokenness from his second marriage.

Matt's clear judgment becomes shrouded in the clouds of this wishful image. Glaring red flags telling him to stop and turn around are unheeded. His relationship with Christ is in its infancy during this time, and Jesus is not the center of Matt's life. And so, he ignores the blaring warning signals and pushes forward to try to obtain the healing he desperately longs for through his relationship with Monica.

The red flags begin once or twice a month initially, and then after seven months, they would happen every several days. Despite all this, Matt and Monica share some good times and they decide to move in together. They become engaged to be married as well.

After nine months, the red flag issues become even more dramatic, with higher intensity. But both partners still progress forward toward marriage hoping that these glaring issues would work themselves out.

Matt, in an attempt to prove his level of commitment to Monica, agrees to try to conceive a child with her. In the 11th month of their relationship, they become pregnant with Matt's youngest daughter. After conception, their relationship issues now become even more severe and magnified. Numerous police reports and calls are made against Matt, and he becomes the victim of reverse sexism. These red flags finally lead him to take a step back and postpone the wedding.

He now sits by himself in his office before leaving work for the day feeling the utter brokenness of his relationship with Monica. He buries his face in his hands. The brokenness he feels is palpable in his chest. He longs to fulfill the void and brokenness created by his failed marriages.

But what Matt doesn't realize at this moment is the Man with holes in His hands standing right behind him with arms open wide.

In effect, Matt's course of action thus far demonstrates the attitude of his heart, "No, Jesus, I got this."

He enters into therapy with a Christian counselor but receives no practical guidance, and the issues of his brokenness are never dealt with on a deeper level. And so, Matt continues treading the same dark path and enters into a vicious cycle of separation and getting back together again with Monica.

After a couple of months of the vicious cycle, Matt decides he has had enough. So, he breaks up with Monica for about a month. About a week and a half into this time he finds himself dating another woman in an attempt to repair the brokenness plaguing him. This relationship never becomes sexual but definitely can be classified as an emotional attachment.

And the guilt intrinsic to being with another woman while Monica is pregnant with his child drives him into further despair. Matt thinks to himself while lying awake at night in the dark: *my unborn child does not deserve to be born into such a broken situation.* And so, he calls off the relationship and comes back to Monica to re-engage with her.

And like clockwork, they are right back in the vicious cycle within a matter of days. Matt nurtures himself again with the image of blending their families into a functional cohesive unit.

But he, in effect, gives the stiff arm to Jesus.

Again, his attitude at this point is, "I got this Jesus. Let me take care of this." He goes back again and again to the picturesque, idyllic image he has built up in his mind.

But what Matt doesn't realize at this moment is the Man with holes in His hands standing right behind him with arms open wide.

His daughter, Myra, is born in January of 2018. Even the five days spent overnight at the hospital proved to be utterly rancorous for him and Monica. Relationship conflict intractably hounds them in the midst of what would otherwise be a joyous and rapturous occasion: God's miracle of life being brought into the world.

With Myra's birth comes additional challenges to their relationship. Now Myra is utilized as a weapon against Matt because she is so precious to him. Matt's absolute and unconditional love for his child creates a profound vulnerability in him. As they enter into the separation part of the cycle, Matt's sweet and precious baby girl is withheld from his fatherly embrace.

The withholding of Myra from him paternally stings and cuts deep. Matt's brokenness becomes even more amplified. And the next progression to the brokenness is lawsuits involving custody battles for Myra. In response to this, Monica and Matt decide to get married, but marriage proves to be no silver bullet for the intractable problems they continue experiencing.

During this time period, Monica files for divorce three times and each divorce becomes non-suited, meaning that both parties agree to try to reconcile. When the boundary of calling the authorities for a non-emergency situation is crossed again Matt decides enough is enough and files for a divorce. A final separation between him and Monica takes place, and Matt once again embarks on his journey toward unbrokenness.

Matt has just turned 40 years of age. He sits in his leather wingback chair in his office. Looking at the trees and nature outside his window, he considers his life and pays special consideration to the broken marriage relationships left behind in the wake of his past, like observing the wooden fragments of a sunken ship drifting along at sea. He resolves at this moment to set his focus on Jesus instead of himself.

And suddenly Matt turns and realizes the Man with holes in His hands has been standing right behind him with arms open wide this whole time.

At this moment, the realization brings his head downward into a bow, not from shame, but because of the gravity of Christ's redeeming grace becoming firmly embedded in his soul. He would later come to realize through reading Scripture and prayer that the voice of condemnation for all of his sin and brokenness was not Christ's voice, but was the voice of shame afforded by his legalistic church upbringing. He now perceives the redemption of Christ in this moment of clarity and resounding truth.

In his office, Matt grabs a legal notepad and writes down goals for himself. His first goal is to grow closer to Christ by reading the Bible from cover to cover. The next goal he sets for himself comes from an encounter he had previously with his pastor, Bill Cornelius, who told him about a 100-hour-long prayer challenge.

So, over the next months, Matt devotes 100 hours of focused time in the presence of God, seeking Him earnestly. Matt realizes early on during these 100 hours that Christ has been there in his story the whole time. As Matt prays and seeks after Jesus, he becomes reminded of all of the "coincidences" of provision and things working out exactly as they did.

The totality of evidence points to Jesus working in his life this whole time. He remembers how the Lord faithfully provided work and projects for him even though he had stepped away from his previous employer right before the pandemic.

Jesus also provided Susan to Matt as a co-worker who connected him with her husband, David. He recalls the first life-giving encounter he had with

David, and now Matt understands that was all Jesus moving chess pieces into their proper place to guide him toward unbrokenness; to guide Matt to the Man with holes in His hands standing right behind him with arms open wide the whole time beckoning his repentance.

For Matt, David would become the example of Jesus and His love to him. He never felt judged by him throughout the entirety of his three failed marriages and subsequent divorces. His approach has always been, "I'm here for you, brother." And then it's up to Matt to follow through and come to him. And to this day, David is still there for Matt as an ever-present reminder of the grace and love of Christ. Every time they meet, he is there with open arms and ready to pull Matt in and give him a big ole bear hug saying, "Come here brother!" And then he speaks the gospel to Matt. He remains the Christ-like example among the men in Matt's life.

Years have passed since Matt met David at his counseling office. They have met periodically in a discipleship/counseling capacity following their initial meeting at the church. Matt now pulls into the Black Rifle coffee shop to meet David for coffee and hot chocolate.

Matt enters, and once again he greets him with a big ole bear hug. They sit down and begin catching up. David looks at Matt and sees in his countenance a new man in Christ. Matt shares with him the new lens he's looking through in life—to live for Jesus. He then updates him on his involvement in his local church, including being mentored by his pastor and looking at starting a new ministry for those going through relational brokenness, especially those who have been divorced.

David smiles at Matt, leans back in his chair, and feels elated about the transformation he sees in his friend. It's all because of Jesus. He sees that the Lord has truly taken hold of Matt's life. He's no longer talking to David about his failed marriages, but rather he is overjoyed to share his new purpose in life.

Moving Forward

Jesus has infused Matt's life with a new purpose. Matt's broken past no longer defines him because of Jesus. He no longer lives in shame because he realizes the extravagant grace of Jesus covers all of his shame and makes him whole again. Now, Matt wants to share this incredible gospel of Jesus with others who are broken and in despair like he was.

Matt is starting a ministry called "Unbrokenness" to serve and care for people who are broken from relationship trauma. His ministry will seek to connect people with Jesus who do not yet have a relationship with Him. His ministry will also seek to care for those who already know Christ but need Jesus to become the center of their life. He will be using social media to fill the void media already seeks to fill, but his ministry will do so in a godly, Christ-centered way. The goal is to get people connected to a faith community through which they can encounter Jesus.

Matt's Takeaways

As Matt began reading his Bible seriously, he realized a few things. The people in the Bible we look up to so often come from deep places of brokenness. When he read the book of Ruth, he suddenly realized that Ruth came from intense trauma. She becomes a widow in the very first chapter. And not only Ruth but her mother-in-law, Naomi, is also ravaged and impoverished by widowhood in that first chapter. These two women were profoundly broken.

And then we come to Boaz. Some Bible commentators point out that he too was likely widowed before ever meeting Ruth. Broken people are found on every single page of Scripture.

But every page of Scripture points us to our true and better Kinsman Redeemer. Every page of Scripture points us to the One who came from the lineage of broken Ruth and Boaz. His whole family line recorded in Matthew chapter one is littered with brokenness upon brokenness. And because of Him . . . because of Jesus, we can become whole. Jesus leads us to unbrokenness because He became utterly broken for *our* sins on the cross.

And with His resurrection, He reveals to us His triumph over all our sin and brokenness. Jesus, the risen Lord, gloriously shows us what unbrokenness in Him will be like one day for all who put their trust in Him so that He would be the center of all our lives and have first place in everything. Jesus is the firstborn from the dead:

".. . He is the beginning, the firstborn from the dead, that in everything he might be preeminent" (Col. 1:18b).

17

What the Bible says about Divorce / Remarriage

Before we delve into what the Bible says about divorce, and by implication remarriage, I would like to remind you that we are looking at these different aspects of life through the heart of Jesus, which is inherent to the gospel lens. In other words, before I share the words of Jesus about divorce, I want you to glimpse His heart for you.

This will be especially important for those of you who are already divorced, are considering divorce, or who have someone close to you going through a divorce. Listen to what Dr. Dane Ortlund has to say from his book, *Gentle and Lowly*, about the heart of Jesus concerning certain areas of the Christ follower's life that are particularly broken and difficult to handle:

> "We all tend to have some small pocket of our life where we have difficulty believing the forgiveness of God reaches. We say we are totally forgiven. And we sincerely believe our sins are forgiven. Pretty much, anyway. But there's that one deep, dark part of our lives, even our present lives, that seems so intractable, so ugly, so beyond recovery. 'To the uttermost' in Hebrews 7:25 means: God's forgiving, redeeming, restoring touch reaches down into the darkest crevices of our souls,

those places where we are most ashamed, most defeated. More than this: those crevices of sin are themselves the places where Christ loves us the most."[15]

In this excerpt, Dr. Ortlund is drawing out the implications of Christ's heart for us in Heb. 7:25 which says, "Consequently, he is able to save to the uttermost those who draw near to God through him, since he always lives to make intercession for them." This is the glorious reality of Jesus being our high priest who intercedes on our behalf before God the Father.

His heart is for you, especially in your brokenness. If divorce or a broken relationship is the "small pocket" in your life where you experience shame most acutely then hear this single solitary truth again before we move any further: divorce and brokenness "are themselves the places where Christ loves us the most."[16]

Now that we have seen the heart of Jesus for us in our brokenness let us receive the words of truth Jesus speaks regarding divorce. Let's consider three texts closely: Matt. 5:31, 32, Matt. 19:3–9, and 1 Cor. 7:13–16 (all NASB).

Matthew 5:31, 32

"It was said, 'Whoever sends his wife away, let him give her a certificate of divorce'; but I say to you that everyone who divorces his wife, except for the reason of unchastity, makes her commit adultery; and whoever marries a divorced woman commits adultery."

In Matt. 5:31 Jesus references Deut. 24:1 regarding the Old Testament practice of divorce. In Deut. 24:1 (NASB), Moses gives a much broader permissibility for divorce than Jesus does here in Matt. 5:32 because Moses says a man can divorce his wife if "she finds no favor in his eyes because he has found some indecency in her." Jesus reinterprets the Mosaic Law for us when He utters the contrastingly powerful words, "But I say to you . . ." His words here in Matthew 5 serve to uphold the cause of women in the patriarchal-dominated Jewish culture of the 1st century.

---

15. Ortlund D (2020), *Gentle and Lowly*, Crossway, 83.
16. Ibid.

Deut. 24:2–4 gives us more insight into the Mosaic Law regarding remarriage. These verses reveal that divorce frees the woman to remarry, but if her second husband divorces her, she is not permitted to return to her first husband because "she has been defiled" (Deut. 24:4 NASB).

But Jesus avoids many of the problems incurred by divorce and remarriage by making divorce allowable under one circumstance: "*the* reason of unchastity" (Mt. 5:32 NASB). What does the word "unchastity" mean? The Greek word used here is *porneia* which is where we get our English word "pornography." This word can also be rendered as "fornication" or "sexual immorality." *Porneia* is the committing of any sexual impurity outside the boundaries of marriage such as adultery or marital unfaithfulness. In creating this one exception, He then explains that divorce or remarriage for any other reason is to be considered adultery.

My position on this very difficult verse is that unbiblical, but legal, remarriage remains valid in the eyes of God. I also believe that the adultery incurred by such a remarriage is not an enduring state but occurs once at the joining of the individuals in the action of remarriage.

What is Jesus doing here in His famous Sermon on the Mount by narrowing down the permissibility of divorce so much? *He is revealing our brokenness.*

Jesus knew then and He certainly still knows now how many unbiblical divorces and remarriages would take place after He uttered these enduring and weighty words. He is skillfully raising the bar of righteousness, so we would be driven into a deeper need for Him amid our brokenness. In another place, during the Sermon on the Mount, He declares, "You therefore must be perfect, as your heavenly Father is perfect (Matt. 5:48 NASB)."

Still, as always, Jesus reveals His heart through Scripture when Paul writes of Him in Rom. 5:20–6:2 (NASB), "The Law came in so that the transgression would increase; but where sin increased, grace abounded all the more, so that, as sin reigned in death, so also grace would reign through righteousness to eternal life through Jesus Christ our Lord. What shall we say then? Are we to continue in sin so that grace may increase? May it never be! How shall we who died to sin still live in it?"

At every turn during His sermon in Matthew chapters 5–7, Jesus ups the ante and asks more of us than we could ever possibly deliver. He takes the Mosaic Law and re-explains the commands in light of a person's heart. He's asking us to have 100% purity of heart in all that we say, think, and do. How could we expect anything different than such narrow permissibility when Jesus teaches us about divorce and remarriage?

Jesus is showing us our deep need for Him and the salvation only He can provide. This is why we must cling to the crux of the sermon, which I believe is found in Matt. 5:17 (NASB), "Do not think that I have come to abolish the Law or the Prophets; I have not come to abolish them but to fulfill them." Jesus is the ultimate fulfillment of the Law and the Prophets. He is our only righteousness before God. We must see our desperate need for His righteousness and salvation.

If we cannot see our desperate need for His righteousness and salvation through His Sermon on the Mount then we are probably not reading it carefully enough. This is why the first beatitude in Matt. 5:3 is, "Blessed are the poor in spirit, for theirs is the kingdom of heaven." In other words, only those who realize they are completely and utterly spiritually bankrupt apart from the saving work of Christ can enter the kingdom of heaven.

If you are divorced or are in the midst of a broken situation then this is your moment to be poor in spirit before Jesus and see how His heart is ever so drawn out to you, especially in your brokenness. If you are not in a broken situation and believe you have no need for Christ's saving grace and righteousness, then how great is your brokenness!

Now let's look at Matt. 19:3–9 (NASB) briefly for additional teaching on divorce and remarriage.

Matthew 19:3–9

> "*Some* Pharisees came to Jesus, testing Him and asking, 'Is it lawful *for a man* to divorce his wife for any reason at all?' And He answered and said, 'Have you not read that He who created *them* from the beginning MADE THEM MALE AND FEMALE, AND SAID, 'FOR THIS REASON A MAN SHALL LEAVE HIS FATHER AND MOTHER AND BE JOINED TO HIS WIFE, AND THE TWO SHALL BECOME ONE FLESH'? 'So they are no longer two, but one flesh. What therefore God has joined together, let no man separate.' They said to Him, 'Why then did Moses command to GIVE HER A CERTIFICATE OF DIVORCE AND SEND *her* AWAY?' He said to them, 'Because of your hardness of heart Moses permitted you to

divorce your wives; but from the beginning, it has not been this way. And I say to you, whoever divorces his wife, except for immorality, and marries another woman commits adultery.'"

What I want us to see here is how Jesus deftly avoids being ensnared by the Pharisees' testing of Him. Whenever He is confronted with a situation, His mouth speaks from that which fills His heart: Scripture.

He takes the Pharisees back to God's original design for marriage in Gen. 1:27 and 2:24. In doing so, He's taking us back to the God-given, pre-fall design for marriage between one male and one female. He establishes the permanence of the male and female being joined together as one flesh. And Jesus concludes that we should let no man cut asunder that which God has brought together as one.

The Pharisees retort and try to make Jesus back down from His permanence view of marriage by quoting Moses to Him, but He replies by telling them their root problem is their "hardness of heart." He again reinforces that "from the beginning it has not been this way" (Matt. 19:8 NASB). In so doing, He takes us back to the original God-given, pre-fall design of marriage. Jesus doesn't budge, not one bit when tested by the Pharisees.

His view of marriage is so lofty. Indeed, the disciples stagger at His words and respond in Matt. 19:10 (NASB), "If the relationship of the man with his wife is like this, it is better not to marry." The same thing is happening to the disciples here that are supposed to happen to us when we read the Sermon on the Mount in Matthew 5–7. Jesus ups the ante and leaves us reeling when we glimpse the unattainably high standard He expects us to reach. He concludes the passage by telling His disciples, "He who is able to accept *this*, let him accept *it*" (Matt. 19:12 NASB).

We can accept Jesus's words only when we receive Him into our lives as the perfect fulfillment of the Law and Prophets. He is our only righteousness. We can receive Him when we see how gentle and humble His heart is toward us broken and weary sinners:

"Come to Me, all who are weary and heavy-laden, and I will give you rest. Take My yoke upon you and learn from Me, for I am gentle and humble in heart, and YOU WILL FIND REST FOR YOUR SOULS. For My yoke is easy and My burden is light" (Matt. 11:28–30 NASB).

But how can His yoke be easy and His burden be light when His standards are so high for marriage, divorce, and remarriage. Answer: everything hinges on *how we come to Him.* Do we come to Jesus like the Pharisees trying to test Him and press Him into categories we are comfortable with or do we come to Him weary and heavy-laden seeing how far we have fallen from His unattainable standards of righteousness? Do we come to Jesus admitting our desperate need for *His* grace and righteousness?

Lastly, here are the Apostle Paul's words on divorce in 1 Cor. 7:13–16 (NASB):

> "And a woman who has an unbelieving husband, and he consents to live with her, she must not send her husband away. For the unbelieving husband is sanctified through his wife, and the unbelieving wife is sanctified through her believing husband; for otherwise your children are unclean, but now they are holy. Yet if the unbelieving one leaves, let him leave; the brother or the sister is not under bondage in such *cases*, but God has called us to peace. For how do you know, O wife, whether you will save your husband? Or how do you know, O husband, whether you will save your wife?"

The main crystallized thought we must grasp as we look at divorce and remarriage through the gospel lens is how we can have an eternal mindset about these controversial topics. Did you notice what Paul does in 1 Cor. 7:14?

He is looking at a broken relationship between a husband and wife through the lens of seeing how the unbelieving spouse can be won over to Jesus through the believing spouse. He repeats this eternal mindset in verse 16 when he asks, "For how do you know, wife, whether you will save your husband?" This indeed is the heart of Jesus. He is the friend of sinners (see Matt. 11:19). "For the Son of Man came to seek and to save the lost" (Luke 19:10).

The phrase "consents to live with" in 1 Cor. 7:13, 14 when the unbelieving spouse agrees to stay with the believing one implies the situation is consensual, and I believe safe for the whole family. The Greek word for "consent" used here means "to agree" and connotes the mindset of striving toward reaching goals and solving problems with the other spouse.

I do *not* believe 1 Cor. 7:13–16 refers to a volatile situation where abuse is present, and the home is not a safe place for the abused spouse or children. In such cases, safety is prioritized, separation is advised, and support from the church family for the abused spouse and children is paramount. It is the high calling and responsibility of the pastor and elders of the church to shepherd the flock with great care and diligence to protect those who need protection during such times of dire need.

An Additional Scriptural Permission for Divorce

1 Cor. 7:15 adds one more Scriptural permission for divorce (in addition to sexual immorality as detailed earlier). Verse 15 says, "Yet if the unbelieving one leaves, let him leave; the brother or the sister is not under bondage in such *cases* . . ." Here we see that abandonment is a biblical reason for divorce. The phrase "not under bondage" implies that remarriage is a permissible possibility, but the Apostle Paul applauds the prospect of remaining unmarried because "one who is unmarried is concerned about the things of the Lord, how he may please the Lord" (1 Cor. 7:32 NASB).

And later in the passage, he reiterates a similar eternal mindset by stating, "This I say for your own benefit; not to put a restraint upon you, but to promote what is appropriate and *to secure* undistracted devotion to the Lord" (1 Cor. 7:35 NASB). The gospel lens is applied to every situation. Look at life through an eternal mindset and the heart of Jesus.

Looking to Remarry

If you find yourself divorced, understand whether you do or do not have the gift of celibacy, "I wish that all were as I myself am [*single*]. But each one has his own gift from God, . . . (1 Cor. 7:7 NASB)." If you do not have this gift, you can look to remarry as Paul states in 1 Cor. 7:2 (NASB), "But because of temptation to sexual immoralities, each man is to have his own wife, and each woman is to have her own husband." There are, however, a few important questions:

"Have you come before the Lord with your first marriage, seeking repentance, if needed?"

"Have you come before the Lord seeking His will, to bring Him the glory, regarding remarriage?"

"Have you considered if remarriage is biblically permissible in light of Scripture?"

Once you have been walking in oneness with Christ (discipleship) and understand He is your first love, your faith will grow in Him. You will come to see that "all things have been created through Him and for Him" (Col. 1:16b NASB) and your life is really about Jesus and not about you (see 2 Cor. 5:15). When you keep Jesus as your first love, at *His* timing, He can orchestrate an opportunity for remarriage if He wills (see 1 John 5:14).

You will see your spiritual fruit bringing love, joy, peace, patience, kindness, goodness, faithfulness, gentleness, and self-control (Gal. 5:22, 23) to others and yourself. You will also be able to recognize spiritual fruit in a potential spouse. As Scripture shares, "So then, you will know them by their fruits" (Matt. 7:20 NASB). You will develop "deal-breakers" on what is vital; for example: does he or she have a heart for discipleship with Christ? For a reference, go to amazon.com and review, *Date Smart to Marry for Life: Divorce Prevention for Single Christian Women*, Westbow Press, 2010.

A Word about Remarriage

If you are divorced and remarried for a reason other than sexual immorality or abandonment, I pray that you do not feel condemned by this chapter whatsoever. God often blesses unbiblical remarriages because He is so very gracious. Look no further than David and Bathsheba. David and Bathsheba both committed adultery and then David had her husband, Uriah, killed so he could take Bathsheba to be his wife. The offspring of this unbiblically initiated marriage was Solomon, from whom Jesus the Messiah would descend. And, not only is Solomon in the lineage of Christ but so are the adulterers, David and Bathsheba (see Matt 1:6). Our God is staggeringly gracious!

Therefore, God certainly does not wish for you to become divorced from an unbiblically initiated marriage. He tells us in Malachi 2:16 (NASB), "For I hate divorce." Plain and simple. His heart, the heart of Jesus, is for you to remain faithful to your wedding vows to illustrate the glorious gospel display of Christ's marriage to the church, His bride. The biblical view of marriage is to take every step necessary to *encourage reconciliation*, prevent divorce, and remain as one flesh with your spouse. This pleases the Lord.

But what if you are divorced? What if this chapter highlights the shame you have gone through in your past? Again, I would like to redirect your attention to the heart of Jesus for you.

Embrace His heart for you. Embrace His forgiveness!

I'll close by again drawing your attention to what Jesus did with the Samaritan woman at the well in John 4. When He encounters her, He comes to her gently and lowly in heart and says, "Give Me a drink" (John 4:7). He then reveals that He has living water to give to her. After a brief interchange, she then says to Jesus, "Sir, give me this water, so that I will not be thirsty or have to come here to draw water" (John 4:15). To this Jesus responds with the non sequitur, "Go, call your husband, and come here (verse 16)." She denies having a husband. And then Jesus unveils His supernatural knowledge of her broken situation by saying, ". . . You are right in saying, 'I have no husband'; for you have had five husbands, and the one you now have is not your husband. What you have said is true" (John 4:17, 18).

What is Jesus doing here to this five times divorced woman who is living with a man who is not her husband?

He's pursuing her with His gentle and lowly heart of redemption.

He knows the full extent of her brokenness regarding divorce and remarriage, and yet He does not lecture her on His permanence view of marriage. Instead, He offers her living water.

He also does not deny or minimize her brokenness, for He plainly reveals to her His intimate knowledge of how broken she is. And yet, the fact that He knows the depths of her sins makes His offer of the living water to her all the sweeter. Can you see His heart for her? Can you see His heart for you?

The Samaritan woman says to Him at the end of their dialogue, ". . . I know that Messiah is coming (he who is called Christ). When he comes, he will tell us all things" (John 4:25).

"Jesus said to her, 'I who speak to you am he'" (John 4:26).

This woman became transformed because she encountered *the heart* of Jesus Christ at that moment.

His heart beats for our redemption. His heart is drawn out to us, especially amid our deepest shame and brokenness.

18
Parenting

His name is Reuben. His son is Micah.

Father and son sit together just beyond the front entrance of their family's tent looking out eastward upon the horizon as a gentle breeze rustles the branches of an olive tree nearby. Reuben takes a deep breath to inhale the fresh morning air. Sun rays begin to climb up over the mountain peaks in the distance beyond to shine upon father and son mildly warming their faces amidst the crisp dawn air.

"Son, can you recite the *Shema* for me?"

Micah, still groggy from his fitful sleep last night, mumbles: "'Hear, O Israel! The Lord is our God, the Lord is one!' That's all I remember, papa."

Reuben replies, "That's okay, son. Let me help you finish the rest. Repeat after me . . ."

> "Hear, O Israel: The Lord our God, the Lord is one. You shall love the Lord your God with all your heart and with all your soul and with all your might. And these words that I command you today shall be on your heart. You shall teach them diligently to your children and shall talk of them when you sit in your house, and when you walk by the way, and when you lie down, and when you rise. You shall bind them as a sign on your hand, and they shall be as frontlets between your eyes. You shall write them on the doorposts of your house and on your gates" (Deut. 6:4-9).

Micah looks up at his dad and asks, "But, papa, what does the *Shema* mean when it says to love the Lord with all the heart and soul and might?"

"That's a great question, son," Reuben says smiling affectionately at his boy. He puts a hand on Micah's shoulder and responds, "Loving the Lord your God with all that you are begins with remembering . . . remembering who we are and from where our forefathers have come. Do you remember how many years they were enslaved in Egypt?"

"400 years," Micah answers.

"That's right, son. 400 years! And do you remember how they were rescued from slavery?"

"The Lord did many miracles through Moses. And then God parted the Red Sea to bring our people out safely on dry land."

Reuben beams at Micah, "Right again, my son! 'And the Lord brought us out of Egypt with a mighty hand and an outstretched arm, with great terror, with signs and wonders'" (Deut. 26:8).

Reuben continues, "So we first remember how God delivered us from slavery and gave us this good land flowing with milk and honey. The Passover feast helps us remember our deliverance from slavery as well. We sacrifice a lamb to remember how God had our forefathers sacrifice a spotless lamb, so the firstborn of the household would be spared."

"And then we thank Him by obeying the commands Moses received from the Lord on Mount Sinai. That's why the *Shema* says 'And these words that I command you today shall be on your heart.' And that's why I shall teach them diligently to you. We will talk of them 'when you walk by the way, and when you lie down, and when you rise.' The more we think and talk about this good law Moses has given us the more we will love the Lord. And that's what it means to love the Lord your God with all your heart and with all your soul and with all your might."

And now in the present day, I can clearly remember my dad doing the same thing with me as Reuben did with his son, Micah. When I was about ten or eleven years old my dad would drive me down the street in his tan Toyota Corolla and sit and wait with me at the bus stop. He brought along Scripture verse cards and taught me how to memorize Scripture.

I remember vividly the day he brought his faded light brown Bible and taught me how to memorize Psalm 23. He trained me up in God's Word diligently. And some 20 years later the Lord is still speaking to me and revealing

Himself to me through the verses my dad taught me while waiting at that bus stop.

He discipled me and showed me who Jesus is as the Lamb of God, and how He has delivered us from our ultimate slavery to sin at the cross and in His triumph over the grave. How could I have understood God's word unless someone guided me? This is the essence of discipleship, and it's also the essence of viewing parenting through the gospel lens.

His name is Bachos.

The wind ripples through his coarse hair as his horse-drawn chariot trundles down the road from Jerusalem to Gaza. He cannot stop thinking about his visit to Jerusalem for worship. A certain pang of rejection simmers inside as he recalls the temple official denying him entry to the assembly of the Lord.

The official had recognized Bachos as the eunuch in the court of Candace, queen of the Ethiopians. Upon Bachos attempting access to the assembly, the temple official replied, "No one who is emasculated or has his male organ cut off shall enter the assembly of the Lord" (Deut. 23:1 NASB).

In his own right, Bachos had turned from the man feeling the heat of shame and rejection rise up into his face as Jewish onlookers stared at the scene. He had quickened his pace to escape further embarrassment, and just as Bachos was about to exit the court of the Gentiles a young boy had run up to him and given him a scroll of Scripture.

"Sir, would you read this before the day is over?" the boy had said.

Now, Bachos glances down at the scroll sitting next to him in the chariot. His curiosity urges him to stop the chariot at once. He picks up the scroll, opens it, and begins to read, "He was led like a sheep to slaughter; And like a Lamb that is silent before its shearer, so He does not open His mouth. In humiliation His justice was taken away; who will describe His generation? For His life is taken away from the earth" (Isa. 53:7, 8 NASB).

". . . Do you understand what you are reading?" (Acts 8:30). The voice startles Bachos out of his concentration, and he turns to see a man looking intently at him gently stroking the head of the horse harnessed to the chariot.

Regaining his footing Bachos answers, "How can I, unless someone guides me?" (Acts 8:31). "Come up and join me, sir. What is your name?"

"My name is Philip, and what is yours?" the evangelist replies as he climbs up to sit next to the Ethiopian.

"I'm Bachos, it's a pleasure to meet you, Philip."

"Why don't you read the passage again so we can take a closer look?" Philip suggests.

Bachos reads the Scripture from Isaiah aloud again, turns to Philip, and asks him, "About whom, I ask you, does the prophet say this, about himself or about someone else?" (Acts 8:34).

A light breeze gently blows over the two men as Philip smiles at the Ethiopian man and answers, "Bachos, have you ever heard of Jesus of Nazareth?"

"I have heard stories that He was a prophet mighty in word and deed."

"Would you be surprised if I told you that this Jesus is more than a prophet?" Philip replies.

"Tell me more about this Jesus," Bachos says with a deep curiosity in his expression.

Philip answers, "Look at the passage again. See this part here about the Lamb silent before its shearer? See how it says 'in humiliation, His justice was taken away' and 'His life is taken away from the earth'?"

"Yes, I see it, but what does this lamb have to do with Jesus of Nazareth, who performed many signs and wonders?"

Philip puts a hand on Bachos' shoulder, "My dear friend, this Jesus, who performed many signs and wonders, *is* the Lamb spoken of here by Isaiah."

Dawning comprehension lights up the Ethiopian's face. "But how can this be?"

"You know the history of the Hebrew people, don't you? You know how we were enslaved to the Egyptians for 400 years, but the Lord God brought our forefathers out of slavery by performing many signs and wonders. The last sign was the death of the firstborn in every household that did not have the blood of an unblemished lamb wiped over the doorframe. Our people were spared from this death because they sacrificed an unblemished lamb in place of the firstborn being killed."

"Like Moses, Jesus came performing many signs and wonders. But unlike Moses, Jesus became the Lamb of God who takes away our sin by His sacrifice on the cross. 'In humiliation, His justice was taken away . . . His life was taken away from the earth' so we could be delivered from death and the slavery of sin forevermore."

One of the horses' whinnies and the chariot begins moving again. Bachos gazes off into the distance and considers what Philip has just told him. He considers the humiliation Jesus must have felt at the cross as His life was taken away from the earth. Suddenly, the humiliation he feels at being denied access to the temple is drowned in the love he now knows Jesus has for him. Bachos contemplates how Jesus can relate to him in a way that no one else can. He also understands that the shame he feels for his own sin has been atoned for by this Jesus who is the Lamb of God.

The chariot lurches on for another kilometer. A glint of sunlight gleaming on a small pool of water just ahead catches Bachos' eye. The Ethiopian looks at Philip and exclaims, "See, here is water! What prevents me from being baptized?" (Acts 8:36).

After halting the chariot, Philip and Bachos climb down and wade into the water. Raising his hand into the air Philip proclaims, "Bachos, because you believe in Jesus Christ, I baptize you, my brother, in the name of the Father, and the Son, and the Holy Spirit." He puts a hand on Bachos' nose, brings him back, and immerses him in the water. Bachos beams in pure elation as he is lifted back up out of the water. The two men emerge from the water, and suddenly Philip vanishes on the spot.

Bachos stares with mouth agape at the space Philip occupied just moments ago. Seconds pass and the Ethiopian looks up at the sky and smiles broadly. With drops of water still running down his face and sunlight illuminating his visage he breaks into laughter . . . his laughter turns into rejoicing and his rejoicing into a song of praise to his God.

What can we take from the above account in viewing parenting through the gospel lens? This passage from Acts 8 gives us the basis of discipleship when Bachos asks Philip, "'How can I [understand this passage] unless someone guides me?'" (verse 31). "Then Philip opened his mouth, and beginning from this Scripture he preached Jesus to him" (Acts 8:35 NASB). The phrase "he preached Jesus to him" is actually one word in Greek: "*euaggelizó.*" This word means "to gospelize" someone.

What a picture of gospel lens parenting! You see, Bachos was in a place of rejection. He had just been denied access to the temple because of his status as a eunuch in the court of Queen Candace. And then the Lord brought Philip into his life to guide him to understand Jesus, who grants forever access into the Father's presence through His sin atoning sacrifice. This also makes sonship status possible. Philip was obedient to the leading of the Holy Spirit, and this opened the door for evangelism and discipleship, which led to salvation.

As parents, we must take extremely seriously the call to disciple our children. They may not be able to articulate to you how much they need you to guide them to understand Jesus, but they will struggle with rejection at one point or another, just like Bachos did. They may feel excluded from the popular crowd at school, they may feel the rejection of not making the team, or they may feel an overall lack of acceptance in their peer group.

In those moments, our children do not need our advice, they need the gospel. We must guide our children to Jesus and His heart in every area of life. Look at what Philip did in Acts 8:35—he began with Scripture. As parents, when God's Word and the gospel of Jesus permeate our own lives, our immediate response or knee-jerk reaction to every issue our children face will naturally be rooted in the good news of Jesus. What does this look like practically?

The discipleship of our children is our second most important ministry, after our first ministry and calling to our spouse. These ministries take precedence over every other obligation: before church, before friends, before career, and any other aspect of life. I confess that I have let lesser pursuits distract me from being fully present with my children at times. In repentance and faith in Jesus, I am called to lay aside all distractions and pursue my family, so they will see Christ in me and the good news of His gospel.

"Therefore, since we are surrounded by so great a cloud of witnesses, let us also lay aside every weight and sin which clings so closely, and let us run with endurance the race that is set before us, looking to Jesus, the author and perfecter of our faith, who for the joy that was set before him endured the cross, despising the shame, and is seated at the right hand of the throne of God" (Heb. 12:1, 2).

Practically, this means that I will get off my smartphone and fully engage in whatever activity the family is doing. Jesus did not pursue me in a distracted manner, but He gave up heaven so He could seek and save me when I was lost without any hope of saving myself. Let us love and pursue our kids like Jesus loves and pursues us.

Two verses are key in gospel-centered parenting: "Having so fond an affection for you, we were well-pleased to impart to you not only the gospel of God but also our own lives, because you had become very dear to us" (1 Thessalonians 2:8 NASB). And "Trust in the Lord with all your heart and do not lean on your own understanding but in all your ways acknowledge Him, and He will make your paths straight" (Proverbs 3:5, 6 NASB). What does it look like practically to impart to your children not only the gospel of God but also your own life? What does it look like to parent while trusting in the Lord with all your heart and leaning not on your own understanding?

His name is Joseph (you met him in chapter 11).

A light breeze blows through the covered patio where he sits hunched over numerous pathology and microbiology textbooks in preparation for becoming a family nurse practitioner (FNP). At this time, Joseph, his wife, and two sons live on the Pioneer Bible Translators (PBT) campus in preparation for mission work in east Africa where he also plans to use his nurse practitioner degree to serve in a medical clinic on the field.

Suddenly, across the campus, an earsplitting scream erupts. Joseph drops his pen and looks up from his textbook. His pulse immediately quickens. He knows that scream. Horror and panic flood his being as he jumps up from the picnic table knocking one of his notebooks to the floor. He sprints in the direction of the scream. He reaches the childcare center where he had dropped off his 18-month-old son, Jackson, earlier that morning. Joseph watches the childcare worker holding Jackson in her arms as he cries and screams in her arms. She's rushing him to the medical clinic on the PBT campus. Joseph looks down and immediately recognizes that his son's hand is red and swollen. With every passing minute, the swelling seems to worsen. From his medical training, he deduces that his son has been bitten by a snake.

The childcare worker, Sarah, tells Joseph that she had moments ago hacked a baby rattlesnake to pieces with a plastic toy lawn mower on the playground by the gutter where the bite had occurred. The ambulance arrives promptly, but the wait feels like an eternity to Joseph. He holds his crying son tightly in the back of the ambulance and sings soothingly to him, "I love you, Lord. And I lift my voice to worship you . . . oh my soul rejoice . . . take joy my King in what you hear . . . may it be a sweet, sweet sound in your ear." The cry turns to a soft whimper as the 18-month-old toddler calms.

Joseph's wife, Lindsey, meets him there at the hospital where they realize that Jackson has received an extensive amount of rattlesnake venom from the bite. Joseph, Lindsey, and Jackson find themselves situated in a small curtained-off area in the ER waiting to be admitted to a room in the hospital. Jackson lays against Lindsey's chest sobbing through the pain. She fights back tears and prays, *I'm absolutely powerless to take his pain away. Lord, please heal my son.*

The impending doom of losing their son affords little sleep for Lindsey and Joseph that night. Morning dawns and the doctor and nurse knock on the door to come in and examine Jackson. Dr. Martinez takes a closer look and palpates his arm leading up to his shoulder and then neck.

"Unfortunately, the swelling is moving up from his hand to his neck. The concern with something like this is Jackson's airway becoming blocked by the swelling," the doctor notifies Joseph and Lindsey gravely. "We will continue blood draws every four hours to evaluate the level of toxicity in the bloodstream."

The nurse adds, "Please let me know if there's anything else I can get for you all or Jackson." With this final word, the doctor and nurse graciously excuse themselves from the room to leave the couple to tend to their precious son.

As promised, the blood draws come every four hours and naturally lead to fierce screams on Jackson's part. All Lindsey and Joseph can do amidst the cacophonous cries is hold their baby boy tight and sing "I Love You, Lord."

Jackson continues to scream "Mommy! Mommy." And Lindsey's heart breaks as she feels powerless to alleviate his pain.

Night comes and Lindsey leaves Jackson in Joseph's arms to go to the restroom. She stares into the mirror looking at her sleep-deprived, bloodshot eyes. She buries her face in her hands and prays, "Lord, I realize there's nothing I can do." A sinking, dreadful feeling envelopes her. She has a profound sense of lacking all control of the situation. And then, not audibly, but in the next moment a word of truth quickens her spirit, "You're right. You're not, but I am." And then, like a movie reel in Lindsey's mind, the Lord reveals who He is to her . . . His attributes: His goodness, kindness, faithfulness, and steadfast love. She takes all this in and reflects on the character of God. Suddenly, the indescribable peace of Christ floods her entire being . . . a peace that surpasses all understanding.

Lindsey comes out of the bathroom and lays down next to Jackson in the hospital bed and she's whisked off into a peaceful sleep. One thought crosses her mind as she dozes off, *I know my husband will stay up playing daddy nurse. I can rest.*

She wakes the next morning and immediately sits bolt upright and looks over at Jackson's hand and arm. Rubbing the sleep out of her eyes she realizes she is witnessing a miracle. The swelling is dramatically improved.

Lindsey jumps out of bed and runs to the nurse's station. "Nurse! Nurse! God has healed my son. Come look at his arm."

A look of incredulity briefly sweeps over the nurse's face. Lindsey goes to the room and turns Jackson loose on the nurse's station. He runs to the front desk where a myriad of wires feed into the telemonitoring system. He begins using both hands to start unplugging the cords of the telemonitors. The medical staff stare at the recovered boy with astonishment.

Within a day Jackson is released to go home after having received a total of 21 vials of anti-venom for the rattlesnake bite. Beyond any doubt, Jesus deserves all the glory for Jackson's rapid recovery and extraordinary resilience to such a potentially fatal bite.

What can be taken from Joseph and Lindsey's experience in regards to gospel lens parenting? The crucial takeaway is realizing, believing, and trusting in the sovereignty of God with your children. They were powerless to stop the rattlesnake bite. I mean what can you do in such a situation? You can't put your children in bubble wrap. As parents, we are not in control.

We have the illusion of control, but only Jesus has that kind of power. "... and he upholds the universe by the word of his power" (Heb. 1:3). We are not in control of our children's salvation. Jesus is. Now, we can and should most certainly pray for the Lord to capture their hearts. We can and should help shape and influence them, but the rest is up to the Lord. Jesus made it clear to Lindsey through Jackson's snake bite that when she released control to the Lord, that's when her heart was flooded with God's peace.

Specifically, this involved Lindsey meditating on the character of God: His goodness, kindness, faithfulness, and steadfast love. In Jeff Vanderstelt's book, *Gospel Fluency*, he outlines a time when his wife, Jayne, was struggling with a lot of anxiety concerning their children. Jeff was able to walk with her through the anxiety and lead her to the confession of her unbelief in God's sovereignty regarding her children. In other words, he reminded her of who God is and what He has done. And the critical point was helping her identify her unbelief in who God is and what He is doing. Next, Jayne was able to confess that unbelief out loud, and then she repented with a confession of faith in who God really is and what He actually does. Jeff sat down with Jayne and asked,

"'What do you believe God is doing or has done, sweetheart?'

"'I believe he has stopped loving me. I believe he has lost control of what's going on with our children. And . . . he's abandoned me,' Jayne said.

"Jeff responded, 'And what do those beliefs tell you about what you are believing God is like?'

"'He's unloving. He's impotent. He is absent,' she said.'"[17]

This was Jayne's confession of sinful unbelief. Pretty gut-level honest right? We need more of this in our daily interactions! The next part of the

---

17. Vanderstelt J. (2017), *Gospel Fluency*, Crossway, 121.

conversation led to Jayne confessing out loud what we know to be true of God from Scripture.

Here's what she came up with: "He is love . . . He is powerful and in control. He is present. Jesus died for me . . . He rose again from the dead . . . I have the Spirit of God in me. I'm loved. I'm not alone . . . I am more than a conqueror through him."[18]

By tracing her anxiety about her children to the roots of her unbelief in who God is and what He's doing, Jayne was able to confess her unbelief out loud. Then she was able to confess out loud who God truly is, what God has done, and who she is in light of His character and activity. This led her out of anxiety into peace, joy, and hope because of the good news of Jesus.

We desperately need to surrender control to Jesus when it comes to parenting. We will only do this when we repent of our sinful unbelief about who God is and what He is doing with our children. We need to confess the daily attributes and actions of God as recorded in Scripture. This will keep us grounded in the truth of the gospel rather than what we feel or see in the midst of our circumstances.

This grounding in the truth of who God is and what He has done for us in the gospel also frees us up as parents to become transparent about our sins with our children. This vulnerability preaches a living gospel of God's grace to our kids. Remember 1 Thess. 2:8 (NASB)? "Having so fond an affection for you, we were well-pleased to impart to you not only the gospel of God but also our own lives . . ."

Lindsey remembers a time when she had a horrible day with her children. She had ended up losing her temper and yelling at them. Later that day, Lindsey gathered her children around for "Tea Time" (a time where they drink tea, read a Bible story together, and then discuss it). Of course, by God's sovereignty, the passage for the day was John 21 where Jesus reinstates Peter after his three denials of Christ. Lindsey and the kids discussed how they needed to be restored to God and to one another through Jesus just like Peter.

The biblical narrative took on a powerful lesson for them that day because Jesus had come right into their shame and restored them just like Jesus entered into Peter's shame, showed him grace, and brought restoration to him. On that day, Lindsey's children and the girl from across the street, Ruby, experienced

---

18. Ibid., 126, 127, 128.

Jesus meeting them in their brokenness through His Word. On that day, the Word of God had palpable, real-life implications for them.

God's Word "is living and active, and sharper than any two-edged sword, piercing to the division of soul and spirit, of joints and marrow, and discerning the thoughts and intentions of the heart" (Heb. 4:12).

Now, let's consider some practical takeaways for looking at parenting through the gospel lens.

19

Parenting:
Practical Applications

What are the practical takeaways for parenting with the gospel lens? For Lindsey and Joseph, they practice daily gospel rhythms that I believe are worth sharing. Joseph begins every morning with the family by discussing a passage from the Bible during breakfast to hide God's Word in the hearts of his children. But before this, Joseph wakes up early to do "spiritual foraging" for his family by reading, praying, and meditating on God's Word *by himself*.

Why is this so important? As fathers, we are all discipling our children in something. We are either pointing them to Jesus and His Word or we are discipling our children to be self-centered. The issue is not *if* we influence our kids, but rather *how* we influence our kids. We have tremendous influential power in our children's lives, and how we steward that power will largely impact the trajectory of their lives. The gospel must be the main influencing power in your parenting.

Joseph has said that to make disciples you have to first be a disciple yourself. As parents, we need to continue being a disciple of Jesus and read the Bible for ourselves before we have something to give to our children. Here is the list of priorities he filters his life through:

1. Being a disciple of Jesus
2. Being a husband
3. Being a father

Joseph intentionally chooses a Scripture or memory verse that he will teach to his children at breakfast or lunchtime. The most critical aspect of this

Bible study time is daily consistency and faithfulness. This does not have to be an extravagant hour-long time of intense Bible study with your children, but a little bit each day will add up and have far-reaching effects by the Spirit activating His Word in the lives of our children at an early age.

Parenting through the gospel lens is helping your children look at life through the heart of Jesus. A great question to ask during Bible study with your kids is, "How do we see Jesus and the gospel in this passage?" And a follow-up question can be, "How does this help us see the world around us differently because of Jesus and the salvation He gives to us?"

Daily reading and focusing on God's Word are the keys to unlocking gospel lens parenting. This is the long-term plan. You can choose a meal during which you also spiritually nourish your children. You never know what spiritual gems might come out of this time.

The other day, Joseph was doing morning devotionals with his three kids and he asked, "What is a mediator?"

His youngest daughter Junia, almost four years old at the time, piped up matter-of-factly, "It's a dinosaur who eats meat!"

◍

What kind of mother or father do you want to be? In other words, what do you want your children to say about you at your funeral? In J.D. Greear's presentation, *God as Our Everlasting Father*[19], he gives 4 common types of fathers:

1. *"The never satisfied father"* (never gives a compliment . . . leads children to perfectionism)
This contrasts with the gospel because we are in Christ and the Father delights in us because of Christ's perfection and the forgiveness we have in Him. We have received Christ's righteousness. If we are daily connecting with our perfect heavenly Father, we will see how His delight in us (because of Jesus) leads us into more intimacy with Him. This will lead us to rightly encourage our children to point them to Jesus, so they will also know the Father's delight. We

---

19. *Everlasting Father*. (2019, December 12). JD Greer Ministries. https://jdgreear.com /broadcast/everlasting-father/.

will then begin to delight in our children, not because of their performance or good behavior, but because they are simply a gift of God's grace.

2. "*The distant father*" (around but never really engaging . . . leads children to seek affection elsewhere or to be aimless or directionless)
This contrasts with the gospel because God our Father is intimate with us by revealing His heart to us in the Scriptures. He relentlessly pursues us through Jesus Christ our Good Shepherd, "I am the good shepherd, I know my own and my own know me" (John 10:14). Are you relentlessly pursuing your children the way Jesus has pursued you? God the Father was so interested in seeking after us that He chose to send His own Son. As the old hymn, *Hark! the Harold Angels Sing* articulates so well, "Veiled in flesh the Godhead see, Hail the incarnate Deity." The incarnation of Christ needs to inform the kind of nearness we seek with our children.

God is not distant. He always has time for us. We can approach His throne of grace with confidence at any time, "Let us then with confidence draw near to the throne of grace, that we may receive mercy and find grace to help in time of need" (Heb. 4:16). The Psalms also portray a relationship with God where we can share our raw emotions with Him and pour out our hearts before Him, "Trust in him at all times, O people; pour out your heart before him; God is a refuge for us." (Ps. 62:8).

Are you always on your phone or mesmerized by a screen when you're around children? Such behavior shows that you are not looking at your children through the gospel lens. I am guilty of this as well. I find that distractions such as my smartphone, laptop, and television can tend to rob me of quality time with my children. My kids long for my attention. Is it exhausting to give them my undivided attention when I'm with them? Yes! Absolutely! But I also know that when I do give them my undistracted focus and attention, they are being valued above lesser pursuits, and this reflects the heart of Christ and His gospel.

3. "*The absent father*" (not present and leads children to seek love elsewhere)
This contrasts with the gospel and the ever-present Father. As alluded to earlier, Jesus is Immanuel, God with us. "I will not leave you as orphans; I will come to you" (John 14:18). And Jesus also says, "And I will ask the Father, and he will give you another Helper, to be with you forever," (John 14:16). The presence

of the Holy Spirit in the life of the believer is further confirmation, in addition to Christ's incarnation, that God's heart is bursting with longing to be near us.

Paul proclaims to the people of Athens that God "... made from one man every nation of mankind to live on all the face of the earth, having determined allotted periods and the boundaries of their dwelling place, that they should seek God, and perhaps feel their way toward him and find him. Yet he is actually not far from each one of us," (Acts 17:26, 27). He is not far from each one of us! He is near to us because of Jesus. He has come for us. Jesus also says this about nearness with Him, "And if I go and prepare a place for you, I will come again and will take you to myself, that where I am you may be also" (John 14:3).

In the way you spend your time, do your kids feel your loving presence with them? Your very presence with your children on a consistent, daily basis will demonstrate the following aspect of the gospel: God's sheep have gone astray and He will stop at nothing until they are safe in His arms enjoying the delight of His presence. "For the Son of Man came to seek and to save the lost" (Luke 19:10).

4. *"The ticking time bomb father"* (leads children to have anger issues themselves or to cower in fear)
This contrasts with the gospel, "The Lord is gracious and merciful, slow to anger and abounding in steadfast love" (Ps. 145:8). Do you ever feel tempted to blow up when your children act out or do something very irritating? Your response at that moment will proclaim the gospel more than any sermon they hear. Do they see righteous indignation in you or loss of control in those tense family moments?

The other night I was reading the *Jesus Storybook Bible* to my son in the rocking chair. He had a micromachine toy car in his hand, and he decided to run the car over the pages of the open book. Well, the car kept blocking the words so I couldn't read them. Annoyed, I gently moved his hand and the car off the page and continued reading. He continued to do this and block the words with his toy. This went on until I lost my temper, snatched the micromachine out of his hand, and chucked it out of the room. My wife, Kelley, saw this and very lovingly told me this wasn't a good example for our children. I apologized for my actions.

By God's grace and the power of the Holy Spirit, we must be slow to anger and abounding in steadfast love with our children. We must not only tell them the gospel with our words, but we must also live the gospel with our reactions and responses. How do we do that?

When the steadfast love of Jesus sinks into the core of our being, we will be empowered to respond with His love in those tense moments. We will become slow to anger when we remember how Christ took, not just God's anger for our sin, but His divine wrath for us on the cross . . . the wrath we fully deserved. How can we be reminded of this love?

This remembrance will only happen when our minds are saturated with Scripture and we are filled with the Spirit to bear His fruit, "But the fruit of the Spirit is love, joy, peace, patience, kindness, goodness, faithfulness, gentleness, self-control; against such things there is no law" (Gal. 5:22, 23).

At the end of the day, you need to ask yourself this question: what do I want my kids to be like when they are 18 and ready to fly the coop? As the saying goes, "Begin with the end in mind." In other words, what is your end goal for your children? The end goal you have in mind for them will determine everything you do for them . . . the very trajectory of your parenting. If your end goal is for them to get into Harvard or Yale your parenting will reflect this aspiration.

But what if your end goal for them is based on the gospel of Jesus Christ? What if your end goal for your children is for them to become fully devoted disciples of Christ who love Jesus with all of their beings? How would such a lens change the way you look at your kids and every parenting situation you encounter with them?

Do your children know that you believe life is all about Jesus? They will know by the way you spend your time, your money, and your energy. It's all about Jesus. "For by him all things were created, in the heavens and on earth, visible and invisible, whether thrones, or dominions or rulers, or authorities—all things have been created through him and for him" (Col. 1:16).

"All things have been created through him and for him" means that Jesus needs to be at the very center of everything we teach our children. This is why my wife, Kelley, and I hold a strong conviction that homeschooling our children will be the most biblical option for us. Biblically, parents are called to be the primary disciplers of their children (see Deut. 6:6–7 & Proverbs 22:6). No one else should be primary. Education is discipleship, and we want Jesus to inform every aspect of their worldview. He must be central in everything they learn. And one day they will leave our home to live out their calling to follow Jesus.

"And going on from there [Jesus] saw two other brothers, James the son of Zebedee and John his brother, in the boat with Zebedee their father, mending their nets, and he called them. Immediately they left the boat and their father and followed him" (Matt. 4:21, 22).

Jesus is so amazing and His call to follow Him is so compelling that these two sons "*immediately*" left all they ever knew, including their own father, to follow Christ. *This* is the end goal of parenting. And so shall it be with our children.

But how do we shepherd the hearts of our children for them to see how amazing Jesus is? In word and deed, we must demonstrate the very heart of Jesus to them.

In his book *Gentle and Lowly*, Dr. Ortlund poignantly shares that our goal as parents is to "make the tender heart of Christ irresistible and unforgettable"[20] to our children.

Let us behold, alongside our children, the beautiful excellence and loveliness of Christ's heart. Through our parenting, may our children feel the tenderness of His heart for them, especially amidst their sins and sufferings.

May Christ's loveliness draw them ever nearer to His heart.

---

20. Ortlund, *Gentle and Lowly*, 100.

Part 6

The Gospel Lens and Suffering

"He must increase, but I must decrease"
(JOHN 3:30).

20

Suffering (Acts 16)

Their names are Paul, Silas, Luke, and Timothy.

The four traveling companions find themselves in Troas, an ancient Greek city overlooking the Aegean Sea. Night has fallen, and Paul lies on his bed exhausted from the day's labors. After drifting off to a fitful sleep he suddenly wakes when a light breeze blows against his face. His bed creaks as he swiftly sits bolt upright and looks around.

In the next moment, a man is standing before him as clear as day. The man pleads with Paul, "Come over to Macedonia and help us" (Acts 16:9). Paul stares at the man in astonished excitement, and before he can say a word in reply the vision of the man vanishes before his very eyes like a vapor.

Paul gets out of bed, quickly walks over to his three companions and, one by one, nudges them awake, "Silas, Timothy, Luke, we must leave at once. I've just seen a vision of a Macedonian man pleading for us to come help him and his people. I have no doubt that God has called us to preach the gospel in Macedonia."

Silas and Timothy, still feeling groggy, begin to wipe the sleep out of their eyes. Luke begins packing up his clothes, parchment, and writing materials.

"I will speak with the captain as soon as he wakes. We can sail a straight course to Samothrace and reach Philippi by way of Neapolis. Lord willing, we leave at first light," Luke announces to his companions.

Her name is Lydia.

She is from the city of Thyatira and is a very successful businesswoman. Her trade is in selling purple fabric, a very expensive commodity in the world of the first century. She grew up as a Gentile, honoring and revering the Hebrew Scriptures. She is known as a God-fearer by those who are well-acquainted with her.

Lydia is organized, strong in her opinions, and persuasive as she is head of operations in her industry guild. However, she is also empty. Her life is buttoned-up and very moral, but she can't help but feel that there's a deep nagging hollowness in her soul, an unnamed longing unfulfilled, an eternal thirst never quite quenched.

The journey to Philippi is uneventful. After arriving, Paul, Silas, Timothy, and Luke spend the first several days in the leading Macedonian city, recovering from their journey and making several acquaintances, but see little in the way of receptivity to the gospel. Silas and Timothy on their part begin to question why they have been sent to Macedonia.

The Sabbath day arrives. Clear, cloudless skies afford much sunshine to fall upon the four travelers as they take a morning walk outside the city gate to a verdant riverside. Silas notes the rhythmic sound of the water gently lapping against the riverbank's edge when they come upon a group of women gathered for prayer.

"Peace upon you," Paul greets the women warmly.

They kindly return his greeting and ask, "Where are you men from?"

"I am from Tarsus. But my companions and I have come here from Troas. I was trying to lay down to sleep six nights ago when a man from Macedonia appeared to me in a vision pleading for us to come here and help him and his people. We concluded then that the Lord has called us to preach the gospel in Philippi. We supposed this beautiful riverside was a place of prayer, and so we came here to seek the Spirit's guidance for our journey."

The women listening to Paul stare at him speechless.

Lydia speaks up first, "What is this gospel you speak of?"

"The gospel is the good news of Jesus the Messiah. Have you heard of Him?" Paul inquires.

"I've heard rumors that He was a prophet, mighty in word and deed, who came to show us the way to God. Tell me what you know of this Man." Lydia speaks with boldness and directness toward the Apostle. But an unmistakable longing can be heard in her voice.

Paul replies, "All my life I thought I knew who God was. I had everything figured out. I sought to become righteous by keeping God's law. But now I realize that no flesh will be justified by the works of the law."

There's a pause, and Paul's words sweep through the gathering of women at the riverside like an abrupt gust of wind.

Lydia speaks up, "But what does this have to do with the prophet called Jesus?"

"Everything. Let me explain," Paul continues. "My zeal for the law overtook me, and I persecuted many people belonging to the Way. I thought I was obeying God in all of this, but one day Jesus revealed Himself to me. While on the Damascus Road, heading to arrest more followers of Jesus, a light brighter than the sun shone upon me and knocked me off my horse. A voice from heaven spoke to me as clear as day. He said, 'Saul, Saul, why are you persecuting Me? It is hard for you to kick against the goads.' I replied, 'Who are you, Lord?' The heavenly voice spoke again, 'I am Jesus whom you are persecuting'" (Acts 26:14, 15 NASB).

"Jesus then told me, 'But get up and stand on your feet; for this purpose I have appeared to you, to appoint you as a servant and a witness not only to the things in which you have seen Me, but also to the things in which I will appear to you, rescuing you from the Jewish people and from the Gentiles, to whom I am sending you to open their eyes so that they may turn from darkness to light, and from the power of Satan to God, that they may receive forgiveness of sins and an inheritance among those who have been sanctified by faith in Me'" (Acts 26:16-18 NASB).

The women process these words in awe and puzzlement wondering what they might mean.

Lydia again, as the spokesperson of the gathering, urges Paul onward, "What happened next?"

"I was blind for the next three days, but Jesus sent a man named Ananias to heal me so I would regain my sight. He then baptized me, and I received food to recover my strength."

Paul goes on, "I told you earlier that I thought I had everything figured out. But Jesus showed me that day that I had nothing figured out. All my life, I had diligently searched the Hebrew Scriptures thinking that in them I had eternal life. But after Jesus revealed Himself to me on the Damascus Road, He also opened my eyes to see that all the Scriptures testify about Him. I re-examined the books of Moses, the Psalms of David, and the Prophets. Suddenly, I saw Jesus on every page."

"This Jesus is the Christ who came to suffer for our sins on the cross so we may receive forgiveness through faith in Him. We are justified through faith in Christ and in Christ alone, not by the works of the law. And there's more.

Jesus did not stay in the tomb, but He was raised from the dead on the third day showing He had conquered sin and death. I now count all things as loss compared to knowing Christ Jesus my risen Lord."

Lydia listens intently to all of Paul's words and testimony. An internal dialogue ensues, *I'm just like Paul. I always thought I had the Scriptures figured out and that my righteousness is gained by the works of the law, but I know I've fallen short. I need this Jesus he speaks of with such power and wonder.*

And at this moment the Lord opens Lydia's heart to the beauty of Jesus and His gospel.

She returns home from the gathering and shares this message with her whole household, and they also believe in Jesus for salvation. The following day Paul baptizes her and her family in the river near the place of prayer. After coming out of the water Lydia embraces the four traveling companions and urges them, "If you have judged me to be faithful to the Lord, come to my house and stay" (Acts 16:15).

Paul begins to object to this, but Lydia prevails upon the four missionaries. From then on, Lydia's house becomes the base of operations for their ministry in Philippi.

The next days are filled with much excitement as the freshness of Lydia's faith serves to invigorate Paul and his companions. One day, they begin walking on their way to the riverside place of prayer when a demon-possessed slave girl approaches them clothed in an assortment of filthy rags, and she shrieks, "These men are servants of the Most High God, who proclaim to you the way of salvation" (Acts 16:17).

At first, the missionaries decided to let this proclamation go unchecked. But after days of the girl continually harassing them, Paul loses his patience. He abruptly rounds on her in the middle of the marketplace and declares in the presence of several bystanders, "I command you in the name of Jesus Christ to come out of her" (Acts 16:18).

The girl falls to the ground with a jolt and writhes in the dirt for several moments until an inhuman voice croaks out of her, "You will suffer for this!"

And suddenly the writhing stops and the girl looks like a lifeless corpse. But Paul walks over to her, kneels down, takes her by the hand, and lifts her up. She stands on her feet staring at Paul, wide-eyed and amazed. It's as if she is opening her eyes for the very first time, and the world is full of vibrant colors and contours. She throws her arms around Paul and tears of joy mixed with relief stream down her face. Like a sunrise breaking through the dead of night, a new day begins to dawn in the girl's heart. Where once her soul was shackled and her body exploited, now she is set free in Christ. A few moments pass as her new reality washes over her.

She lets go of Paul. A wave of panic flashes across her face. "What's wrong dear child?" the apostle asks her.

"My masters will beat me for this. I'm supposed to be a fortuneteller, and now I am not who I was. I cannot tell fortunes anymore."

"You have a new Master now. His name is Jesus. He will never take advantage of you. You have nothing to fear, not even death."

What transpires next happens fast.

"What do you mean you will not tell fortunes anymore?"

The voice is laced with fury. The girl swiftly turns around to see her old master standing just feet away fuming. Apparently, he had overheard her declaration of freedom. He begins moving toward the girl and reaches a hand out to grab her forcefully by the arm, but Paul and Silas interpose and stand in between the girl and her former master.

"She is no longer your slave, sir," Paul interjects as he locks eyes with the man intensely.

"The magistrate will hear of this!" the master sneers back at Paul.

A moment passes and suddenly the master is standing in between two of his business partners. The two men step forward and seize Paul and Silas. They forcibly drag them across the town square kicking up dust as they go. The men throw Paul and Silas to the ground before the magistrates, seated loftily in their seats of honor overlooking the marketplace. The missionaries look up from the ground and see the chief magistrate open his mouth in outrage.

"What is the meaning of this?" he roars.

The masters of the slave girl step forward. "These men are Jews, and they are disturbing our city. They advocate customs that are not lawful for us as Romans to accept or practice" (Acts 16:21).

Suddenly, a cacophony of jeering erupts from the crowd rapidly gathering around the scene. In a matter of moments, the people of Philippi viciously cry out, "Away with these Jews . . . these scum of the earth!"

The chief magistrate stands up from his seat and utters his pronouncement over Paul and Silas.

The crowd quiets down to hear him, "They will be beaten with rods and thrown in prison."

The Philippian mob erupts with cheers of approval.

Two Roman soldiers step forward at the command of the magistrate and rip off Paul and Silas' tunics and upper garments. The missionaries sink to their knees and their faces press into the dust of the marketplace grounds; their bare backs exposed to the open air. Paul turns his head to see his ministry companion mentally preparing for what comes next. With great poise and courage, Paul stretches out his hand and grabs Silas by the arm. Squinting through the dust in his eyes, Silas turns to look at Paul. They nod at one another in solidarity.

The soldiers each brandish a metal rod and whip them through the air as if to put on a show for the mob of onlookers. With bloodlust in his eyes, the first soldier approaches Paul, and in one swift movement, he raises and brings the rod swiftly down on his bare back. CRACK. The sound is audibly heard by all the spectators in the marketplace. Paul's right posterior rib is fractured and redness spreads across his back. The Apostle shrieks in agony as his body sinks lower into the dirt.

Silas is next. The second soldier raises his rod and wallops Silas with two successive blows. Searing pain spreads across his back. He screams in pain and blinks back tears. Silas glances over to see more blows being inflicted upon Paul. Both men cry out in agonizing pain as they suffer multiple rib fractures, contusions, and superficial open wounds slowly oozing blood. Both soldiers stagger from the fatigue of the beating they have just inflicted.

After receiving these blows, Paul and Silas are dragged by four Roman soldiers to the chief jailer. The missionaries' backs are still exposed and appear black and blue from extensive bruising. The drainage from the open wounds strewn across their upper bodies has slowed to a trickle allowing the blood to dry and scab.

The soldiers shove Paul and Silas down before the jailer's feet. They groan in pain as they fall face down before the man.

One of the soldiers addresses the jailer, "The magistrate orders the incarceration of these men. Keep them under secure guard."

And with this charge, the soldiers swiftly turn and exit the prison. The jailer, an ex-military man, looks down at Paul and Silas with a hardened, unfeeling gaze.

With a merciless tone, he gives the command to two of his servants, "Put these men in the inner prison and fasten their feet in the stocks."

Paul and Silas are forcefully taken to the inner prison and thrust onto their backs. The jailer's servants splay the missionaries' legs wide open to the extreme end range of motion until they are stretched well beyond discomfort. The servants then fasten wooden stocks securely around their ankles leaving Paul and Silas to extreme confinement and agonizing pain. Silas exhales forcibly to assuage the pain. His eyes begin to close from sheer exhaustion, but then he's abruptly startled by several hairy rats scurrying across the jail cell. Paul, on his part, begins to feel nauseated by the stench of human feces permeating the inner prison.

Around midnight both men suddenly lock eyes with one another and instantly recall the vision Paul had of the Macedonian man asking for help. They experience the unmistakable presence of the Holy Spirit come upon them. They begin praying and giving thanks to the Lord, overflowing with joy unspeakable. Paul remembers the words Jesus had spoken to Ananias during his own conversion, "For I will show him how much he must suffer for the sake of my name" (Acts 9:16).

Paul prays, "Jesus, all of this is for the sake of Your name."

Being mutually encouraged by one another's resilience in faith, a song of praise erupts from their hearts. Their song starts low and then grows in strength. And one by one the prisoners begin listening to their song of praise. The convicts across the corridor each lift their heads and gaze in wonderment in the direction of Paul and Silas.

What transpires next is nothing short of incredible. From out of nowhere, the iron bars of the prison began to shake. Paul, Silas, and the other prisoners palpably feel a vibration in the ground. This vibration turns into a rumble which then becomes a great earthquake. The noise of the rumbling is thunderous as the prison continues to violently shake until a metallic clanking sound of shackles breaking apart can be heard. With one final blast of shaking, the prison doors fly open, and all the prisoners' chains fall off. As suddenly as it had come the earthquake stops. Silence ensues.

And then only one sound can be heard: the unsheathing of a sword. The jailer closes his eyes and takes a deep breath. He raises his weapon with the sharpened blade pointing toward his chest as he prepares to fall on his sword.

Paul musters all of his strength and cries out, "Do not harm yourself, for we are all here" (Acts 16:28).

The next sound that can be heard in the black of night is the clanking of metal on the prison floor after the jailer drops his sword with trembling hands.

He calls to his servants, "Quick, bring me the torchlight."

After receiving the torch, the jailer runs to Paul and Silas' cell and falls down before them, his whole body with a tremor reminiscent of the violent earthquake that just occurred. The jailer grabs Paul and Silas and brings them out of their jail cell. The question he asks them leaves Silas thunderstruck.

"Sirs, what must I do to be saved?" (Acts 16:30).

The missionaries reply, "Believe in the Lord Jesus, and you will be saved, you and your household" (Acts 16:31).

And the jailer takes Paul and Silas out of the prison and brings them into his home. After lighting a lantern, the jailer has his wife, children, and the household servants all gather around Paul and Silas in the living room.

"These men have a message to share with us." The jailer announces to his household.

And Paul and Silas proclaim the good news of salvation in Jesus Christ to the jailer and his whole household. After they finish sharing the gospel, the jailer then calls for a basin of water, and he washes their wounds. The once callous and brutal man now kneels to wash their bloodied and bruised backs. As Paul and Silas flinch with every wipe and cleansing, the jailer suddenly becomes overwhelmed with compassion for them. In his mind's eye, he envisions the sufferings of Christ that Paul has just preached about.

The image pierces him like the spikes driven through Christ's hands and feet. The jailer understands at this moment that Jesus gave up His life to pay for all of his sins. The callousness of his heart melts away as he grasps the Savior's immeasurable love for him. He then considers the resurrection of Jesus and comprehends the answer to his question, *what must I do to be saved?* he thinks to himself: *Absolutely nothing but believe in Jesus just as they said. Jesus has done it all.*

Great joy comes upon him and everyone present, and at that very hour of the night, the jailer and his whole household are baptized in the river at the place of prayer. In celebration, they all return to the jailer's house and a feast is set before Paul and Silas.

After the feast, Paul and Silas accompany the jailer back to the prison where they wait for morning's first light to dawn.

At the break of day, the Philippian magistrates send for the clandestine release of Paul and Silas, but Paul will have none of it. He responds, "They have beaten us publicly, uncondemned, men who are Roman citizens, and have thrown us into prison; and do they now throw us out secretly? No! Let them come themselves and take us out" (Acts 16:37).

After receiving profuse apologies from the magistrates for the injustice done to them, Paul and Silas forgive them and leave the prison grounds.

A wide grin spreads across Paul's face as he chuckles to Silas, "Did you see the look on their faces when they found out we were Roman citizens? They were terrified of us!" Silas smiles in return as they make their way back to Lydia's house.

There they greet Lydia, Luke, Timothy, the Philippian jailer's family, and the girl who received deliverance from slavery. Paul considers Lydia, the former slave girl, and the jailer . . . all of them so diverse in every way. All of them captured by Jesus and His love for them. A joy overflows his heart. A new church has been born.

⁂

Years pass and Paul finds himself imprisoned yet again; not in Philippi this time but in Rome where he is waiting to stand trial before Caesar. A soft gleam of sunlight shines through a small crack in the wall illuminating the chains fastened securely around his wrists and ankles. He looks down at his chains and smiles.

He thinks of Lydia, the jailer, and the girl who was delivered from her master's fortunetelling trade. Paul remembers the times of sweet fellowship he had with the Philippian church in Lydia's house. The joy of the Philippian believers is indelibly etched on his heart.

Paul picks up a quill, dips it in ink, and writes these words, "I thank my God in all my remembrance of you, always in every prayer of mine for you all making my prayer with joy, because of your partnership in the gospel from the first day until now" (Phil. 1:3-5).

He then writes, "I want you to know, brothers, that what has happened to me has really served to advance the gospel, so that it has become known throughout the whole imperial guard and to all the rest that my imprisonment is for Christ. And most of the brothers, having become confident in the Lord by my imprisonment, are much more bold to speak the word without fear . . . Yes, and I will rejoice for I know that through your prayers and the help of the Spirit of Jesus Christ this will turn out for my deliverance, as it is my eager expectation and hope that I will not be at all ashamed, but that with full courage now as always Christ will be honored in my body, whether by life or by death. For to me to live is Christ, and to die is gain" (Phil. 1:12-14, 18–21).

One of the only things that can never be taken away from you in this life is your attitude. In the narrative of Scripture outlined above from Acts 16 and Philippians 1, we see that *it is possible* to look at suffering, discomfort, misery, inconvenience, and isolation *as means*, not obstacles, by which we can say with Paul, "what has happened to me has really served to advance the gospel" and "now as always Christ will be honored in my body, whether by life or by death." The question I want to explore with you throughout the coming chapters is how can we have such a perspective? How can we have such an attitude?

Briefly, I want to highlight a few practical takeaways from Paul and Silas in Acts 16. Firstly, we see that they bathed their suffering in prayer and praise. They rejoiced in the midst of their suffering, "About midnight Paul and Silas were praying and singing hymns to God, and the prisoners were listening to them" (Acts 16:25). In the midst of agonizing pain, unbearable confinement, and nagging exhaustion they prayed and praised God.

Are you suffering right now? I urge you to bring your suffering to Jesus in prayer. Call out to Him! "The Lord is near to all who call on Him, to all who call on Him in truth (Ps. 145:18 NASB). The presence of Jesus is so sweet and so intimate to those who are brokenhearted: "The Lord is near to the brokenhearted and saves those who are crushed in spirit" (Ps. 34:18).

Prayer is not only our access to the presence of the living God, but prayer is also how we can honestly process our raw emotions in the midst of suffering. In prayer, we can take our anger, our confusion, our frustrations, our bitterness, our doubts, and our questions and bring them before our compassionate Savior who all too well knows with great intimacy what we are going through.

Jesus, in His time on earth, experienced the full range of human emotion. He descended to far greater depths of suffering than any human has or will ever know. "For we do not have a high priest who is unable to sympathize with our weaknesses, but one who in every respect has been tempted as we are, yet without sin" (Heb. 4:15). Therefore, if we pray through our suffering in light of Jesus and His suffering, He can lead us to praise.

And so, we see that Paul and Silas were singing songs of praise (or *hymns* as the Greek denotes). Their praying seems to overflow into hymns of praise. There is something so special about music. Have you ever imagined a universe where music does not exist? It's unimaginable! The Lord gave us music as a good gift to uniquely minister to our hearts and channel His praise. Singing and making music capture and captivate the human heart unlike anything else. Singing and making music also connect us to the living God amid our suffering. Praise leads us to take the focus off ourselves while suffering and sets our gaze on Jesus and His beauty.

When you sing in times of suffering, people will take notice. Acts 16:25 says, ". . . and the prisoners were listening to them." The Greek word for "listening" here literally means "to listen attentively." The prisoners were thunderstruck and, at the same time, very attracted to the way Paul and Silas handled their suffering. Suffering with prayer and praise will demand an explanation. Suffering in this way is to suffer with purpose. And this leads to our second takeaway from Acts 16.

Secondly, by the grace of Jesus, they did not disconnect their suffering from the overarching purpose and mission of Jesus. Their journey to Philippi was all about Jesus and connecting people with Him. After being miraculously sprung from jail, they preached the gospel to the Philippian jailer and his family. Their horrific circumstances and pain furthered the advancement of the gospel instead of hindering it. Are you quick to complain about your circumstances or, by the grace of Jesus, do you connect your circumstances to your calling and the overarching mission of Jesus for your life?

They also suffered in community, not in isolation. Paul and Silas must have had the sweetest brotherly fellowship while chained up with their ankles spread out in the stocks. We see, after they are released from prison, that they return to Lydia's house and continue connecting and communing with other believers. Do you tend toward isolation and exclusion from the body of Christ in times of suffering, or do you press even deeper into the relationships you have with your church body? Maybe you need to put this book down right now and call a believer in Christ you can trust and share your suffering with them.

Lastly, we can remember that Jesus is the Hero of this story, not Paul or Silas. Jesus is the One who first suffered for us on the cross to pay for *all* of our sins because of His immeasurable love for us. He then was raised from the dead on the third day to become our living hope in our darkest hour. It is this Jesus who sent these missionaries out to Philippi in the first place. And because Jesus has all authority in heaven and on earth, He sovereignly allowed the brutal flogging and unjust imprisonment of Paul and Silas.

We see that Jesus saved the jailer and his whole household *because* this injustice was done to Paul and Silas, not despite it. Jesus is so amazing because He redeems the most painful of circumstances to advance His kingdom through them. And not only that, but Jesus also promises that He is with us in our sufferings even to the end of the age as we go and make disciples of all nations (see Matt. 28:19, 20). Are you quick to forget about the death *and* resurrection of Christ in the midst of suffering, or do you remind yourself daily of the love and living hope you have in the risen Christ? And do you remind yourself daily of Christ's sovereignty over all our circumstances?

I work as a physical therapist at a large hospital in South Texas. The other day, I was working with a patient in the Intensive Care Unit (ICU). Something dawned on me at the end of the session. After getting the patient out of bed and into the bedside recliner, I wrote down exercises on the marker board for her to do during her hospital stay. As she looked at the board, I asked her if she could read what I had written.

She replied, "All I see is black smears and smudges. Hold on, wait a second. Let me put on my glasses." I handed her glasses to her. She put them on. "Ah yes. I can read the exercises clearly now."

I wonder if most of us look at the suffering we endure in this life and see only "black smears and smudges." We must remember that the death *and* resurrection of Jesus are the basis of our living hope and these truths must be brought to bear on the suffering in our lives. I contend that if we were to put on gospel lenses and then look at our sufferings, we would see them with a Christ-exalting clarity. No longer would our suffering be devoid of significance, but our pain would have a purpose, our misery would have meaning, and the prisoners around us would be listening as we meet our trials with a deep abiding joy that only Jesus can give.

In the coming chapters, I will introduce you to Sean, Lisa, and David. We will look at their stories through the lens of the gospel and answer the question of how we can have a gospel-enriched perspective in the midst of deep suffering.

21

Chronic Suffering

His name is Sean.

It's April 6, 2008, Sunday night. The cloudless night sky gleams with the light of a crescent moon. The moonlight illuminates an oak tree situated behind the youth building of the First Baptist Church of Magnum, Texas. At the base of this oak tree is a small circular wooden deck inlaid with a sitting area where parishioners may gather under the tree.

Sean, at age 16, has just returned from a concert performed by one of the members of the youth group in the Silver Canyon area of San Antonio. Sean's friend gave him a ride back from the concert and dropped him off at the area behind the youth building. Sean now waits for his brother, Gerald, to return as well from the concert because they decided to ride back separately.

Boredom inspires Sean to climb up the oak tree surrounded by the wooden deck. He climbs higher. And higher. A gentle breeze blows against his cheek afforded by the higher elevation. Satisfied with his feat of climbing he begins making his way down, the moonlight illuminating his footholds. On his way down, he steps on a singular branch while still about 15 feet above the ground. The branch creaks as he puts his full weight on it, and in the blink of an eye the branch snaps.

Sean falls.

The thud of his body hitting the wooden deck resounds and can be heard from the parking lot behind the youth building. Sean's neck and arms bear the brunt of the initial impact on the deck when he lands. And the world goes dark.

Brenda, a mother with children in the youth group, partially witnesses Sean's fall from the tree. She hears the crack from bone colliding with the wooden deck. She runs from the parking lot and finds him there unconscious and reflexively writhing in pain. Brenda's mind races. *What to do . . . what to do?* She instinctively grabs her cell phone and dials 911.

"This is 911, what's your emergency?" the operator asks with a calm but firm tone.

"There's a boy here." Panicked sobs escape from Brenda's quivering voice in between each sentence. "He's fallen from a tree. He's badly hurt."

"Where are you, ma'am?"

"I'm at First Baptist Church of Magnum."

"Can you tell me specifically where this accident has occurred?"

"We're behind the youth building. There's a tree behind the youth building. Oh, please send help quickly. I don't know what to do for this young man," Brenda pleads.

"Please remain calm. Take a deep breath and compose yourself. Does it look like his neck has been hurt by the fall?"

"Yes. And his arms are bent awkwardly."

"Okay, ma'am this is very important. Do not try to move him. Leave him right where he is. I have already dispatched EMS, and they are headed your way. Ready yourself to flag down the EMS workers and lead them to this young man. They will take care of him from there. Help is on the way."

"Okay. I'll stand by the parking lot and flag them down." Brenda responds, slightly reassured but still horrified by the scene that lay before her.

The wait for EMS is agonizing to Brenda. Finally, she spots them. Sirens blare. Red and blue lights flash. An ambulance and fire truck arrive. The medical workers run to the scene and immediately realize the severity of Sean's condition. They secure his neck in a brace and load him on a gurney. The EMS team lead radios the call in for Sean to be life-flighted to University Hospital (UH), a level-one trauma center. The volunteer fireman chief directs his team to have the firetruck positioned strategically with the red lights flashing and the headlights illuminating a makeshift landing pad in the church parking lot.

Within seven minutes, the helicopter arrives. The beating whir of the propellers resounds in the parking lot. The branches of the tree from which Sean fell whip back and forth due to the wind current produced. The EMS team carefully loads Sean onto the chopper, and he is flown to the hospital. He is admitted directly to the Intensive Care Unit (ICU).

Her name is Lisa.

Her cell phone buzzes and rings. She picks up on the third ring. It's Rocky, the church youth pastor, on the other line.

"Lisa, you need to get to the church. Sean fell from the tree behind the church . . . he's hurt badly . . . I'm so sorry to tell you this."

"What?" Lisa replies stunned.

She thinks he's joking. But then a whirlwind of emotion and panic seizes her as she realizes he's completely serious. Both Sean's mother and father pile into their Ford Explorer and travel at a high rate of speed through their neighborhood heading toward the church.

On their way, Lisa's phone rings a second time. It's Rocky again. And this time his voice quivers from the gravity of the situation.

"Lisa, they are life-flighting Sean to University Hospital. He's still breathing, but you need to head straight there," he says gravely.

At the phrase "life-flighting," a new level of panic and fear overwhelm her.

"Oh no," she stifles into the phone. "Scott, go straight to University Hospital. Rocky says they're life-flighting Sean now."

Scott makes a swift right turn to redirect their course toward the hospital.

Lisa hangs up. Tears fill her eyes. She begins begging God in prayer.

"Lord, please spare my son's life. Oh, please let him live. Jesus, please. Jesus, please." Lisa pleads.

A torrent of emotions and thoughts overwhelm her as she tries to process the current situation. Questions batter her mind like breakers beating against a ship, one after another. She thinks to herself, *is my son going to live through the night? How did he fall from that tree? Why is this happening? Will he survive the helicopter ride to the hospital?*

Scott and Lisa's car screeches to a stop in the hospital parking lot. They get out and run straight for the Emergency Room entrance. A receptionist dressed in a red jacket directs them to the admitting area. The lady retrieves a clipboard with several papers to be filled out on it.

With the paperwork completed, Scott and Lisa are taken to see Sean in the ICU. The sliding glass doors are open leading to his room. Both parents' hearts are racing as they enter the room and wonder what scene will unfold before them. Several lines are attached to Sean. Oxygen tubing is in his nose. A monitor displaying his heart rate and rhythm along with his oxygen saturation looms overhead. Sean's arms are bandaged and bent at unnatural angles. His neck is secured in a white rigid neck brace.

"What took y'all so long to get here?" Sean asks his mom and dad as they enter the room.

"Oh, we're so sorry, Sean. We got here as fast as we could. They had us fill out paperwork before taking us to see you," Lisa replies.

"Don't worry son. We're here now, and we're not going anywhere. We will be here for you from here on out." Scott reassures his son.

Sean drifts off to sleep within the next hour. Scott and Lisa's pastor, Earl Strafford, comes to comfort and console them. The tears begin to stream down both of their faces as the pastor and several other family friends gather around to offer support and prayer.

Monday comes. Sean is taken to the operating room to undergo surgery to stabilize the fractures in his neck. He receives 2 rods and 14 screws to bolt the hardware into place. A week of uncertainty begins as Lisa and Scott are not sure whether their son will survive this trauma or not.

For the next five days, Sean's condition waxes and wanes. His vitals are up and down. One area of his clinical presentation would improve while another would decline. The doctors prescribe him morphine to control the pain, but this also causes Sean to have several bouts of hallucinations. Lisa watches her son with mounting anxiety and stress as he writhes in the hospital bed. She wonders if the hardware in his neck will somehow come loose from all of the squirming and twisting in bed.

"I'm trapped! The building is on fire! Get me out of here!" Sean begins to scream as he wriggles his shoulders and upper body violently in bed. Lisa rushes to the bedside and puts a hand on Sean's shoulder.

"Honey, you're having hallucinations right now from the morphine they're giving you. There is no fire. You're not trapped. You're in the hospital. You fell from a tree and broke some bones. You need to rest and relax right now," Lisa says firmly but soothingly to deescalate Sean's frantic behavior. For the moment, he relaxes and sinks back into a fitful sleep.

The next few days pass in a blur for Scott and Lisa. Friday comes. Dr. Patel, the intensivist, enters the room and approaches them. He is not satisfied with Sean's clinical course thus far. He cuts straight to the point with the shaken parents.

"There are two main points of concern for Sean here. The first point is his respiratory status. He has not been stable from a respiratory standpoint, and so we recommend that Sean receive what's called a tracheostomy. This is where we would create a hole in the base of his neck and place a tube there for ease of ventilation and oxygen support."

"The second point is Sean's nutrition status. He's not able to take in enough calories at this time to adequately nourish his body as it tries to heal itself. So, we also recommend a feeding tube to be surgically placed in his stomach," Dr. Patel shares.

"Can we have some time to think about these options?" Lisa asks. "They sound pretty invasive."

"Yes, just let us know as soon as you can. Thank you."

"Thank you, Doctor." Scott and Lisa respond.

They begin praying that such procedures would not be necessary for Sean. At this time, Lisa and Scott are the Sunday School teachers for Sean and his fellow sophomore year classmates at First Baptist. Lisa's phone rings again. It's Amber, one of the girls from the Sunday School class.

"Hi, Mrs. Baker. How is Sean doing? We've been praying for him."

"It's pretty touch and go right now. He's not doing all that well, and the doctors are suggesting more invasive procedures. Please pray that he'll be okay and not need these procedures."

"Yes, ma'am. We will pray."

That Friday afternoon, Amber sends a text to the whole sophomore Sunday School class telling them to meet at Rocky and Jane's house that night for an all-night prayer vigil for Sean.

"C'mon in y'all," Rocky says welcoming the sophomores into his home. "So glad you could come on such short notice." A total of 11 guys and girls trickle in throughout the night to pray for Sean.

Sparks fly up as the fire crackles in the cozy fire pit behind Rocky and Jane's house. The sophomore faithful gather in a circle around the fire to pray for Sean. Amber speaks up first.

"Thank y'all so much for coming. Sean really needs our prayers right now. I spoke with his mom earlier today, and it sounds like the doctors are considering some more intense procedures. She asked us to pray specifically that he would not need these to happen. Who can start us off in prayer?"

One of the sophomores named Justin prays first.

"Father God, I pray right now that you heal Sean so that he would not need these procedures. Please show up. Please be glorified in this. Let us see Your glory. I pray for Mr. and Mrs. Baker to feel your peace during this chaotic time at the hospital not knowing what will happen next to their son. I pray all this in the name of Jesus Christ. Amen."

On and on, the sophomores labor in prayer for their friend and brother in Christ throughout the night.

Saturday morning comes. Dr. Patel's physician assistant, P.A. Montgomery, comes to see Sean while making her rounds. She cannot believe her eyes. She is amazed at the miraculous clinical improvement Sean has made overnight, especially regarding his respiratory status. She is so taken aback by Sean's progress that she leaves the room immediately to bring Dr. Patel in to witness the improvement firsthand. Ordinarily, she would simply add a progress note to Sean's chart, but this progress is worth the doctor's attention.

Lisa and Scott witnessed this miracle.

"Praise be to God! Thank you, Lord Jesus. You are so good. You've answered our prayers," Lisa exclaims while sitting next to her husband in Sean's room. She would later find out what her Sunday School class did for her son over the previous night.

Needless to say, Sean would go on to never need a tracheostomy or a feeding tube for that matter. There's no doubt in Lisa's mind that God answered the prayers of those students that Friday night.

In the second week of Sean's hospital stay, he undergoes surgery on both of his arms due to the fractures sustained by the fall.

During this time, Sean is still in and out of lucid thinking due to the pain meds and surgeries he has received. For the first time since he has been at the hospital, he considers what will become of his life. As he lays in the hospital bed he looks over at his mom and sees her nodding off in the recliner where she sits. He then looks down at his arms, both of them covered by casts. His eyes trail down toward his feet. He cannot move them. Next, he thinks to himself, *I'll be back playing baseball in like a year.*

The next day a hard reality comes from the neurosurgeon regarding his condition. Dr. Wilcox walks into the room with a white coat donned and a surgical cap adorning his head. His manner is nonchalant but caring. He stands at the foot of the bed alternating glances at Sean and his parents at the bedside.

Dr. Wilcox delivers the news, "Sean, we are able to diagnose that you have what's called an incomplete spinal cord injury at C-5, that's the part of your neck that was fractured by the fall. The injury is incomplete, which means that your spinal cord was not completely severed, so the information highway going from your brain to the rest of your body is still partially intact. This will allow you some movement in your arms, but there is no telling how much muscle movement or sensation you will regain. I know this is hard to hear, but that's why your rehabilitation process will be so crucial in the coming days and months, and even years. If you are clinically stable, we are going to transfer you to a good rehab facility within the next day or so."

"Will I walk again, doctor?" Sean asks.

Dr. Wilcox pauses and then replies, "The chances are not very likely because your injury is so high on your spinal cord."

The words hang in the air for a moment. Sean diverts his gaze downward again at his motionless feet. Tears well up in Lisa's eyes. Scott looks solemnly off at an unspecified point in the room. The tense moment passes when the doctor makes a few conclusive remarks.

"But Sean, that is why it's so important that you give it your all at rehab. Let's focus on what you can regain through physical and occupational therapy. Your therapists at rehab are going to become your best friends. You'll find that the human brain is an amazing organ. Our brains can adapt and find new ways to make our muscles work so we can move. Let's see how much movement you can regain. Okay?"

"Thank you, Dr. Wilcox," Scott speaks up on behalf of his son who lies there, still processing the information.

The surgeon nods compassionately and exits the room.

By the grace of Jesus, Sean's clinical condition stabilizes over the following days, and he is transferred to the Texas Institute of Rehabilitation and Research (TIRR), where his parents would be initially trained on how to care for him until he would begin his subsequent courses of rehab to maximize his independence. Sean would go on to complete three different courses of rehab at TIRR.

His initial return home was not easy after his first stay at TIRR. Lisa and Scott poured themselves into ensuring Sean had everything he needed to adapt to life at home (and they still do so to this day). In the early days of his return home, Sean's care proved to be overwhelming for Scott and Lisa. He still remained in a neck brace and both arms were in casts. Sean needed assistance with nearly every single daily living task you can imagine. Both parents had to check on him and administer medications every three to four hours.

This round-the-clock care afforded very little sleep for them. They used to joke that they no longer slept at night but rather took short naps. They kept a monitor by their bed to listen for Sean if he needed anything throughout the night.

∞

During the second course of rehab at TIRR, Sean begins physical and occupational therapy for three hours each day. The training is grueling and exhausting for him. The therapists put him through rigorous physical exercise and train him on accomplishing everyday life activities such as getting to the edge of the bed from a lying position and transferring from the bed to the wheelchair while watching out for autonomic dysreflexia. He also learns to operate his electric-powered wheelchair at this time.

One particular day, Sean is in the rehab gym working with his therapist on sliding board transfers when he looks up and notices a commotion going on at the other end of the gym. It's one of the other patients; a boy that looks to be around 10 years old is in a wheelchair with his left leg amputated. His face is red as he raises his voice at the therapist trying to motivate him to do occupational therapy. The boy's mother stands by for support and encouragement. He begins wailing and gesturing rapidly with his hands in agitation. Sean can hear every word of the tantrum being thrown.

"I don't wanna to do this! This sucks! Take me back to my room, now!"

"Ricky, that's not how you talk to this kind therapist lady, trying to help you get stronger." Ricky's mom, Debra, interjects in a firm but soothing tone. "Just give this a chance and see how much strength you can get back."

"NO! I DON'T WANT TO DO THIS ANYMORE!" Ricky yells enunciating each word clearly so that everyone in the gym can hear.

Debra's face flushes with embarrassment at the scene as nearly everyone turns to spectate. The therapist reaches out and puts a hand on her shoulder to comfort her. She then turns to Ricky making herself eye-level with him.

"Ricky, I know you're frustrated. I know this must be extremely hard for . . ."

"NO, you don't know!" Ricky interrupts. "You have no idea what it's like to be in this wheelchair, unable to walk."

"You're right. I don't. But there's only one way for you to get better. Let us help you, please, Ricky."

"NO! Take me back to my room!"

"Okay then, let's take you back to your room," the therapist says in resignation.

And with that, the therapist wheels Ricky out of the gym, his mother trailing behind staring at the floor in shame. The other therapists and patients resume their activities restoring the gym to its normal hubbub. Meanwhile, Sean finishes his therapy session giving an extra concerted effort to follow his therapist's instructions.

Later that day, Sean stops by Ricky's room on his way back from therapy. Ricky's mom, Debra, sees him at the entrance and walks over to him. Sean introduces himself telling her that he's the patient who is just across the hall.

"Would it be okay if I talk with Ricky for a few minutes?" Sean asks.

"Oh yes, please. Come on in."

Sean parks his chair at Ricky's bedside. The boy lays on his adjustable bed with his amputated limb wrapped in an ACE bandage. He's watching Toy Story 2 on the TV. He barely notices Sean. After a quick glance, he resumes watching the movie and does not take his eyes off the screen.

"Hey Ricky, would it be okay if I chatted with you for a few minutes?" Sean asks.

"What about?" Ricky responds curtly.

"Well, you know both of us are here in the same boat. We're both stuck in wheelchairs for now. We're both in tough spots. We have to look out for each other. So, I'm curious . . . what's your story? How did you end up here?"

The young boy hesitates and eyes Sean as if to consider whether to answer or not. And then, in the next moment, he decides to let his guard down.

"I was riding in the backseat when my dad was driving one night. My sister was in the front passenger seat. Our car crashed and rolled. My body was wedged under the seat from the crash, and they had to amputate my leg. My dad and sister passed away in the accident."

Ricky's words hang in the air for the next several moments. Sean takes in his story and considers what to say next. Ricky's mother stands next to the other side of the bed with tears streaming down her cheeks.

"I am sorry, Ricky. I'm so sorry, ma'am," Sean says comfortingly to the mother and son.

"Thanks. What happened to you? Why are you here?" Ricky asks Sean to relieve the somber tension filling the room.

"Oh, I fell from a tree and landed on a wooden deck, breaking my neck. I'm paralyzed in my legs and have limited use of my arms."

"I'm sorry." Ricky reciprocates in a monotone voice.

"Thanks. I appreciate you sharing your story with me. That means a lot. You have been through so much at such a young age. I understand now why this therapy thing is so hard for you. Please, don't give up. You must give your best effort. Your mom needs you right now. Be strong for your mom. You're all she has left."

"But I just don't wanna do it."

"There are days when I don't want to either, but that doesn't mean we shouldn't keep going. I want to ask you another serious question, Ricky. Do you have any faith background?"

"What do you mean, 'faith background'?"

"Do you believe in God?"

"Well, yes. Of course, I do. But why would He let this happen to me?"

"I don't know the answer to that question. But I believe He has kept us alive for a reason. Ricky, I believe in Jesus. I know that He loves us. He loves us so much that He died on the cross to forgive our sins."

These words, though familiar to Ricky, have a greater impact on him coming from Sean at this moment, in this context. He begins to open up more to Sean.

"But why would God let these bad things happen to us if He loves us so much?" Ricky asks genuinely.

"As I said, I don't know why things happen the way they do. But I do know this: in Jesus, we have a new purpose for our lives. We can live for Him and do what He wants us to do. He has shown that He was willing to suffer for us, so we can find hope when we suffer. He loves you, Ricky. He really does."

"It's hard to understand all of this," Ricky concludes after a moment of thinking about what Sean just said.

"I don't understand it all either. But you need to know that we are in this thing together. Jesus can help us even though it's hard. You can come to see me in my room anytime. I'm right across the hall," Sean offers.

"Thanks."

"I'll see you around, Ricky."

And with that, Sean uses his electric-powered wheelchair to turn around. He starts to go back to his room, but Debra's voice calls out to him. He stops and turns his wheelchair around.

"Sean, you have no idea how much that means to me what you just did. All of this has been so overwhelming for me. I can't help but think that God sent you to encourage my son," she confides with tears filling her eyes.

"Of course, ma'am. You and Ricky have both been through such a terrible ordeal. I can't imagine your loss. I'm so sorry."

The tears begin flowing down her cheeks. After a few moments, Debra dries her eyes and adds, "Thank you." And she slips back into her son's room.

The next day Sean notices Ricky in the rehab gym with his occupational therapist. His attitude has done a 180. He's completely different. Ricky is cooperative and attentive to the instructions from his therapist, and he gives a maximum effort to carry out the tasks during the session. Sean smiles at the transformation he sees and quietly prays, "Thank You, Jesus. You're so awesome."

He looks up to find Debra beaming as she witnesses the transformation in her son as well. She glances across the room at Sean, and he can see her mouthing the words, "Thank you so much!" with her hands together moving up and down. Sean smiles back at her and nods genially.

๛

By the grace of Jesus, both Scott and Lisa advocated for Sean and ensured he received everything he needed throughout his recovery process. The summer after his junior year he obtained his driver's license and was gifted a wheelchair-accessible modified minivan. He was able to drive himself to school his whole senior year.

Also, by the grace of Jesus, Sean graduated high school and even did so in the top ten percent of his class. He was on the principal's advisory committee as well as his high school's Honor Society. He would go on to be accepted into the school of business at Texas A&M. Sean was cautioned against attending A&M because of his disabilities. But Sean went anyway. To this day, he does not regret this decision, even though the adjustment to living on campus the first two semesters proved extremely challenging. Again, by the grace of Jesus and against all odds, Sean graduated from Texas A&M's Mays College of Business in 2016.

In 2019, the Lord opened up a job opportunity for Sean to begin working at an IT company. He's very thankful and pleased to have his job as an IT specialist. Lisa and Scott's dining room has since been converted into Sean's office space, which now functions as the company's help desk.

Because of this job, Sean is able to shine the light of Jesus into his workplace and especially into the life of those who remain skeptical toward Christians and view many of them as hypocrites. Sean has the unique opportunity to represent Jesus and what a life sincerely devoted to Christ looks like to those individuals. The grace of Jesus has been poured out lavishly on Sean even though his life did not end up the way he thought it would.

Lisa recalls how a chaplain came to see them when they were at University Hospital after the accident initially occurred. The chaplain shared with them, "Sean's story is not the story Sean thought it would be, but he still has a story to tell." Sean is still telling his story. Jesus has prepared Sean's story to impact lives for eternity. His story brings glory to the name of Jesus.

The Hero of Sean's Story

Jesus was, is, and will remain the hero of Sean's story. He had a purpose in allowing that branch to break leading to Sean's spinal cord injury and paralysis.

The purpose of Jesus continues to be lived out in Sean's life to this day.

How do we know Jesus has a purpose for such a horrific life-altering event? Lisa realized something about the orchestration of the timing of when Sean's accident occurred. Her husband, Scott, worked as a contract employee for AT&T from 2006 to 2008. Amazingly enough, his contract job ended the Friday before Sean's accident occurred on Sunday night.

Being jobless allowed Scott to have the freedom to pour his time, energy, and efforts into caring for his son while Lisa continued her employment to financially support the family. Jesus knew this injury would happen to Sean at the exact time it did, and He orchestrated all of the intricate details so Sean would receive the care he needed.

Prayer and faith in Jesus are what kept Scott and Lisa going through those long and arduous initial days of recovery. Their family, church community, friends, Sean's baseball team, and strangers across the nation fervently joined the prayer effort. Even the local radio station lifted Sean up in prayer. Scott and Lisa's church went as far as opening up an online prayer portal for Sean and his recovery.

Lisa found herself overwhelmed by the outpouring of Christ's love through the prayer entries on the church website. As she read each entry, she sensed the grace of Jesus consoling her heart in those dark days. She does not doubt that Sean's accident increased the prayer life of many people in her community and beyond.

The Healing is Not Complete

One day several months after returning home from TIRR, Sean propelled himself into the kitchen where he observed Lisa sitting with her back to him, her face buried in her hands. She was crying. He could see her shoulders moving up and down as she sobbed into a tissue.

"What's wrong, mom?" Sean inquired concernedly.

"We've been doing everything we can and then some to reach our goal to see you walk again, son. I just want to see you walk again. I feel discouraged," Lisa confessed through the tears clouding her vision.

"Mom, I may never walk again but that's okay," Sean concluded with resolve.

Such a response indicates that Jesus had been working in Sean's heart. Jesus gave Sean peace about his future, and Jesus spoke through Sean to Lisa's heart at the moment that she needed to have such peace and trust in God too. What Lisa has realized is this: at the end of the day, it is not about us, but rather how our lives will bring glory to God.

And this doesn't mean that Sean is free from struggles. No, not at all. To this day, every day is a grueling, uphill battle. I'll let him tell you in his own words what he goes through daily.

"Every morning I wake up at about 6:30 AM and get in my shower/commode chair to do my daily bowel program because I don't have control of my faculties anymore. I then shower upon completion followed by getting dressed and then transferring into my chair so I'm ready for work. Because certain muscles in my arms don't work or are extremely weak, I require assistance getting back in bed and getting dressed. I take pills 3 times a day for various reasons, but the bulk is related to my spinal cord injury. I also self-catheterize throughout the day about every 6 hours. My parents/caregivers perform all meal prep because I lack the fine motor skills in my hands to cook for myself. I constantly have to problem solve on a daily basis to find the best and most efficient way of doing things because of my physical limitations."

Such tenacity and perseverance come from God. Indeed, Jesus is the One who gives Sean the strength every day to endure as he does.

Not only does Sean struggle with day-to-day physical limitations and setbacks, but one of the greatest challenges for him is the social barriers that separate him from everyday interactions that non-disabled people easily take for granted. Sean's primary love language is physical touch and affection. But being in a wheelchair does not afford him the ability or opportunity to walk up to a friend or family member and experience an affectionate embrace. Additionally, before his injury, Sean was an avid baseball player. He would use his athleticism to spark conversation, but now he cannot do so. Without any doubt, life-long physical disability comes with a set of multifaceted limitations. The loss is real.

Seeing Sean's World through the Gospel Lens

How does the gospel of Jesus speak into this loss? The gospel tells us that when we experience loss we can and should grieve the loss. The shortest verse in the Bible tells us our Lord did just that when He was confronted with the death of His friend, Lazarus.

"Jesus wept" (John 11:35).

We can picture the tears streaming down our Savior's face as He empathized with Mary at the loss of her brother. But what we know, and what Jesus certainly knew at the time, is that He would raise Lazarus from the dead a few moments later.

"But when Jesus heard this, He said, 'This sickness is not to end in death, but for the glory of God, so that the Son of God may be glorified by it'" (John 11:4 NASB).

Therefore, our grief is not without hope. We put our hope in the glory of God. We put our hope in the glory of Jesus. Sean can look forward, through the gospel lens, to the day when he will *run* with his glorified body into his Savior's arms and experience the warmth of His embrace. He will be utterly enveloped in a love that surpasses knowledge . . . the love of Jesus Christ. Sean will be completely healed one day in heaven when he is face to face with his Savior. But for now, he can live on this earth with a renewed perspective.

Jesus has shown Sean how privileged he is to live life from two different perspectives. He spent the first 16 years of his life as a healthy, gifted, and athletic individual. He was able to walk and had control over his body and took so many of the simple blessings of God for granted while being completely oblivious to those who live life with disabilities. Able-bodied people don't generally think to make more room for those in a wheelchair and allow them more time for simple everyday maneuvers.

But now, Jesus has given Sean a unique perspective. He can identify with both the able-bodied and those with disabilities because he has lived in both worlds. Through this perspective, he can relate to a different demographic of people on a deeper level. He understands now how to not overlook those he had previously overlooked. This has broadened his mind and perspective for the better.

We can be reminded that Jesus can uniquely identify with us because of His incarnation, "And the Word became flesh, and dwelt among us, and we saw His glory, glory as of the only begotten from the Father, full of grace and truth" (John 1:14 NASB).

Through the gospel lens, Sean and Lisa don't have to ask, "Why did this horrible thing happen to Sean?" Rather, the gospel lens empowers them to ask, "How can Jesus be glorified through all of this?" Life is not about Sean. It's not about Lisa. And it's not about you or me either. It's all about Jesus.

The Purpose of Jesus in Our Lives

Without the purpose of Jesus in his life, Sean would never have met Ricky and his mom. He would not have been able to sow gospel seeds to make an eternal impact on their lives. Without the purpose of Jesus in his life, Sean would not have been blessed with the job he currently has where he can represent Jesus in his workplace for the glory and honor of Christ's name. Sean would never have been able to traverse these unforeseen roads and come in contact with these overlooked people if not for the purpose of Jesus in his life.

Because after all, our lives are all about Him.

22

The Silence of God

His name is David.

He sits at his desk reviewing the papers he has just filled out. Lamplight bathes the words on the front page: *Missionary Journeyman Application (1981–1983)*. The letterhead at the top of the page reads, *Southern Baptist Convention International Mission Board (IMB)*. He taps his pen rapidly on the desk, and the ticking noise echoes in his bedroom as a nervous excitement pulsates through him. He longs to serve Jesus overseas. The next day, he mails out his application. It is February of 1981.

Months pass and no response in the mail comes. The month of May arrives, and David nonchalantly walks to the mailbox to do a routine postal check. He thumbs through the envelopes addressed to him, and the fourth one stops him dead in his tracks. His pulse quickens. Could it just possibly be? The letter is from the Mission Board. He quickly tears open the envelope and extracts its contents. His eyes dart back and forth across the paper as he reads it. The letter reads as follows:

> *Congratulations! You have been accepted by the International Mission Board as a Missionary Journeyman along with 80 other applicants from a nationwide selection process. You will be serving in Zambia, Africa as a religious educator in two government secondary schools.*

A smile breaks across his face, and he looks up from the letter. He walks with a spring of elation in his step back to the rented house where he is staying. It is May of 1981.

After a two-month summer missionary training program, David is prepared to be a journeyman with the IMB.

August arrives and he makes the flight from Lubbock to Dallas, Texas, and then to Atlanta, Georgia. From Atlanta, he flies to London, England. After a layover in London, he travels to Africa and finally arrives in Lusaka, Zambia on August 21, 1981.

In the fall of 1981, David begins teaching at two government secondary schools under the British system. While in Zambia, he also develops and leads five men's discipleship programs. One of these programs takes place at Mandabvu Baptist Church.

His name is Clement. He is a quiet and studious bespectacled young man in his early twenties. He is a native of Lusaka, and he faithfully attends Mandabvu Baptist Church. One Sunday his pastor, Reuben Nkhata, stops him on his way out the front door of the sanctuary and tells him about a discipleship program beginning later in the afternoon around 2 PM.

"The program will be led by a missionary from the United States. His name is David. The program will be twelve weeks long . . ." Pastor Nkhata pauses and adds, "Clement, I highly recommend that you attend. It will be good for your growth as a follower of Christ," the pastor says clapping Clement encouragingly on the shoulder.

"I will go, Pastor Nkhata."

Later that day, David leads the first session of the discipleship program in a classroom located behind the main sanctuary of the church. He stands at the front of the class with great excitement building up in him. He is passionate about training young men to follow Jesus and to know His Word. As he begins teaching Module One, *An Introduction to Discipleship*, he looks out across the young Zambian men seated before him, poring over their open Bibles. So many of them are hungry for God's Word and many of them looking to deepen their relationship with Jesus Christ. But as the sessions continue, one disciple stands out to David as particularly devoted to Christ and His calling over his life: Clement Lungu.

David leads the same twelve-session discipleship program at the International Church in Lusaka. As the weeks go by at this location, another disciple stands out to David as especially zealous for the Lord through the discipleship process. His name is Stephen Kabamba.

He perceives that both Clement and Stephen are not only passionate disciples of Jesus, but they also demonstrate a yearning to become disciple-makers themselves. So, David selects both of these men to accompany him in traveling to a church in Kabwe, Zambia about an hour and a half north of Lusaka, one way. In selecting these two young men, he plans to model the teaching aspect of the discipleship process.

Every Saturday David would drive Clement and Stephen in a white single-cab Isuzu truck to Kabwe. They would leave in the morning and return to Lusaka later in the afternoon. The rides up to Kabwe would be filled with rich spiritual conversation.

David begins, "Clement and Stephen, let me tell you about a spiritual discipline that has helped me in my prayer life. You can personalize Scripture and turn it into fuel for your prayer life. Take Psalm 23:1 for example, "The Lord is my Shepherd, I shall not want." You can personalize this verse and pray the words back to the Lord, "You, O Lord, are my Shepherd, I shall not want."

"I like this," Clement responds. "Let me try . . . I have been crucified with You, Jesus, and it is no longer I who live, but You, Christ, live in me. And the life which I now live in the flesh I live by faith in You, the Son of God, who loved me and gave Yourself up for me."

"Excellent, Clement! Galatians 2:20 is my life verse!" he says in affirmation, with a huge grin on his face. In great eagerness, both disciples continue to sharpen iron with David week after week.

The Sunday after the sixth session with David, Clement approaches Pastor Nkhata at the end of the service.

"Pastor Nkhata, I want to tell you something," Clement confides after embracing him.

"Yes, brother Clement. I also would like to know how the discipleship training process is going with the American missionary."

"That's actually what I wanted to talk to you about, Pastor Nkhata. I have learned much from David. Jesus has become real to me through the discipleship I have done under him. The Lord has moved in my heart, Pastor. I want to devote my life to full-time Christian ministry. There's nothing else I would rather do with my life."

"This is excellent news. Alleluia! Praise the Lord, brother!" Pastor Nkhata gives another warm hug to Clement.

Three weeks pass quickly, and week 9 of the discipleship program arrives. The date is November 6, 1982.

David, Clement, and Stephen have just finished an enriching session on Module 9, entitled *Fellowship*. David, exhausted from pouring himself out in teaching and leading the program, says not a word to either of his disciple-makers-in-training on the way back to Lusaka from Kabwe. The truck lurches up after hitting a bump in the road, and both Clement and Stephen perk up a little.

They approach a curve in the road. While driving around the curve, David loses control of the truck completely. In the flash of a moment, the truck begins to roll. The momentum from going around the curve carries the truck through two complete revolutions. The sound of metal clanging against pavement resounds in the cab of the truck. The force of impact causes the windshield to pop out all in one piece. The glass shatters but remains enclosed and held together by the rubber gasket. The truck nearly completes the third revolution but comes to a halting stop with one loud bang when it collides with the road.

All three passengers are thrown through the windshield frame out onto the road. Blood drains from their head wounds and scraped arms and legs.

Mangled and bleeding from his head, David lays face up on the side of the road looking up at the blue African sky. Abruptly, he stands to his feet. The world around him spins and becomes dim. His eyes begin to close. He collapses to the ground. A group of schoolboys playing soccer nearby witness him falling to the ground.

David, Clement, and Stephen lay on the side of the road battered and bruised, wounded and bloodied. The truck they were in lays on its side a few feet away from them with the wheels off the ground.

Suddenly, a flatbed truck skids to a stop, and the driver, a native Zambian man, jumps out. He runs up to the scene and surveys three unconscious men laying on the road. He then proceeds to load each unconscious body onto the bed of his flatbed. Next, he drives to Kabwe Hospital taking care not to injure his precious cargo.

Four days later, pilot Walt Garret and Dr. Giles Fort fly in a Mission Aviation Fellowship plane to Kabwe to pick David up and take him to Harare, Zimbabwe for specialized medical surgeries and care of his closed-head injury. This is due to the fact of Kabwe Hospital's limited medical supplies and resources.

Eight days pass. After four closed-head injury surgeries, David awakens from his semiconscious state at a hospital in Harare. He opens his eyes and surveys the room. Completely disoriented, he has no idea where he is or what has happened. He looks to his left and observes a window. Pressure on his bladder alerts him of his need to use the bathroom.

He gets up out of bed and ambles over to the restroom. He then notices three other men in their beds all bandaged up in the room with him. At first, he is surprised that he intuitively knows where the toilet is located in the hospital room. The bathroom door creaks slightly as he opens it, and upon entering he sees himself in the mirror for the first time in many days.

The left side of his face is completely swollen. His left eye is swollen shut. The tissue surrounding his eye is red and inflamed impairing all vision in that eye. Half of his head is completely shaven from the center to the left side. Both cheekbones are fractured along with his left jawbone. And two 2-millimeter rods protrude out of his temples on the left and right, being internally connected to braces on his top teeth. The rods have been placed there to approximate the fractured bones together in their proper places. The top of his right ear is missing, having been severed off during the wreck.

Emotionally, David is unable to feel shocked or disgusted by the man he witnesses before him. Through his one good eye, his right eye, he simply gazes at the figure, dazed and emotionally blunted by the horrific sight in the mirror. He is completely numb to the affective world.

After going to the restroom, he returns to bed and waits. Hours pass and the sunlight fades in the room. Night begins to fall. Suddenly, someone is at the entrance of the unit directly across from the nurse's station. David's missionary friend, Micky, enters the room.

"How are you, David?" Micky inquires with a tone of compassion ringing through his voice as he absorbs the appearance of his friend before him.

"I'm here," he replies with a flat affect. "What happened?"

"You were in a truck wreck."

"What happened to Clement and Stephen?" David asks.

Micky looks at him and pauses, not knowing how to formulate his next sentence. His pulse quickens. The words come out suddenly.

"Clement died. He died the night of the wreck from loss of blood due to a head injury. They tell me the hospital was not medically equipped to care for him and give him what was needed to save his life." Micky pauses again and quickly adds, "Stephen is fine though. He should have a swift recovery from all of this. He's already left the hospital and gone home."

The news of Clement's death does not register emotionally for David. He turns his head to the left and stares out the window into the fading evening light. The affective fog would linger for months to come.

Micky converses with David for a few minutes more, sharing news about the other missionaries mutually known by both of them. He then shares a parting word of condolence concerning Clement's death and exits the room.

After one more surgery to remove the rods from both temples, David is discharged from the hospital, and he goes to live with Dr. Giles and Dr. Wanna Ann Fort in Harare, Zimbabwe.

He stays with the Forts for the next three weeks for physical and medical recovery. Both doctors show him the utmost compassion and loving care during the post-acute stages of his recovery. During this time, the affective fog remains heavy upon David and extends to cast a spiritual fog over him as well. One evening he turns to his left and observes a Bible on the nightstand next to his bed. He thinks to himself, *I don't need to read that. I already know about that book.*

In December 1982, he returns to Lusaka, Zambia to finish his missionary work teaching religious education in the two government high schools there. During this period, David begins trying to piece together the whole timeline of the truck wreck, Clement's death, and all the people involved in his recovery process.

Early January arrives. A knock comes at the front door of David's lodging in Lusaka. He walks to the foyer and opens the door. Pastor Nkhata stands before him. The pastor opens his arms, steps forward, and wraps him up in a warm brotherly embrace. He releases the missionary and puts a hand on his shoulder.

"David, there's something I want to show you. Come with me."

The pastor conducts him to his car and within moments they are riding side by side away from the house. Within twenty minutes they arrive at a cemetery. David gets out and follows Pastor Nkhata on a paved path in between rows of mounds of graves. Suddenly he stops and steps aside and ushers him to stand in front of Clement's grave.

Pastor Nkhata tells David to say whatever he wants and allows him time alone at the grave of his deceased friend and disciple. He looks down and observes the grave. Amid the flowers laid down on the gravesite mound, is a blue cup, a keepsake of Clement's from childhood. A soft breeze whisks through the air and gently blows against David's emotionless face. He simply stands there looking on with nothing to say.

He feels nothing.

The affective fog, consequent of his closed head injury, still lingers over him and bars him from any kind of emotional response. Tears that may have fallen do not come. Sorrow for what has been lost eludes his human experience.

Three months pass by as David continues teaching religious education at the two government high schools.

April 21, 1983, arrives. He stands outside on the gravel driveway of the mission house. A Zambian policeman dressed in the customary gray uniform approaches David.

"I am Officer Mulenga with the Lusaka Police Department," he tells him. The policeman states this perfunctory greeting while holding up his badge for him to see it. He swiftly goes on, "Can you confirm that you were driving the vehicle that crashed leading to the death of Clement Lungu on November 6, 1982?"

"Yes."

"You are under arrest for causing death by dangerous driving. You can either remain here under house arrest, or I will take you into custody where you will remain in the Lusaka jail system until the date of your court hearing before the judge."

David, still dealing with the residual brain fog, hears these words fall on his ears like a silent jackhammer.

Next, the officer extracts an official document from a portfolio tucked under his arm and reads out the condition of the charges:

"If you are found guilty of the above-stated charges you will be sentenced to five years in prison and will be liable to pay a 1,000 Kwacha fine."

The officer finishes delivering the memorandum of charges firmly and professionally. David elects the house arrest option, and the encounter with the police officer draws to a close.

The days leading up to the court hearing passed at an agonizingly slow pace for him. During this time the IMB secures a defense attorney for him as he remains under house arrest.

At last, the date of the conviction trial arrives, May 26, 1983. The trial is carried out under the customary practices of the British criminal justice system. David sits in the defendant's box. The Zambian judge sits elevated above the courtroom surveying the scene before him. His dark skin contrasts sharply with the ivory-colored wig situated upon his head. He's cloaked in a black robe. As the judge is also the stenographer of the court proceedings, he holds a ballpoint pen in his right hand ready to record all that transpires during the hearing. He looks down at David in the defendant's box. He observes the scars on his face. But what he cannot see are the scars on his heart that would impact him for decades to come.

With a swing of his gavel, the judge pronounces, "This hearing is now in session."

He then clearly states the case for all in the courtroom to hear him: "The prosecution for this case is the nation of Zambia versus the defendant who stands charged with causing death by dangerous driving. Let us proceed with our first witness."

Witness after witness comes to the stand. Stephen Kabamba, being one of the passengers involved in the wreck, is among them. Each witness is cross-examined by the prosecution and, correspondingly, by David's defense attorney. This goes on for three and a half hours.

Still steeped in his affective fog, he witnesses all of these proceedings as an emotionless bystander. The expression on his face is remote and distant. His countenance betrays the gravity of the scene before him. He has little affective understanding that he could actually go to prison and languish in the Zambian criminal justice system for five years. The final word spoken by the judge will decide his fate.

The cross-examination of witnesses draws to a close.

The judge pronounces, "And now time for closing arguments from the prosecution and then the defense." Within fifteen minutes both sides have said their piece.

With another swing of his gavel, the judge declares, "This court is adjourned for the present. I will review the evidence and pronounce the verdict over this case when we reconvene." The judge stands and exits the courtroom.

He returns within twenty minutes and takes his seat again. He thuds his gavel and states, "This court is now in session. I have reached my verdict for this case."

He pauses and reads aloud the following written statement:

"After reviewing all of the evidence and testimonies of the witnesses, there is no record of any mechanical inspection of the truck involved in this accident to see if there were any mechanical failures that could be deemed responsible for this wreck. Therefore, we find the defendant innocent of all charges. He is from this day forward exonerated of all charges."

The date is May 26, 1983.

June of 1983 arrives. Having finished his missionary work and being an exonerated man, David returns to the United States. He moves to Arlington, Texas, and rooms with another missionary journeyman during this time.

Also in June, the residual affective and spiritual fog is lifted, and he becomes emotionally perceptive for the first time in months. One of the catalysts of this lifting is a heartrending breakup with the girlfriend he had before leaving for Africa two years prior.

David is broken. He is broken emotionally from the breakup. He is broken physically, awaiting a cornea transplant for his left eye scheduled in September. He is broken financially, being jobless upon his return home. This jobless state is exacerbated by the fact that he is not allowed to begin working until his cornea transplant is performed. And he is broken spiritually, having no direction and little hope. His only hope is in seeking Jesus. He is sustained by this seeking of Jesus during his stint in Arlington from July 1983 through January 1984.

David begins to think that God has forsaken him and placed him in a spiritual darkness. One morning he is reading Oswald Chambers' devotional *My Utmost for His Highest*.[21] Suddenly, a phrase from the devotional leaps off the page at him and resonates deeply with his distressed soul. He circles the phrase "discipline of darkness." He hangs onto the succinct description of this phrase and the vivid power of loss he feels. But worse still is the fact that he feels forsaken by God. He cries out in desperation to God both day and night.

And God is silent.

Day after day, David wakes up automatically around 6 AM, and his mind kicks into gear racing in a frenzy. He lies in bed staring up at the popcorn ceiling of his two-bedroom apartment, his roommate in the other room. Wave after wave of pulse-quickening questions batters and buffets his mind, flooding him with a barrage of anxiety. *How am I going to find a job like this? What does the future hold for me? Why do I feel like God has forsaken me when I was doing His work in Africa? "My God, My God why have you forsaken me?"*

He prays this silently as recalls Psalm 22:1. Each successive question intensifies the anxiety he feels in his innermost being. David begins to feel like a rocking chair; a flurry of motion in his mind with absolutely zero forward progress.

He rolls over in bed and his eyes fixate on the burgundy leather-grained 1977 New American Standard Bible he bought as a seminary student. It sits

---

21. Chambers O. (1935), *My Utmost for His Highest*, Feb. 14th.

there on his nightstand. He reaches out, takes the Bible in hand, jumps out of bed, kneels down on the floor, and opens to the book of Psalms. He begins poring over the Psalms starting in chapter one. When he comes upon Psalm 9, verse 10 jumps off the page at him and begins to resonate in his soul.

"And those who know Thy name will put their trust in Thee; For Thou, O LORD, hast not forsaken those who seek Thee."

And so, he begins seeking Jesus earnestly. The idea of God's silence, feeling forsaken, and simply lost without experiencing His presence is the epitome of loneliness. Not ever knowing any earthly father, David begins to feel like he has lost the only Dad he's ever known. For years he has felt cheated out of having a dad to raise him, and now he feels his heavenly Father has turned away from him as well.

In these dark days, the Psalms are the only spiritual food that sustains him. His soul is nurtured by reading and praying the Psalms, especially the Psalms of lament that conclude with stanzas of victory.

David kneels in his 10 by 12-foot bedroom with the lamp on the nightstand turned on. It is 11:03 at night. He cannot sleep. Every time he tries to lay down for rest the anxiety kicks in, and the sinking feeling of being alone, forsaken, and directionless floods his senses. His restlessness has driven him to his knees once again this night. His burgundy Bible lays open on the carpet to Psalm 13 (NASB) on page 508. Lamplight illuminates the words on the page, but the Spirit of God makes them come alive to his soul. He cries out to God:

How long, O LORD? Wilt Thou forget me forever?
How long wilt Thou hide Thy face from me?
How long shall I take counsel in my soul,
Having sorrow in my heart all the day?
How long will my enemy be exalted over me?

Consider and answer me, O LORD, my God;
Enlighten my eyes, lest I sleep the sleep of death,
Lest my enemy say, "I have overcome him,"
Lest my adversaries rejoice when I am shaken.

But I have trusted in Thy lovingkindness;
My heart shall rejoice in Thy salvation.
I will sing to the LORD,
Because He has dealt bountifully with me.

He prays the third stanza seven or eight times over rapidly until he is breathless. He pauses and takes a deep breath. He exhales and then prays silently, *I trust in Your love, Lord Jesus. My heart rejoices in Your salvation, Lord Jesus. I don't have a song to sing to You right now. Why haven't You dealt bountifully with me yet?*

It is late winter of 1983. In the midst of the throes of God's silence, the Lord provides a faithful friend to David; his best friend from childhood, Darrell Carey. Darrell begins calling him during his lunch hours at work. At this time, Darrell is working for Pioneer Natural Gas in Amarillo, Texas while David is in Arlington. Darrell takes time out of his lunch break to discuss career opportunities in Amarillo and how he can help Darrell finish building his house.

And so, Darrell convinces him to move to Amarillo to search out potential job openings. He allows David to stay with him and his wife, Linda, for a few months until he secures a job and gets back on his feet.

On February 14, 1984, Jesus provides a job for him at the Catholic Family Service as a counselor in Amarillo. And the silence of God is finally broken after over 15 months. David finally experiences a sense of renewal in his relationship with Jesus through the Lord's provision of this job. The silence of God is over.

But the moral injury and soul wound of having such a large responsibility for the death of another human being still weighs heavily upon his scarred soul.

The Gospel Lens and the Healing Process

Ten years pass. It's the year 1994. David is now married with a wife and three children. He works as a director at the Family Guidance Center in Dallas, Texas. On this particular day, a therapist has come to the Center to train about twenty other therapists on using psychodrama as a form of therapy for their clients.

The training therapist stands at the front of the room, and the therapists are seated amidst five rows in front of her.

"Does anyone have a trauma in their past and wouldn't mind being a volunteer for a psychodrama demonstration?"

Silence ensues. The therapist trainer looks across the audience. No one is raising their hand.

"I'll do it," David announces raising his hand.

"Excellent! Thank you so much. Would you mind telling me your name?"

"I'm David," he says as he walks forward to the front of the room.

"David, would you mind telling everyone your story of trauma? And then we will reenact the event and walk through the trauma with you."

He retells his story to the audience in a space of five minutes. Afterward, the trainer calls for her assistant to help present a dramatic reenactment of the truck wreck. David watches as the assistant sprawls out on the floor after reenacting coming through the windshield of the truck. His eyes fixate on three imagined bodies lying on the grass and asphalt with flashes of the real wreck running through his mind like a movie scene played in slow motion. He can see Clement's motionless body and his head injury as he lays unconscious on the Zambian road. David begins to weep. The tears trickle down his face as he reimagines the traumatic event.

The trainer then asks, "David, how would you like to have seen this event played out differently?"

Silence follows amidst the audience as he pauses before answering.

"I would rather it had been me that died instead of Clement."

Several audible gasps escape from the therapists in the audience at this statement. They are amazed that he would willingly give his life for someone else.

This experience is one of several touch points in David's life that would aid him in working through the trauma and feelings of regret over Clement's death. Jesus remains the orchestrator of the circumstances leading up to this touchpoint. The next touchpoint He provides for healing comes years later.

∷

It's the year 2006. David finds himself in Magnolia, Texas. He sits in a leather swivel chair in his office. The office is situated in the back left corner of the house. Several windows allow natural light to shine through and illuminate the room. Once again, his thoughts journey back to that day in November of 1982. A pang of regret nags at his soul. The moral injury simmers and festers inside him.

Suddenly, the Lord brings a thought across his mind. David immediately recalls the event of a fellow missionary named Ed Miller who was driving one night in northern Zambia where there were no street lamps or lights to illuminate the road. A drunk Zambian man had stepped out in front of Ed's car. He had no time to swerve out of the way. The incident happened so fast. The man was instantly killed by the impact of the vehicle on his body.

Due to the African custom of "instant justice", Ed could not stop and render aid. Instant justice is where an incident like the one mentioned above is met by an African crowd gathering around the car responsible for the death and then pulling the driver out of the car and beating him to death, thus executing instant justice.

David remembers Ed's story vividly as he sits in his office chair. So, he decides to contact him via email to ask him how he dealt with helping create the loss of a life. He types the following email to Ed and hits send:

02/21/2006
Hi, Ed,
This is David, 1981–83 Missionary Journeyman in Lusaka. I requested your email from Mary Small, with who I keep in frequent contact. She was gracious enough to give it to me. I still remember that adventurous trip you, Fred Allen, and I made to South Africa in December 1981 making the delivery run for the mission station. I had only been on the mission field for a short time and everything was so exotic and fascinating. I even got to drive back the Isuzu truck that I, unfortunately, totaled on Nov. 6, 1982.

This brings me to the main reason for the email. If memory serves correctly (cannot remember if I was still in Zambia or back in the States), you were driving one night and hit a Zambian on the road. Cannot remember if he died, but I do remember you were unable to get out to help because of the Zambian "Instant Justice"; and concern for your own life. Here are my questions: do you think of it often and, if you do, what are the spiritual dimensions you wrap around it for "the peace that surpasses understanding"?

As you know, 21-year-old Clement Lungu died from the vehicular accident I had while driving as we were coming back from a discipleship training I developed and was leading at Tom Small's church in Kabwe. Life is so precious and vital to me and my heart has stayed saddened these years that God used me to help bring Clement home. No depression, yet saddened at his loss and responsibility I still feel. Any spiritual medicine or theological cure would be helpful. My concern is I may be trying to find a finite answer to an infinite question.
In Christ's love and mine,
David G.

The next day he receives the following response from Ed.

02/22/2006
Dear David,

We do remember you and appreciate the ministry you had while in Zambia. We were on furlough when you went back to the states and we never got your address.

Regarding the accident I had . . . I fretted and worried about it also, but I gave it to the Lord. While not pleased at having the accident, I did realize that it was just that, an accident. I would not have taken his life for any reason, but we are not always in control of the situations we live in. I know the Lord's grace is sufficient for you. Pray you will find peace in your memory and forgive yourself.

I appreciate your ministry here and investment in people's lives. I trust you're finding fulfillment in serving the people you counsel and are able to encourage them.

Also, in the same place where you had your accident, there were several other accidents at the same spot. There was something unseen about the road that made it a difficult area outside Kabwe. I don't know exactly what it was, but they did some work on the stretch of road because of the number of people who had accidents there. Linda and I were on furlough when you had your accident. We did not see you after that time to express to you our love and concern. I pray you will have the peace of God.

One thing that spoke to me is that God is using this life to prepare us for eternity. I'm grateful that you and the young man you worked with were prepared for eternity. You had a part in his life though it was short by the world's view. You were used by the Lord to prepare him for his eternity.

Life on earth is short no matter how long it is lived. We are just to be a tool in the Lord's hand. God's grace is sufficient. Even your sad experience, though tragic as it was, has been a blessing that you could minister to others who had never lived through such an experience. God is at work in all things to make us a blessing. I trust you will be able to forgive yourself and recognize that you do not have to be weighed down by that experience or events.

Blessings on you and your family. Glad to know you are faithfully serving the Lord in the part of His vineyard He has called you to.

Yours, Ed Miller
Again, thanks for writing. Hope to hear more from you.

Before David reaches the halfway point of the above email, tears begin welling up in his eyes. He keeps reading. In the next moment, a torrent of emotion bursts through the dam of composure that has been begging to crumble for years. He leans forward placing his elbows on his chestnut rolltop desk. He buries his face in his hands. Violent sobs begin shaking his body. The floodgates have opened. He stands up. He begins pacing around the house from room to room trying to regain composure. After 23 years of bottled-up emotion, the barrier has finally come crashing down, and the relief is overwhelming.

After several minutes he returns to his desk and continues reading Ed's email, having nearly recovered his composure. A singular sentence provides special relief to him. He reads the following lines a second and third time:

"While not pleased at having the accident, I did realize that it was just that, an accident."

Waves of relief and comfort wash over his soul at these words. There in his office chair on February 22, 2006, the love and consolation of Jesus bring healing to the 23-year-old moral injury that has plagued his soul. He experiences the healing balm of Christ to his soul wound.

In processing the comfort from Ed Miller's email, one question bothers David. He ponders to himself, *why could I not get this relief of burden from God's words in Scripture instead of Ed's email? It's not like I haven't sought Him for relief.*

In future correspondence with Ed, David puts this question to him and Ed's response is, "It just shows we all need each other. As a part of the body of Christ, when one hurts, it weakens the whole body."

˙˚

The Gospel Lens and the Continued Healing Process

How can we look at the silence of God and the healing process through the lens of the gospel? Upon reviewing the panorama of the entire narrative, we can perceive that Jesus was orchestrating every single event for His glory and his greater good.

When David was lonely, physically broken, financially insecure, jobless, spouseless, and spiritually destitute, Jesus was right there. When he was on his knees day after day, night after night poring over the Psalms, Jesus was right there. When the silence of God was utterly deafening, Jesus was right there. When David was placed under house arrest, Jesus was right there. When the judge pronounced his final verdict over him, Jesus was right there. How do we know Jesus was right there? The truth of Scripture tells us so:

"I have been crucified with Christ; and it is no longer I who live, but Christ who lives in me; and the *life* which I now live in the flesh I live by faith in the Son of God, who loved me and gave Himself for me (Gal. 2:20 NASB)."

Not only does Scripture show us that Jesus was right there, living in David through all of this, but divine orchestration of life events points to Jesus being there as well. You will recall that he was placed under house arrest on April 21, 1983. This day was no coincidence by any stretch of the imagination.

Exactly three years later to the day, David's only daughter was born (April 21, 1986). Her name is Lindsey. You have already read part of her story regarding her son's rattlesnake bite and subsequent healing by the Lord.

You will recall that he was exonerated by the judge on May 26, 1983. Remember, the judge stated that no inspection of the truck had been done to know for sure if a mechanical malfunction was the cause of the wreck.

This exoneration day was no coincidence by any stretch of the imagination. Exactly seven years later to the day, David's youngest son was born (May 26, 1990).

I am that youngest son.

My full name is Jonathan Clement Griffin. By the grace of Jesus, Clement's legacy lives on in me. And his legacy will continue to live on in my firstborn son whose name is Jett Clement Griffin. From beginning to end, Jesus has orchestrated every single event in the healing process.

Jesus was also the One who orchestrated the psychodrama performance as a touchpoint of healing for David at the Family Guidance Center. Jesus was the One who orchestrated Ed's accident, the healing process, and eventual correspondence with him to bring to bear the healing balm of Christ on his soul. But you know what? Balm wears off eventually.

The Healing is Not Complete

It must be stated that even though David has experienced immense relief and healing through the above-mentioned divine orchestration of events, he still has flashes of recurring moments of regret over the death of Clement. His narrative highlights the fact of God's nurturing tenderness at different points in our lives, but at the same time leaves room for the reality of the believer's ongoing struggle on this side of heaven. Scripture reveals this as well:

> "For we know that the whole creation has been groaning together in the pains of childbirth until now. And not only the creation, but we ourselves, who have the first fruits of the Spirit, groan inwardly as we wait eagerly for adoption as sons, the redemption of our bodies" (Rom. 8:22, 23).

And so, David waits and groans. The groaning lessens as he continues to be gripped by the steadfast love and grace of Christ.

The Gospel Lens and the Hero of this Story

Jesus is the Hero of this story.

Life is not about you, and it's not about me either. From beginning to end, it's all about Jesus. Jesus Himself tells John on the island of Patmos in the book of Revelation, "Fear not, I am the first and the last" (1:17). What an astounding truth! Jesus is the first and the last.

All of life is about Jesus.

And therefore, the final door of healing for our suffering is unlocked only when the Holy Spirit reveals this truth to us: our lives are all about Jesus, not about us. Looking through the gospel lens at our suffering ultimately leads us to ask the following question:

"How can Jesus be glorified through my suffering?"

The same Jesus who called David to the mission field to prepare Clement Lungu for eternity also called him to be a Christian counselor when he was 16 years old. Through the gospel lens, we can perceive the numerous lives Jesus has touched through David's work as a Christian counselor to bring the healing and hope of Christ to the hurting and broken (you may recall David's involvement in Matt's story from chapter 16). By the grace of Jesus, his suffering in the truck wreck has afforded him greater empathetic capacities with many who are in the throes of their own traumas.

For this is written in Scripture:

"Blessed be the God and Father of our Lord Jesus Christ, the Father of mercies and God of all comfort, who comforts us in all our affliction, so that we may be able to comfort those who are in any affliction, with the comfort with which we ourselves are comforted by God" (2 Cor. 1:3, 4).

Indeed, Jesus has empowered David to walk alongside many in their suffering to bring to bear the richness of His mercy and comfort. Only those who have been truly broken in the past can empathize with the truly broken in the present. Jesus used Clement's death to uniquely equip and prepare him as a Christian counselor. God did not orchestrate David's healing process for his own sake, but ultimately to magnify the name of Jesus in the numerous lives he has walked alongside over the years.

Here is an overview of what Jesus has shown David through his "discipline of darkness" and searching for answers during his healing process.

Understanding Suffering (as seen through the gospel lens): Learnings Through the Spiritual Journey

"and He died for all, so that they who live might no longer live for themselves, but for Him who died and rose again on their behalf" (2 Cor. 5:15 NASB).

1. *God is Sovereign. He has chosen to permit evil and suffering and has entrusted us with trials of various kinds through a divine destiny for every believer who has walked the face of His earth.*
2. *For those in Christ, nothing can separate us from His love.*

3. *Jesus Christ became a curse for us and was forsaken—separated from His Father—so we will never have to endure being cursed or forsaken. And Christ loves us even more than that.*

4. *From the eating of the forbidden fruit until the marriage supper of the Lamb, there will always be evil and suffering. However, God, in His infinite wisdom, has given us a choice on how to react and respond to suffering.*

5. *How we use our suffering is one way Christ has predestined us to live out His will, to make Him the Hero of our stories.*

6. *Humility is an outcome of suffering and grows exponentially the more we see God's big picture for our suffering.*

7. *Jesus Christ will reveal His truths when we are ready to capture His understanding regarding our own suffering. He will restore our soul in His timing as we wait and hope in Him.*

8. *Walking with Christ, letting His word richly dwell within us, believing the Holy Spirit is at work, and godly fellowship with other believers all play life-defining roles in our healing, and later, helping others heal.*

9. *Our lives are not about us . . . they are about Jesus Christ. Understanding this truth unlocks the final door in the healing process.*

Seeing Jesus in Suffering

Now many years have passed since David's "discipline of darkness" and feeling of God's silence as he pored over the book of Psalms. After having grown deeper in his relationship with Jesus, he can see Jesus revealed in the Psalms. For example, the only way we can say that "our cup of blessing overflows" in Psalm 23:5 is because *Jesus* has drunk the cup of God's wrath that we as sinful humanity fully deserve. Jesus drank this cup so we could receive a cup of blessing that overflows for all eternity.

David experienced suffering, but Jesus experienced *the* suffering to secure eternal salvation for all who would put their trust in Him. "And those who know Thy name will put their trust in thee; For Thou, O LORD, hast not forsaken those who seek Thee" (Ps. 9:10 NASB). Even though he *felt* forsaken by God, he never was. In Heb. 13:5 (NASB) God tells us, ". . . I WILL NEVER DESERT YOU, NOR WILL I EVER FORSAKE YOU."

Jesus was literally forsaken by God at the cross and screamed out quoting Ps. 22:1, "My God, my God why have you forsaken me?" In His suffering on the cross, Jesus Christ experienced the horrific silence of God and was forsaken so we, who put our trust in Him, would never be forsaken nor endure the eternal silence of God. If we behold Jesus with eyes of faith, we can see *Him* drinking the cup of wrath we deserve, being forsaken as we deserve, and experiencing the silence of God as we deserve. On the cross, Jesus received what we deserve so we could receive what *He* deserves. What does Jesus deserve?

Indeed, if we put our trust in Jesus we will stand before God the Father holy, blameless, and free from any accusation of sin. This is what Jesus deserves. And we will receive the embrace of Christ and the Father's delight in us through Him. And we will declare with the psalmist, "I will bless the LORD at all times; His praise shall continually be in my mouth" (Ps. 34:1 NASB).

As David sees Clement's death through the lens of the gospel he sees Jesus, and he is being set free.

Part 7

The Gospel Lens
and the Heart of Jesus

"... for I am gentle and lowly in heart ..."
(MATT. 11:29).

His name is Jesus.

Oh, that precious name. There is no sweeter name than the name of Jesus. There is no higher name than the name of Jesus. Would you take a few moments and consider Jesus with me? Let us ponder and meditate on Him . . . on His greatness . . . on His majestic lowliness . . . on His glorious gentleness. There is no one like Him.

Come with me. I would like to take you along with me as we enter into three different scenes of His life recorded in the gospels: the garden, the cross, and the empty tomb. In each scene, we are going to place ourselves right there beside Him. Through vivid visualization, let's try to breathe the air He breathed. Let's see what He saw, hear what He heard, smell what He smelled, taste what He tasted, and perhaps attempt to feel what He felt.

Our goal here is to glimpse the heart of Jesus for us.

Thereby, we may witness His inexorable loveliness and beauty. Let's begin.

23

The Garden

It's an eerily quiet night. Clouds creep across the sky ominously veiling the moon from illuminating Jesus and His disciples as they walk softly across the ravine of the Kidron. Darkness envelops them. But Jesus has taken His disciples to this place so many times before that they need no guiding light to illumine their path. The Light of the world leads them onward. They make their slow ascent up the Mount of Olives and enter the Garden of Gethsemane. Olive trees are interspersed throughout the garden affording more shade from the already weakened moonlight. The walls surrounding the garden are overtaken with vines and foliage.

As soon as they enter the garden, a stabbing feeling of unease grips Jesus in His chest. The hairs on the back of His neck stand straight up like sentinels guarding their post, wary of impending doom, an unspeakable destiny. A chill runs down His spine, icing His very soul.

He warns His disciples, "Pray that you may not enter into temptation"[22] (Luke 22:40). He glances at each of their exhausted faces with a shepherd's protective concern on His face. This Jesus, who knows the full weight of treachery laying ahead of Him, considers not Himself at this moment, but the well-being of His disciples instead.

"Peter, James, John, come over here with Me." He motions for the three men to come closer to Him away from the other disciples.

Jesus confides to them, "My soul is deeply grieved, to the point of death; remain here and keep watch with Me" (Matt. 26:38). He shares His heart as He fights the dread and anguish.

---

22. All Scripture used in chapter 23 is from the New American Standard Bible (NASB 1995).

The three disciples of the inner circle sit down together and begin keeping watch, offering up prayers amongst themselves.

Jesus, on His part, trudges about a stone's throw beyond them deeper into the garden, deeper into the darkness of the night. He drops to the ground, His knees thudding against the earth. He falls on His face. The dry soil, dirt, and grass press against His wearied face. The pleasant scent of the olive trees is masked by the smell of sweat profusely trickling down His face, moistening and mingling with the dirt. His body shudders with apprehension.

"Father, if You are willing, remove this cup from Me; yet not My will, but Yours be done" (Luke 22:42).

At the mention of the "cup" in His prayer, Jesus glimpses in His mind's eye the fierce, fiery furnace of His Father's wrath against all of humanity's sin that will soon be His to bathe in completely and utterly. The prospect of drinking down to the dregs the chalice of God's wrath elicits an acute terror in the Son of God during this moment.

He is utterly horrified. He is overwhelmingly petrified.

An angel, a warrior of light, appears at Jesus' side placing a luminescent hand on His trembling shoulder. The darkness shrouding and surrounding Jesus leaps back momentarily, as the Son of God receives strength in His time of need.

Strengthened, yes. Relieved, no. Jesus feels even more so now the deep anguish of His soul. He is being tempted and tested in every way as we are. He's beginning to experience the weight of Calvary before Calvary happens. This is His moment to back out or to carry to full completion the will of His Father. The Father's will is the mission and heart of Jesus. The Father's will is the salvation of sinners.

With the vice grip of agony closing tightly around His soul, Jesus prays "very fervently; and His sweat [becomes] like drops of blood, falling down upon the ground" (Luke 22:44). The medical condition of hematohidrosis has set in.

Imagine yourself kneeling down on the ground next to Jesus at this moment. You watch as His body tremors in agony and anguish. You witness the sweating drops of blood dripping off His face and hitting the ground. The liquid grief of His impending forsakenness moistens the dirt. A guttural cry of despair mixed with relentless resolve resounds from His mouth:

"Yet not My will, but Yours be done." Our glorious Savior prays these words thrice and victoriously on your behalf and mine. The first Adam failed the test in the Garden of Eden resulting in condemnation for all, but here we see the Second Adam resolutely triumphing in the Garden of Gethsemane, meriting salvation for all those who would call upon His name.

Jesus gets up from the ground, His legs nearly trembling under the weight of what He knows comes next. He ambles over to His disciples. He finds "them sleeping from sorrow" (Luke 22:45).

"Why are you sleeping? Get up and pray that you may not enter into temptation" (Luke 22:46). The question and command are not uttered harshly by the Savior. Again, a concerned protective shepherd's countenance registers on the face of Christ. Here, we see Jesus at His greatest hour of need and agony, and He comes upon His disciples having given way to dereliction of duty. They could not keep watch for even one hour, and yet the Son of God, being under tremendous duress, does not deal with them in a harsh reactionary way. Instead, He instructs them to pray for protection from temptation.

The beauty of Christ's character is a wonder to behold: while handling the immensity of His own last temptation, Jesus still exhibits utter selflessness in humble consideration of His disciples' needs. He's staring down the barrel of imminent death . . . an avalanche of God's wrath bearing down on His soul, *and He's still thinking of others.*

Before Jesus can finish His sentence, a rhythmic cacophony of clanging metal and marching footsteps invades the solace of the garden. A crowd of men quickly comes through the entrance, Judas Iscariot leading the way. Torchlight now illuminates the immediate vicinity of Jesus and His disciples. All they can glimpse are faces faintly illumined by firelight, but they mainly just see silhouettes of swords, clubs, lanterns, torches, and the men holding them. The crowd is thirsty for blood.

Jesus walks up to the mob of men. The agony of His prayer time still weighs on Him, but He is fearless in the face of His accusers.

Judas approaches Jesus and declares, "Hail, Rabbi!" (Matt. 26:49).

And he grabs Jesus by both shoulders and kisses Him on each cheek. The feeling of the lips of His betrayer, the man He has poured into for three years straight, cuts to His heart. A sign of warmth and affection, now maligned and distorted, becomes a sign of betrayal. Here we see the plunging of the knife into the Messiah's back, and now Judas twists the knife with a kiss. This betrayal compounds the agony He already feels from His time with His Father in the garden.

But He must stay focused on His mission.

Jesus asks the crowd, "Whom do you seek?" (John 18:4).

One of their number stammers out, "We are looking for Jesus the Nazarene."

"I am *He*" (John 18:5).

At these awesome words, the men standing in front of Jesus are immediately jolted back and fall to the ground. The men's swords, clubs, and lanterns clatter and clang with the thud of their bodies on the garden soil. They quickly get up to regain their footing. The mob instinctively steps back a few paces from Jesus as they now realize the gravity of His presence, the Son of God standing before them.

"Whom do you seek?" (John 18:7).

A foolishly brave soul in the crowd stammers again, "Jesus the Nazarene" (John 18:7).

"I told you that I am *He*; so if you seek Me, let these go their way" (John 18:8).

We can take note here of the absolute poise of Christ. Being fully submerged in the anguish of His foreknowledge of the cross and bearing the betrayal of Judas, Jesus the Christ remains resolutely thoughtful and protective of His disciples. He truly is the good shepherd.

He is now, with perfect integrity, embodying the very words He spoke to His disciples in John 10:11-14:

> "I am the good shepherd; the good shepherd lays down His life for the sheep. He who is a hired hand, and not a shepherd, who is not the owner of the sheep, sees the wolf coming, and leaves the sheep and flees, and the wolf snatches them and scatters *them. He flees* because he is a hired hand and is not concerned about the sheep. I am the good shepherd, and I know My own and My own know Me,"

Jesus utters the words, "'let these go their way,' to fulfill the word which He spoke, 'Of those whom You have given Me I lost not one'" (John 18:8, 9).

At this point, the servant of the high priest, Malchus, comes to his senses after being awed by the power of Jesus and moves forward to apprehend Him. Peter, in anticipation of the arrest, takes swift action. He brandishes his sword and strikes the servant, cutting off his right ear. Malchus immediately puts his hand up to the side of his head to staunch the blood, but a steady trickle continues to flow onto the garments over his shoulder. He shrieks in pain.

"Stop! No more of this" (Luke 22:51). The voice of Jesus echoes in the garden as He lays a hand on Peter and guides him back to stand by the other disciples.

"Put your sword back into its place; for all those who take up the sword shall perish by the sword. Or do you think that I cannot appeal to My Father, and He will at once put at My disposal more than twelve legions of angels? How then will the Scriptures be fulfilled, *which say* that it must happen this way?" (Matt. 26:52-54)

Here we glimpse the majestic meekness of Christ, His glorious gentleness. Again, with perfect integrity, He embodies His own words in the Sermon on the Mount, "Blessed are the gentle, for they shall inherit the earth" (Matt. 5:5). At this moment facing arrest, Jesus has infinite and unspeakable power at His disposal, and yet He deliberately withholds from exercising it, demonstrating perfect self-restraint and self-control. And His majestic meekness is not meaningless but has a divine purpose: the fulfillment of Scripture to accomplish His Father's will. This is the heart of Jesus.

He then walks over, bends down, and picks up the servant's ear. It is cold in His hand. Next, Jesus strides over to Malchus and places the severed ear back on the side of his head. Miraculously the flow of blood stops, and the ear is completely healed and intact. Malchus guardedly puts a hand up to his head and gingerly feels his healed ear now. He brings his blood-soaked right hand in front of his face and stares at it, noting the absence of fresh blood. Malchus then looks up at Jesus, steps back, and stares at the Christ with mouth agape.

In the face of His enemies, those who come to arrest Him, Jesus displays perfect compassion. His tender heart of compassion is demonstrated towards Malchus, a person of low birth and inferior rank, a servant of the high priest. Here, Jesus perfectly embodies His own words in the Sermon on the Mount again, "You have heard that it was said, 'YOU SHALL LOVE YOUR NEIGHBOR and hate your enemy.' But I say to you, love your enemies and pray for those who persecute you," (Matt. 5:43, 44).

Another man comes and seizes Jesus. He binds His hands with rope. The rope is pulled taut binding both of Christ's hands together in front of Him. The rope is rough on His wrists, irritating the skin.

"Have you come out with swords and clubs as you would against a robber? While I was with you daily in the temple, you did not lay hands on Me; but this hour and the power of darkness are yours" (Luke 22:52, 53).

❀

Over the next day, Jesus is unjustly examined by the Sanhedrin, then by Pontius Pilate, thirdly by Herod, and then sent back a second time to Pilate. He is falsely accused of blasphemy and then sedition. Pilate tries to have Jesus released, but the chief priests, the rulers, and the people demand Barabbas to be released and for Jesus to be crucified.

Through this divinely orchestrated miscarriage of justice, Jesus is condemned to death: "And Pilate pronounced sentence that their demand be granted. And he released the man they were asking for who had been thrown into prison for insurrection and murder, but he delivered Jesus to their will" (Luke 23:24, 25).

This is the gospel. You and I are Barabbas. We go free and Jesus takes our rightful place on the cross.

24

The Cross

The weight of the cross is unbearable for Jesus. He is outside the city gates now and struggling as He makes the ascent up the hill leading to Golgotha, the Place of the Skull. With every step, He winces. The rugged vertical beam of the wooden cross digs deeper into His fresh wounds afforded by His cat-o'-nine-tails scourging. The flesh of Christ's back is laid bare, and every step exacerbates His agony. The friction is excruciating.

Suddenly, Jesus stumbles and the weight of the cross does not allow Him to regain His balance. He collapses to the ground and the cross thuds as it lands next to Him. The Roman soldiers escorting Christ to Calvary quickly grab a man from the onlooking crowd and forcefully enlist him to bear the cross to assist the wearied Savior. His name is Simon, a man of Cyrene.

Here we see Jesus, with perfect integrity, embodying His own words in Luke 14:27, "Whoever does not carry his own cross and come after Me cannot be My disciple."[23]

And the fact that the Son of God is not able to bear the weight of His own cross without the assistance of another person stands as a strong argument for us to bear our crosses in the context of a Christ-following community. What an intimate experience to come alongside other brothers and sisters to help them bear their crosses. Paul commands the churches in Galatia to "Bear one another's burdens, and thereby fulfill the law of Christ" (Gal. 6:2).

With Simon's help, Jesus reaches the top of Golgotha. He stares up at the sky, and dread becomes a deluge on His soul. His moment has come. The consummation of the ages is at hand.

---

23. All Scripture used in chapter 24 is from the New American Standard Bible (NASB 1995).

The soldiers come and strip Jesus completely naked of His garments. Christ feels an intense weight of shame as He stands completely exposed to the mocking crowd surrounding Him. The Romans divide His garments up and cast lots to decide who will keep them.

They give him wine to drink noticing how parched and thirsty He is from the ascent to Golgotha. The wine is mixed with gall and tastes extremely bitter. Jesus spits out the remainder of the liquid, His thirst remaining unquenched.

Prior to these events, the soldiers twisted together a crown of thorns. The thorns are about four to five inches in length and razor-sharp. One of the soldiers walks over to Jesus and roughly presses the thorns onto His head. The pain sears Jesus and nearly takes His breath away. Flowing lines of blood trickle down His forehead under each thorn.

The soldiers have Jesus lay down on the cross and stretch His hands out on either side of the horizontal crossbeam; the wounded Messiah completely laid bare measuring with His outstretched arms the width and depth of His love for us. He beckons us into His affectionate embrace, His wide-open arms unveiling the sheer warmth of His heart toward us . . . toward the very people who are executing Him. Can you glimpse the vastness of His love for you?

A Roman soldier bends down bearing a huge metal spike in his hand. He presses the sharp tip of the spike into Christ's right wrist. He lifts a hammer and brings it swiftly down driving the spike through flesh, tissue, vessel, nerve, and bone. Jesus gasps as the iron spike is driven deeper through His wrist into the wooden beam with every blow of the hammer.

The pain takes His breath away.

A loud pinging sound resounds from the metal-on-metal pounding. On His part, Jesus feels agonizing tingling pain as the spike has been driven straight through the median nerve in His wrist. The whole excruciating process is repeated on the left side and then again on His feet. Being nailed to the cross, He cannot move so much as an inch. But a fresh volley of agony commences when the soldiers hoist the crucified Savior's cross to an upright position.

Now He contends against gravity, and every breath is agonizingly painful to take. He has to push up with His legs and nailed down feet to expand His chest enough for inhalation to achieve life-sustaining respiration. Every breath brings excruciating friction as His flesh-exposed bloodied back rubs against the maliciously rugged wood of the cross. Two criminals are crucified along with Jesus, one on His left and the other on His right.

"Father, forgive them; for they do not know what they are doing" (Luke 23:34).

Christ's voice resonates throughout Golgotha, a voice full of breath-taking compassion and immeasurable mercy. His body has been stripped and laid bare on the cross, but now His heart is laid bare for all to see.

Can you see how beautiful His heart is?

His face has been marred beyond recognition. As Isaiah says, "He was despised and forsaken of men, A man of sorrows and acquainted with grief; And like one from whom men hide their face He was despised, and we did not esteem Him" (Is. 53:3). But with these ineffable words of forgiveness uttered from the cross, Jesus displays a beauty beyond bearing, a loveliness that draws in even the most hardened of hearts.

The criminal on Christ's left sneers at Him now, "Are You not the Christ? Save Yourself and us!" (Luke 23:39).

Before Jesus has time to respond, the criminal on Christ's right retorts, "Do you not even fear God, since you are under the same sentence of condemnation? And we indeed *are suffering* justly, for we are receiving what we deserve for our deeds; but this man has done nothing wrong" (Luke 23:40, 41).

The repentant criminal turns to Christ and pleads, "Jesus, remember me when You come in Your kingdom!" (Luke 23:42).

Jesus turns to the man and looking at him with eyes full of forgiveness proclaims, "Truly I say to you, today you shall be with Me in Paradise" (Luke 23:43).

An unspeakable joy floods the man like a torrent, tidal waves of grace overwhelming his soul. A smile breaks out across his face. Tears of elation begin streaming down his cheeks. His whole life he has been running from God, but now, being nailed to a cross alongside the Savior of the world, he can run from Him no more. The beauty and loveliness of Christ's heart have become utterly disarming and arresting to him. Salvation has never tasted sweeter.

It's now around noon time. Suddenly heavy darkness shrouds the sky, completely veiling any light from the sun. The onlookers witnessing Christ's crucifixion feel the weight of an unspeakable gloom descend upon the earth, smothering the very air they breathe. This pitch-black darkness goes on for three hours straight until about 3 pm. At this time, the moment of moments that made Jesus sweat drops of blood in the garden comes upon the Savior.

"MY GOD, MY GOD, WHY HAVE YOU FORSAKEN ME?" (Matt. 27:46).

Jesus screams these words at the top of His lungs. These words resonate throughout the Place of the Skull, allowing everyone to hear the shriek emanating from the Savior. All of the agonies of crucifixion are nothing compared to what Christ is experiencing at this moment. The crucifixion process may have damaged His body, but being forsaken by His Father now ravages His very heart. For all eternity past, Jesus has always known perfect intimacy and love with His Father, but now on the cross, He receives the just punishment, condemnation, and wrath of God for all of *our sins*. This is the only time ever where Jesus *does not* address God as *Father*.

At this moment, Jesus is not treated as God's Son to make possible what the Apostle John would later write about His Savior, "My little children, I am writing these things to you so that you may not sin. And if anyone sins, we have an Advocate with the Father, Jesus Christ the righteous; and He Himself is the propitiation for our sins; and not for ours only, but also for *those of* the whole world" (1 John 2:1, 2). In being forsaken on the cross, Jesus is absorbing the wrath of God to become "the propitiation for our sins." He is satisfying the justice of God the Father, so that we would never be forsaken:

"... for He Himself has said, 'I WILL NEVER DESERT YOU, NOR WILL I EVER FORSAKE YOU,'" (Heb. 13:5).

Jesus suffers completely and utterly in our place. His sacrifice is substitutionary for us. He absorbs exactly what our sins deserve. He takes upon Himself all of the punishment, all of the condemnation, all of the judgment, all of the shame, and all of the wrath we rightfully deserve. God pours all of this on His Son instead of us. Can you imagine a greater love?

And then, the One who offers us living water, tells the soldiers from the cross, "I am thirsty" (John 19:28).

The soldiers offer Him a drink by using a hyssop branch holding a sour wine-soaked sponge. Jesus sucks the wine out of the sponge. The sour-tasting wine moistens His mouth and allows Him to clear His throat. After this, He declares these indelible words that will forever change the course of human history:

"It is finished!" (John 19:30)

These three words are profoundly pregnant with meaning. These three words transform anxiety to peace, condemnation to acquittal, cowardice to confidence, guilt to grace, striving to rest, insignificance to purpose, worthlessness to being treasured, being wounded to being washed, unquenched desire to soul-satisfaction, being lost to being found, and being dead to being alive in Jesus Christ, if we put our trust in Him and Him alone.

Why do these three words mean all of this? The phrase literally means "paid in full." Jesus proclaims at this moment that the just penalty and price for *all* our sins has been paid in full through His finished work on the cross, through the shedding of His own precious blood for us.

Have you received these three words from Jesus? Has He spoken them over your life yet? Have you ceased from striving? Have you, being wearied and heavy-laden, taken His yoke upon you? He is "gentle and humble in heart, and YOU WILL FIND REST FOR YOUR SOULS" (Matt. 11:29).

All because Jesus declared on the cross, "It is finished."

After proclaiming these three history-changing words, Jesus bows His head and breathes His last breath, the perfect atoning sacrifice for sin lifeless on the cross.

And a thunderously loud ripping sound can be heard in the temple as the curtain separating God's presence from man is torn in two from top to bottom. Now, because of Jesus and His finished work on the cross, we can have intimate access to God as our Father.

Jews and Gentiles alike can now be ushered into God's presence: "for through [Jesus] we both have our access in one Spirit to the Father" (Eph. 2:18).

They then take Christ's dead body down from the cross and lay him in the tomb of Joseph of Arimathea. Prior to burial, Joseph and Nicodemus wrap His body "in a clean linen cloth" (Matt. 27:59).

Pilate ensures the tomb is secure and places a governmental seal on the large rock covering the entrance. He sets Roman soldiers to guard the tomb round-the-clock to ensure nothing happens to the body of Jesus. But Pilate fails to realize that greater security of Christ's tomb ensures greater authenticity of a resurrection if the tomb is soon to be found empty.

25

The Empty Tomb

It's early Sunday morning, still dark outside. Mary Magdalene makes her way to the tomb of Jesus weeping as she walks. Her head hangs down and she stares at her feet. Sorrow over her dead rabbi has kept her awake for most of the night. Tears continue to stream down her face as she follows the path leading to the garden owned by Joseph of Arimathea. She enters the garden and looks up at the tomb where she knows Jesus was laid.

Shock registers immediately on her face. She observes that the boulder-sized rock over the entrance has been rolled away. The opening is eerily dark. Fear grips her. So she turns and runs back to the other disciples and singles out Peter and John.

"They have taken away the Lord out of the tomb, and we do not know where they have laid Him"[24] (John 20:2).

Upon hearing these strange words, Peter and John take off in a sprint for their Lord's tomb. John outpaces Peter but comes up short being too afraid to enter the unnerving pitch-blackness of the tomb.

Peter reaches the tomb next and boldly enters, leaving John to look on standing at the threshold. Peter comes to the place where Jesus was laid and marvels. He picks up the linen face-cloth noticing how someone has rolled it up and separated it from the other wrappings and grave clothes of Jesus. Peter smells the face-cloth and is reminded of His Lord.

John ponders the significance of Christ's empty tomb, and after some time both he and Peter decide to return "again to their own homes" (John 20:10).

Mary, for her part, though, is not satisfied. She is incensed that someone would dishonor the burial of her Lord. *How could they disrupt the tomb of Jesus*

---

24. All Scripture used in chapter 25 is from the New American Standard Bible (NASB 1995).

like this? Who would take His body away and roll up His face-cloth and separate it from the burial wrappings? She wanders over to the uncovered entrance of the tomb to see for herself what John and Peter spoke of just moments before. Grief and pain mixed with a tinge of anger are expressed on her face. Her tears keep coming.

Upon entry to the tomb, she immediately notices two men dressed brightly in white and seated, "one at the head and one at the feet, where the body of Jesus had been lying" (John 20:12).

The brightly dressed man at the head compassionately asks, "Woman, why are you weeping?" (John 20:13).

She responds, "Because they have taken away my Lord, and I do not know where they have laid Him" (John 20:13).

Suddenly, another person enters the tomb. Mary turns around and sees a man standing there right in front of her.

Like the brightly dressed man, this man also asks, "Woman, why are you weeping? Whom are you seeking?" (John 20:15). His tone is gentle and kind.

Mary begins to become frustrated at these questions that seem to have obvious answers. She presumes this man is the gardener and expects answers from Him regarding the disruption of her Lord's tomb. Slightly agitated she responds, "Sir, if you have carried Him away, tell me where you have laid Him, and I will take Him away" (John 20:15).

The man, whom Mary believes to be the gardener, responds with one word: "Mary!" (John 20:16)

His voice is personal and filled with familiarity as He utters her name. His voice is tender and resonates with warmth.

She hears the man call her by name and comprehension dawns on her. Suddenly the veil blinding her eyes, keeping her bound up in grief, is lifted. Hearing this man call her by name changes everything.

In a moment, the man before her has gone from stranger to Savior, from gardener to God in the flesh. All because He calls her by name.

> "But now, thus says the LORD, your Creator, O Jacob, And He who formed you, O Israel, 'Do not fear, for I have redeemed you; I have called you by name; you are Mine!'" (Is. 43:1).

Have you heard Jesus calling for you? Have you heard His tender voice telling you He has redeemed you, that He has called you by name, and that

He has made you His own? Listen to His voice calling you through the words of Scripture. His heart is for you to belong to Him.

Months before this encounter with Mary, Jesus uttered these words:

> "Truly, truly, I say to you, an hour is coming and now is, when the dead will hear the voice of the Son of God, and those who hear will live" (John 5:25).

Mary turns to her Savior, her soul overflowing with joy and her grief turned to jubilation.

"Rabboni!" (John 20:16).

She cannot contain her love and affection for Jesus at this moment. She wraps Him up in a warm embrace.

". . . Stop clinging to Me, for I have not yet ascended to the Father; but go to My brethren and say to them, 'I ascend to My Father and your Father, and My God and your God'" (John 20:17).

Jesus shows Mary at this moment that clinging to His physical resurrected body is not needed at this time because it is to her advantage that He goes away:

> "But I tell you the truth, it is to your advantage that I go away; for if I do not go away, the Helper will not come to you; but if I go, I will send Him to you" (John 16:7).

The heart of Jesus is truthful and loving enough to tell Mary what she ought to be doing instead of clinging to Him: she is to tell others about the ascension of the risen Savior.

She nods in loving affirmation and submission to her Lord's command. She runs as fast as she can back to the other disciples. She feels weightless. It's as though she has been reborn after meeting the risen Christ and hearing His tender voice call her by name. Suddenly, the colors of the early morning become brighter and newer and fresher to her. Spring has sprung out of the deadness of winter. Jesus has defeated death itself! And she cannot keep this life-altering news to herself.

"I have seen the Lord" (John 20:18) becomes the anthem her soul sings. She will never be the same.

ॐ

What is the significance of the resurrection with regards to the heart of Jesus? I want you to consider the following three post-resurrection appearances: doubting Thomas, the reinstatement of Peter, and our risen Lord's Great Commission to His disciples.

Doubting Thomas

Ten of the disciples sit solemnly at a table in the upper room and talk quietly among themselves. The doors are shut. The shutters are closed. Fear, sorrow, and anxiety fill the room. The morose atmosphere is palpable. With the death of Jesus, all that they've experienced with Him feels as though it has been for not. The disciples are now purposeless . . . aimless.

Suddenly, Jesus Himself comes and stands in their midst where they are cowering in fear. He is among His ten disciples; Thomas is absent. Jesus looks around at each of their faces, shock registering on their countenances. Then He speaks these utterly soothing and bolstering words:

"Peace *be* with you" (John 20:19).

Christ's words hang in the air for a few moments. His words are an impenetrable life raft floating amid a raging sea of fear. As the reality of their risen Lord and His words of peace are digested into their souls, the morale of the disciples is lifted and buoyed to the surface.

Next, Jesus corroborates the life-changing evidence standing before them by lifting His sleeve to display His wrists, revealing the scars from the nails. A gasp from each disciple is audible. They are trying to process what they are seeing, their minds jumping into overdrive.

"It really is You, Lord," one of the disciples concludes, standing amazed and transfixed.

One by one a huge smile breaks out across each disciple's face. A transcendent joy overflows in the upper room.

Jesus proclaims to them, "Peace *be* with you as the Father has sent Me, I also send you" (John 20:21).

As quickly and mysteriously as He appeared, Jesus leaves the upper room.

A few hours pass and then the secret knocking pattern can be heard at the front door. James lets the newcomer in. It's Thomas.

The disciples rush over to him and grab him by the shoulders.

"We have seen the Lord!" (John 20:25).

A frown forms on Thomas' face. Disbelief intermingled with doubt ensnare his mind and heart like overgrown greenbrier vines.

"Unless I see in His hands the imprint of the nails, and put my finger into the place of the nails, and put my hand into His side, I will not believe" (John 20:25).

Eight days pass. The disciples along with Thomas remain huddled in the upper room with the doors and shutters shut tight.

Suddenly, Jesus walks right through the locked door in the front of the room. Thomas looks up and drops the broiled fish in his hand. His plate makes a clattering sound on the table. His jaw drops, mouth agape. Jesus again stands in the middle of His followers.

"Peace *be* with you" (John 20:26).

Jesus then walks straight up to Thomas. The two of them stare at one another for what seems like a long moment. Thomas, on his part, stares at Jesus with wide eyes pried open by shock.

The risen Jesus looks at His doubting disciple, His heart filled with a deep abiding longing for Thomas to turn and truly believe. Jesus takes a hold of Thomas's hand. The feel of the risen Savior's hand on his hand is warm and familiar yet oddly unfamiliar and glorious at the same time.

"Reach here with your finger, and see My hands; and reach here your hand and put it into My side; and do not be unbelieving, but believing" (John 20:27).

Here we can see the intense longing and desire of Christ's heart. He desires that we believe in Him as the risen Lord and Savior. We can hear the yearning in the voice of Jesus as He tells Thomas to "not be unbelieving, but believing." *Why* does the heart of Jesus long for us to believe in His resurrection so intensely?

I believe the answer is found in John 14:19, "After a little while the world will no longer see Me, but you *will* see Me; because I live, you will live also." We can hang onto these words as an irrevocable promise from Jesus: because He lives, or because He is risen, we will live also . . . we will also be raised from the dead. What a promise! We will one day enjoy eternity forever with our risen Savior because His resurrection ensures our resurrection if we believe in Him.

Even greater still, the resurrection means that Jesus, *Himself*, longs to be with us for all eternity, and this is what our Savior tenderly expresses in John 14:3, "If I go and prepare a place for you, I will come again and receive you to Myself, that where I am, *there* you may be also." The resurrection reveals the heart of Christ to us. He wants us to be right where He is.

But Thomas's response to Christ's passionate pursuit of his belief in the resurrection is most striking of all. In the next moment, Thomas falls at the Savior's feet. He grasps Christ's ankles with both hands. Emotion overtakes Him. Passionate faith in Jesus resonates in his voice:

"My Lord and my God!" (John 20:28)

Jesus pursues Thomas to believe in His resurrection and what is the result? One of the most profound confessions of faith in Christ ever uttered from human lips. By this confession, Thomas goes from doubter to devoted unto death. And instead of a dead rabbi, he now has a risen Lord and Savior. Instead of a mere human teacher, he now has God in the flesh standing right in front of him. Instead of a mere prophet showing people the way to God, Thomas now has *the* Way, *the* Truth, and *the* Life standing right in front of him.

And the risen Jesus, on His part, receives this designation "Lord and God" without raising a single objection.

Peter's Reinstatement and Restoration

Peter has made up his mind. He's going back to his former trade. A stinging regret and shame gnaw at his soul for his three denials of Christ. Not a day goes by without him thinking about the three times he disowned his Lord before people who were perfect strangers to him. In those rare moments when he quiets himself, his soul is chilled by the moment when Jesus looked across the courtyard and made eye contact with him after the third denial. The piercing gaze of Christ remains seared in his memory. So one day he walks up to John and the other disciples to tell them his plan.

"I am going fishing" (John 21:3).

The other disciples agree to come along. They get into a boat and push off into the Sea of Tiberias. Peter and his crew fish all night long and come up desperately empty-handed. They do not catch a single fish. Nagging frustration pricks and closes around Peter's heart like rusted barbed wire. He's exhausted from a toilsome night of fishing, and the fact that his net has nothing but seaweed and barnacles adds insult to his already wearied soul.

Just as his outlook could not seem bleaker the faint light of a soon-to-be radiant sunrise breaks through the darkness of the Palestinian sky, lifting and illuminating Peter's gaze. But he also notices something more than the rays of the sun stretching across the farthest reaches of the horizon. Suddenly, a man is standing on the beach, His true identity being veiled to the disciples looking on from the boat.

Suddenly the man is calling to them. His voice is deep and rich. The natural acoustics of the sea carry His words to the fisherman like a stork swiftly delivering precious cargo.

"Children, you do not have any fish do you?" (John 21:5)

In unison, the disciples answer, "No."

The man replies, "Cast the net on the right-hand side of the boat and you will find *a catch*" (John 21:6).

Exasperated but willing to try anything at this point, the disciples do exactly what the mysterious man on the beach tells them to do. Peter and John eagerly and desperately watch the net they've just cast into the lake float atop the water briefly. And then the miraculous happens.

The weighted ends of the net begin to sink into the water and enclose around a huge school of fish. The disciples start trying to haul in the huge catch, but they cannot because of its immense weight. They watch with eye-popping amazement the myriad number of fish wriggling around inside the net, making wet flopping and thudding noises as their scaly bodies collide with one another. Peter and John look at one another exchanging a wide-eyed expression.

John whispers in amazement to Peter, "It is the Lord" (John 21:7).

Suddenly, a flashback from three years ago washes over Peter's mind. He recalls with distinct clarity a similar miraculous catch of fish. He remembers falling at the feet of Jesus and crying out, "Go away from me, Lord, for I am a sinful man!" (Luke 5:8). The reassuring response of Jesus at that moment replays vividly in his mind, "Do not fear, from now on you will be catching men" (Luke 5:10).

Presently, Peter quickly snatches up his outer garment and throws it over himself. Without a second's hesitation, he leaps out of the boat, diving into the sea. The rush of the cold water does not faze him. Adrenaline has taken over. His arms flail about through the water in an unorthodox freestyle stroke pattern. The other disciples make it to shore before Peter does, staying dry and composed.

When they reach the shore, they can see clearly that this truly is Jesus standing before them. He has already started a charcoal fire with "fish placed on it, and bread" (John 21:9). He motions with His hand for them to come over to Him.

"Bring some of the fish which you have now caught" (John 21:10).

Peter, with some help from the other disciples, brings the net full of the miraculous catch and drags it up next to the fire. They count out 153 fish flipping and flopping around in the net.

After finishing breakfast, Jesus walks up to Peter. His heart longs for their relationship to be made right. He puts a hand on Peter's shoulder, on the one who denied Him three times. Peter cannot bring himself to hold sustained eye contact with Jesus.

"Walk with Me, Peter."

Peter gets up from the sand and dusts himself off. He begins walking beside Jesus along the shore. Feelings of shame and dread rush up inside him like a gust of wind. One-on-one time with Jesus at this point is unbearably awkward. He thinks about saying sorry to his Lord, but the words die on his lips before being vocalized. Apologizing seems so pitifully inadequate for the level of wrong he has done and so unfit for the person who walks alongside him now.

Jesus makes the first move.

"Simon, *son* of John, do you love Me more than these?" (John 21:15)

Peter's heart sinks. *Why did He have to go there first?* he thinks to himself. Jesus gets directly to the point and dives straight to the heart of the matter. In asking this question, Jesus is relentlessly and graciously pursuing Peter's renewal, reinstatement, and restoration.

The word Jesus uses here for love is *agapaó* meaning a love that is wholly devoted and sacrificial, a love that denotes total commitment.

"Yes, Lord; You know that I love You" (John 21:15).

Peter cannot bring himself to use the word *agapaó* to describe his love for Jesus in response. Instead, he uses the word *phileō*, meaning brotherly and affectionate love. He's not ready to declare total commitment to Jesus in light of his recent past.

Jesus then says, "Tend My lambs" (John 21:15).

Peter is disarmed and taken aback. He does not expect this response from Jesus. The good shepherd is calling him to be a shepherd. The risen Christ, at this moment, is graciously calling into leadership the one who denied Him three times. What scandalous grace! What's more is that He's calling Peter to shepherd *His* lambs, the very lambs that belong to Jesus. Here we see the Savior entrusting what is most precious to Him into Peter's hands. Could you ever imagine a more stunning redemption? The heart of Christ is staggeringly gracious.

Again, Jesus asks Peter, "Simon, *son* of John, do you love Me?" (John 21:16)

Peter responds a second time, "Yes, Lord; You know that I love You" (John 21:16).

In this second round of questions and answers between Jesus and Peter, we see the same mismatch in levels of love used by the two men. But this does not seem to concern Jesus one bit.

Instead, He responds, "Shepherd My sheep."

Peter again cannot believe the gracious words of restoration spoken from Jesus to him at this moment. Everything inside Peter is screaming, *but I'm not worthy, Lord!* The shame he feels before Jesus is beginning to vanish, like a vaporous breath exhaled on a cold morning.

A third time Jesus asks, "Simon, *son* of John, do you love Me?" (John 21:17).

This time Jesus does not use *agapaó* for "love" but instead mimics Peter's use of the word *phileō*. This third time questioning Peter's love for His Lord brings grief to his heart. But Peter fails to see that his three denials of Christ are now restoratively met with three questions about his love and commitment to Christ. Jesus is personally and intimately drawing Peter to love Him more than anything, not despite his three denials, but now more than ever *because* of his three denials. The heart of Jesus is most drawn to restore our brokenness. It's who He is. It's what He does.

Fighting back the grief, Peter responds, "Lord, You know all things; You know that I love You" (John 21:17).

Jesus then replies, "Tend My sheep" (John 21:17).

Jesus gives Peter three questions about his love for Him and then calls him to shepherd leadership three times. In a matter of days from this encounter, the church will be birthed through the coming of the Holy Spirit in Acts 2. And then Jesus is going to use Peter to preach the inaugural message to win three thousand lost souls to salvation. By the lavish grace of Christ, Peter indeed will obey his Lord's command to shepherd and tend His sheep, to be the "rock," the foundation of His church (see Matt. 16:18).

How does the resurrection of Jesus show us His breathtakingly beautiful heart? *The reality of the risen Christ displays restoration in action.*

We see Jesus coming back from the dead and then personally seeking out a shame-filled Peter to restore and reinstate him. The grace of Jesus runs so deep that He even calls the man who denied him three times to become one of the foremost leaders in the early church. Jesus fills Peter's life with Christ-exalting purpose and shepherd leadership.

The heartbeat of the resurrected Christ is the *redemption* of our brokenness, the *removal* of our shame, and the *restoration* of our hope. Next, we will see how the risen Christ calls not only Peter but *us* as well, into a thrilling and Christ-exalting purpose instead of self-centered insignificance.

The Great Commission

The Galilean morning air is crisp as the eleven disciples make their journey up to the top of the mountain on which Jesus has chosen to bid them one last farewell. Peter, James, and John look out over the sprawling Palestinian landscape before them and take in the panoramic vista. All of creation seems brighter and newer now that they *know* their Lord is risen from the dead. A thrill of hope surges inside of each of them, eclipsing all of the sorrow they experienced at Golgotha.

As promised, Jesus arrives at the top of the mountain and stands among His eleven disciples. Upon glimpsing their risen Savior, the majority of the disciples fall to their knees and worship Jesus. They bow their heads and lift their hands in awe and wonder. His resurrected body emanates a glory and power that draws them into humble adoration.

But some of them doubt the reality they see before them. The contrast of the worshipers and doubters together on the mountain before the resurrected Christ could not be starker (see Matt. 28:17).

Amidst the intermingled presence of worship and doubt, Jesus opens His mouth and utters these staggering words:

> "All authority has been given to Me in heaven and on earth. Go therefore and make disciples of all the nations, baptizing them in the name of the Father and the Son and the Holy Spirit, teaching them to observe all that I commanded you; and lo, I am with you always, even to the end of the age" (Matt. 28:18–20).

These paradigm-shifting words hang in the air as the risen Messiah stops speaking. The power of His words leaves all of the disciples speechless. Their existence will never be the same. This Great Commission will forever be the new trajectory of their lives. Everything they seek to do from this moment onward will always thread back to these pivotal words.

"All authority has been given to Me in heaven and on earth."

Wow! In this first statement, we see Jesus reveal the full scope of His divine nature. He is God. He has all authority in heaven and on earth! Such a stunning claim has never been legitimately made by anyone else in human history. The resurrection means Christ has all authority, including authority over death.

What does this profound truth mean for us as His followers? It means we should never, ever take Christ's words lightly. We are to come under His authority completely. He is our risen Lord.

Moreover, there is extreme heart-consoling comfort to be felt in these words. If Jesus has all authority, and He does, then we who belong to Him can rest in His sovereign control over everything that comes our way. We can move forward in fearless obedience to Him because the one who has all authority is for us and not against us as we carry out His mission on earth. His heart beats for us to join Him in His mission. So, what is His mission?

"Go therefore and make disciples of all the nations, baptizing them in the name of the Father and the Son and the Holy Spirit, teaching them to observe all that I commanded you . . ."

Here we see that the resurrection of Christ means He infuses our lives with an eternal purpose and significance. This is the heart of Jesus. He longs for you and me to join Him in making disciples of all the nations. His heart is for every tribe, tongue, and nation to know His salvation and hope. And what's mind-blowing about all of this, is the desire of Christ's heart to use broken vessels like you and me to carry out His mission to the nations.

Paul puts it like this, "Therefore, we are ambassadors for Christ, as though God were making an appeal through us; we beg you on behalf of Christ, be reconciled to God" (2 Cor. 5:20).

Did you notice how the Great Commission in Matthew 28 is not about you or me? It's all about Jesus and His plan to reach the nations for His glory. Earlier in 2nd Corinthians 5, Paul puts this fact very poignantly, "For the love of Christ controls us, having concluded this, that one died for all, therefore all died; and He died for all, so that they who live might no longer live for themselves, but for Him who died and rose again on their behalf" (verses 14, 15).

The mark of true Christ-followers is that they "no longer live for themselves, but for Him who died and rose again on their behalf!" The resurrection means that our lives take on a totally different trajectory, being no longer self-centered, *but Christ-centered*. This is all because of who Jesus is and what He has done. We live for Christ as He sends us out to make disciples, baptizing them in the name of the Father, the Son, and the Holy Spirit, and then we are called to teach people to obey what Christ has commanded us.

But you may be thinking to yourself: *this sounds very overwhelming! Making disciples of all the nations, baptizing them, and teaching them to obey what Christ has commanded? What? How am I ever going to do this?*

I'm so glad you asked! Let the last words Jesus declares in the book of Matthew nourish and soothe your soul:

". . . and lo, I am with you always, even to the end of the age" (Matt. 28:20).

The One who has all authority in heaven and on earth has *not* left you to carry out His Great Commission by yourself. You are not alone. He is with you always. Let me say that again: Jesus is with you always, even to the end of the age. He is with you in every gospel conversation. He is with you in every kind deed you do to display the gospel. And He's even with you when you falter and fail to live for Him.

Jesus is with us because He has given us His Holy Spirit. He has also given us brothers and sisters in Christ through His body, the church. Christ never meant for you to do the Great Commission alone. The Great Commission is meant to be carried out in the context of your local church.

In the next section, we will cover the practical implications of the resurrection of Jesus. These include intimate community, radical generosity, and a fearless proclamation of the risen Christ.

26

Practical Implications of the Resurrection

I want to close this section by sharing three practical implications of the resurrection and ascension of Jesus. After Jesus is raised from the dead, He ascends to His Father and then sends the Holy Spirit, the Helper, just as He promised. This happens in Acts 1 and 2. The disciples' lives become marked by the following three realities after the risen and ascended Christ sends the Holy Spirit to them:

1. Intimate Community
2. Radical Generosity
3. Fearless Proclamation of the Risen Christ

Intimate Community

We are told in Acts 2:42[25] the following about the disciples of the risen Jesus:

> "They were continually devoting themselves to the apostles' teaching and to fellowship, to the breaking of bread and to prayer."

---

25. All Scripture used in chapter 26 is from the New American Standard Bible (NASB 1995).

Notice how the coming of the Holy Spirit after Christ's resurrection and ascension leads the disciples to spend time together in the biblical community. They "continually devote themselves" to what we have recorded today in the New Testament. They fellowshipped together, which means they had a common bond and mission together through the risen Jesus and the indwelling of His Spirit. They ate together. They prayed together.

I want to encourage you if you haven't already: please join a Bible-believing church in your local area and get involved as much as you can to experience an intimate biblical community. This is the only way you will be able to effectively look at life through the gospel lens, through the heart of Jesus.

What does becoming involved in a biblical community look like? My church has small groups called discipleship groups or "d-groups." These are groups of about four to five people of the same gender meeting together weekly to study Scripture, confess sin, pray for one another, and encourage one another.

The other night I was meeting with my guys, and we were examining Ephesians 5:1, 2 in greater depth. What happened that Monday night during discipleship group amazed me. We were meditating together on verse 2, a verse I had read many times before, and suddenly two words leaped off the page at me. It was as if the Holy Spirit gave me a spiritual magnifying glass, and He italicized, bolded, and then highlighted these two words as I'd never seen before. Here is Eph. 5:1, 2.

"Therefore be imitators of God, as beloved children; and walk in love, just as Christ also loved you and gave Himself up for us, an offering and a sacrifice to God as a fragrant aroma."

Can you guess which two words in verse 2 jumped out at me? They are incredibly mundane words, but in context, these words pack a wallop of a punch. The two words magnified to me were the words, *"just as."* Absolutely staggering. Paul is calling us to "walk in love, *just as* Christ also loved you and gave Himself up for us..." (emphasis mine). Can you imagine the utter weight of this call to love? The words "just as" are from a singular Greek word that means "corresponding to" or "to the same degree as."

Wow! How could we ever love people as sacrificially as Christ has loved us? The call here is to walk in a love so deep and so radical toward others that they would come away from interacting with us and think to themselves, *wow I feel like I experienced the sacrificial love of Jesus just now.*

What we concluded that night about this weighty call to love is that we will never love to the same degree as Jesus has loved us *until* we begin to realize *just how beloved we are in the eyes of God the Father.* We are His beloved children through Christ! In other words, we must first experience and grasp the sacrificial love Jesus has poured out on us. You cannot pour love onto others from an empty bucket. You have to be filled to overflowing with the love of Jesus for you, His heart for you, *and then* His love will slosh out over the sides of your bucket and spill onto others around you.

These soul-enriching gospel insights came in the context of an intimate biblical community.

Radical Generosity

Secondly, we see the radical generosity of the disciples after the Holy Spirit comes:

> "And all those who had believed were together and had all things in common; and they began selling their property and possessions and were sharing them with all, as anyone might have need. Day by day continuing with one mind in the temple, and breaking bread from house to house, they were taking their meals together with gladness and sincerity of heart," (Acts 2:44–46)

The gospel changes you, even what you do with your time, money, and possessions! The beauty of the risen Savior frees us from the vice-grip of materialism and greed with which this world can choke us out and make us unfruitful:

"And the one on whom seed was sown among the thorns, this is the man who hears the word, and the worry of the world and the deceitfulness of wealth choke the word, and it becomes unfruitful" (Matt. 13:22).

Because Jesus and His mission set our lives on a Christ-centered and Christ-exalting trajectory, we can give our possessions away to share "with all, as anyone might have need" (Acts 2:45).

I can remember one instance very vividly early on in my marriage. Kelley and I did not have a lot of extra cash in our bank account, but we wanted to give towards a disaster relief effort our church was supporting at the time. We decided we would sell some of the movies we kept in a large cardboard box. We started going through the box trying to decide which ones we would sell and which ones we would keep. Semi-overwhelmed by the decision-making process, I left Kelley alone with the box in our bedroom to go do something in the kitchen. After a few moments went by she came out of our bedroom with a look of resolve on her countenance.

She told me, "I think we should sell *all* of our movies."

And that's exactly what we did.

My wife became even more beautiful to me that day because Jesus allowed me to glimpse the beauty of His radical generosity *He* placed in her heart.

I want to encourage you if you haven't already: generosity begins by tithing at least ten percent of your income to your local church, yet we are to do this cheerfully (see 2 Cor. 9:7). If you have to work up to that number, Jesus knows your heart. But ten percent is a great starting place because we should all be growing in sacrificial giving. And do not let ten percent be your limit because "freely you received, freely give" (Matt. 10:8b). The biblical precedent for this is found in Prov. 3:9–10:

> "Honor the LORD from your wealth
> And from the first of all your produce;
> So your barns will be filled with plenty
> And your vats will overflow with new wine."

The radical generosity of Jesus is this: He gave and gave and gave until He poured Himself out to death on the cross and shed His blood for the forgiveness of our sins. Such radical generosity is worth sharing with those around us.

The third practical implication of the resurrection, ascension, and coming of the Holy Spirit is a fearless proclamation of the risen Christ.

Fearless Proclamation of the Risen Christ

Time and time again throughout the book of Acts you see one of the Apostles stand up and boldly declare the good news of the gospel, and *every time* they make mention of the resurrection of Jesus. Take a look at the following verses:

> "This Jesus God raised up again, to which we are all witnesses. There-fore having been exalted to the right hand of God, and having received

from the Father the promise of the Holy Spirit, He has poured forth this which you both see and hear" (Acts 2:32, 33).

"But you disowned the Holy and Righteous One and asked for a murderer to be granted to you, but put to death the Prince of life, the one whom God raised from the dead, *a fact* to which we are witnesses" (Acts 3:14, 15).

"Then Peter, filled with the Holy Spirit, said to them, 'Rulers and elders of the people, if we are on trial today for a benefit done to a sick man, as to how this man has been made well, let it be known to all of you and to all the people of Israel, that by the name of Jesus Christ the Nazarene, whom you crucified, whom God raised from the dead—by this name this man stands here before you in good health'" (Acts 4:8-10).

"We are witnesses of all the things He did both in the land of the Jews and in Jerusalem. They also put Him to death by hanging Him on a cross. God raised Him up on the third day and granted that He become visible, not to all the people, but to witnesses who were chosen beforehand by God, that is, to us who ate and drank with Him after He arose from the dead" (Acts 10:39-41).

All of these statements were spoken by the Holy Spirit-inspired, reinstated Peter. He could not stop proclaiming the risen Christ. Jesus being alive from the dead completely changed his life. He became restored by Christ's resurrection grace. And the Holy Spirit filled Peter to boldly proclaim his Savior to an unbelieving world. When the authorities asked Peter and John to stop proclaiming the risen Jesus, this was their reply:

"But Peter and John answered and said to them, 'Whether it is right in the sight of God to give heed to you rather than to God, you be the judge; for we cannot stop speaking about what we have seen and heard'" (Acts 4:19, 20).

But how can we practically declare the gospel of our risen Savior in today's society? Again, I'm so glad you asked.

Declaring the gospel begins when we slow down our hectic lives and show interest in another person. We can then begin to build a relationship. Jesus perfectly engages with the woman of Samaria in John 4:4–42. He started with a similarity: water. She was drawing water, and He was thirsty. He then asked her for a drink (engaging her in conversation). Soon thereafter, He takes the conversation to a spiritual level by offering her living water. The following is a practical outline on gospel sharing moments.

Gospel Sharing Moments

"Therefore, we are ambassadors for Christ, as though God were making an appeal through us; we beg you on behalf of Christ, be reconciled to God" (2 Cor. 5:20).

i. To share the gospel you will need:
   a. **A deep abiding love relationship with Jesus Christ,** so that His love will overflow from your heart and spill onto others who may face eternity separated from God, condemned to eternal punishment.
   b. **Prayer**: pray before you go out to encounter your neighbor (the one closest to you at that time—see the story of the Good Samaritan in Luke 10:25-37).
   c. **Intent**: be intentional in *declaring* the good news of Jesus Christ to a lost person whenever and wherever you encounter anyone that presents an opportunity.
   d. **Focus**: focus on looking for that opportunity in taking any conversation to a spiritual level. This is often most difficult because it is so easy to be distracted by temporal and empty subjects of conversation.
   e. **Personal contact with others**:
      i. "You are the salt of the earth; but if the salt has become tasteless, how can it be made salty again? It is no longer good for anything, except to be thrown out and trampled underfoot by men" (Matt. 5:13).
      ii. Salt is used as a preservative, seasoning for food, and an antiseptic, it helps maintain body homeostasis, makes you thirsty, etc. Yet salt is unable to work unless it **comes in contact** with the item to be salted. Salt has to be applied or rubbed in for it to take maximal and optimal effect. As Jesus takes salt to the

spiritual level, we, too, need to be in contact with our neighbor (the person closest to us at that time). We can begin by rubbing in or applying the good news of Jesus to our everyday conversations. Jesus has called us to be His salt of the earth. He has called us to make contact with those outside the church to speak His love into their lives. Do not let yourself remain in the salt shaker of the church. We get to experience the joy of walking alongside others as we declare His good news into their lives!

2. **Initiate the conversation: ask questions about your "neighbor."**
   a. Find something, anything to compliment them on to get them engaged in sharing about themselves.
      i. Jewelry, shoes, tattoos, what they do, etc.
      ii. Be sincere.
      iii. Earn the right to share about Jesus.

3. **Build a relationship**, no matter how much time you have. Sincere earnestness is vital, and this can be seen in your countenance. We worship a Savior, who not only freely gives us eternal life (John 3:16, Rom. 6:23), but also abundant life on earth (John 10:10). How could we not want to give the gospel away?
   a. Reduce talking about yourself.
      i. I talk about myself.
      ii. We all talk about ourselves.
      iii. But there is a vast difference between being self-focused and sharing the gospel for eternal consequences.
      iv. Dr. Ortlund puts it best: *"How exhausting is the misery of self. How energizing are the joys of living for another."*[26]
   b. There is a solution to solving this epidemic of talking too much about ourselves. We all tend to have an agenda when someone else is talking. We tend to only think about what we can say next about ourselves. In Christ, we can overcome this self-centered tendency. Through the Holy Spirit, we can **simply listen without coming up with a self-focused response**. We can listen deeper to what they are revealing about themselves.

---

26. Ortlund D. (2020), *Gentle and Lowly*, Crossway *205*.

        i. What are *they* going through? What are *they* experiencing? What are *they* feeling? How can we begin to feel what they are feeling alongside them in solidarity?

    c. After they have finished, respond with something that will continue their story, situation, issue, circumstances, etc. While listening, find a word or phrase that can help take the conversation to a spiritual level. Hear if they are experiencing loss. Jesus can make them whole again. Hear if they are hurting. Jesus can bring healing. Hear what they are seeking. Jesus is the only one who can satisfy their deepest longings.

4. Use their conversation to take it to **a spiritual level** that shows a similarity with the gospel. If nothing comes up, use one of these neutral questions:

    a. "What is your faith or religious background?"

        i. "Was the gospel ever presented to you?"

        ii. If so, "Can you tell me what the gospel message is?"

    b. "Do you worship anywhere?"

        i. If so, "What do they share about the gospel?"

        ii. If no worship attendance, ask if they've ever heard the gospel.

    c. "I was wondering what you think would surprise most people about you?"

        i. "Why?"

        ii. Relate their answer to a spiritual level.

    d. "I was wondering what is your greatest strength?"

        i. "Why?"

        ii. Relate their answer to a spiritual level.

    e. "I was wondering what do you consider to be two major turning points in your life?"

        i. "Why?"

        ii. Relate their answer to a spiritual level.

    f. "I was wondering what you value the most in your life?"

        i. "Why?"

        ii. Relate their answer to a spiritual level.

5. Organically share the gospel of Jesus Christ.

The gospel of Jesus is the good news that Jesus, God's only Son, came to earth and lived the perfect life that we could not live, died the death on the cross for our sins

*that we deserved, and rose again to restore us to right relationship with God our
Father and Creator. By believing in Jesus, we have the free gift of eternal life, and
now we can live out our lives to love, serve, and glorify Him.*

6. Trust that the Holy Spirit will do the saving as you plant seeds.
7. Offer to **pray** for them on the spot.
   a. Ask what they need prayer for and then pray the gospel over them.
   b. I get to do this every day at my work as a physical therapist,
      and every day the mutual blessing of prayer with my patients is
      soul-enriching.
   c. Inviting Jesus into their situation through prayer is key!
   d. It is thrilling to watch the restoring presence of Jesus enter broken
      situations.
8. Humbly and boldly share truth from God's word or Scripture verses
   with them:
   a. God's word never returns void:
      "So will My word be which goes forth from My mouth;
      It will not return to Me empty,
      Without accomplishing what I desire,
      And without succeeding for which I sent it" (Is. 55:11).
   b. Seek to proclaim Christ:
      "What then? Only that in every way, whether in pretense or in
      truth, Christ is proclaimed; and in this I rejoice" (Phil. 1:18).
   c. Share stories from Scripture with them:
      i. The parable of the prodigal son is gripping and easy to share
         (see Luke 15)

What does this look like in real life for you? For example, next time you're at a
restaurant make an intentional effort to learn your waiter's name. We can take
note of how personal Jesus is when He engages with people. He called Mary by
name to reveal to her His true identity after the resurrection. He called Peter
by name three times when He restored and reinstated Him. So it's important
to learn the names of those around us so we can engage deeper with them.

If you notice any tattoos on your waiter you can say, "Nice ink. What's
your story?" Everyone with a tattoo has a story. You can do the same with
any jewelry they are wearing. Listen with interest and allow the Holy Spirit
to guide you in how to take the conversation to a spiritual level.

The other day my dad and mom were dining out at one of their favorite restaurants. My dad noticed their waitress, Kendra, had a tattoo. So, he initiated a conversation with her by asking what her tattoo meant. She replied that it was the Bulgarian word for "hope." Kendra left to go attend to her waitress duties. While she was gone my mom said to my dad that her hope could be in Jesus Christ.

And he said, "Yes! Why didn't I think of that?"

When Kendra returned my dad asked, "So Kendra, may I ask what your hope is in?"

She replied, "I had a difficult upbringing and I had the word put on my arm to have hope in my situation."

My dad responded very intentionally, "Did you ever put your hope in Jesus Christ?"

Kendra's countenance grew somber. "I tried, but He wasn't there for me."

Many people at this point in the conversation would pull back and reticently discontinue the conversation. But that's not who my dad is.

Jesus gave my dad boldness through the Holy Spirit to reply, "I'm so sorry. The heart of Jesus wants to show you how much He really loves you. Will you give Him another chance?"

She paused and then said, "Yes."

My mom exchanged contact info with Kendra and invited her to church. The following Sunday she and her boyfriend, Ed, attended church with my parents and heard a gospel-rich sermon. Afterward, my parents took Kendra and Ed to lunch and heard more of their stories. They hoped to share Jesus Christ and look at discipling them. As my mom and dad made personal contact with them, being salt of the earth, they organically shared more of the good news of Jesus. Gospel seeds were lavishly sown into Kendra and Ed's lives.

They are still being bathed in prayer, and we are watching for what the Holy Spirit is going to do in them.

All of this took place because of a broken situation that led Kendra to tattoo the word for "hope" on her body. The good news of Christ's resurrection is this: *Jesus is our living hope.*

The risen Jesus took ahold of the man who denied Him three times and completely restored him according to God's great mercy. That man, named Peter, penned these indelible words through the Holy Spirit about the living hope of Christ:

"Blessed be the God and Father of our Lord Jesus Christ, who according to His great mercy has caused us to be born again to a living hope through the resurrection of Jesus Christ from the dead," (1 Peter 1:3).

Conclusion

Throughout this book, you have met
several different characters as we have endeavored to look at life through
the heart of Jesus, the gospel lens. I want you to know that these characters
are real people, and by God's grace, I have tried to do justice to each of their
narratives in turn.

In chapter 1, you met Esther from Tanzania. You should have seen the
look on her face when she put on the prescription glasses given to her by
Dr. Byemba. Her smile truly did light up the room. Looking through the
lens of the gospel will brighten your spirit and give you a fresh perspective as
you realize that the lens is the very heart of Jesus, and the focus of the lens is
Jesus Himself.

In chapter 2, you met Mariam, also from Tanzania. Her shattered marriage
and subsequent divorce devastated her. When she tried going to church, she
found only shame to greet her at the door when they said she had to sit in a
red chair separated from the rest of the congregation. But the gospel says all
of us deserve to sit in the red chair because of our radical sin nature.

Thanks be to God for Jesus Christ! Our tender and loving Savior does not
let that happen to us. He takes our shame for us. He did not sit on a red chair
but instead was nailed to a cross that ran red with His precious and perfect
shed blood. We can now be covered in His robe of righteousness to give us
free and intimate access to the very heart of God, our gracious heavenly Father.

In chapter 3, you met Nick, my roommate from college. It was in college
that I saw Jesus take hold of his life. You should have heard the sound of his
voice on the phone after he read the gospel of John a second time through.
Our amazing Savior had completely captured his heart. Nick went from being
a timid college student to a bold proclaimer of the gospel. By the grace of Jesus,

Nick went on to start a Bible study in our dorm called Moore-Hill More Hope. This Bible study would go on for years after Nick graduated from college.

Jesus then used Moore-Hill More Hope to bring a college student named James to salvation. James then shared and lived the gospel out in front of his roommate Rohit, who comes from a Hindu background. Jesus brought Rohit to salvation through the sincere witness James lived out for Christ. Jesus is so good!

By God's orchestration, Rohit and I ended up in the same church after graduating from college because we both moved to the same city. Currently, Rohit is in my discipleship group, the one I mentioned in chapter 26. I had the joy of watching Rohit leave the comfort of his family's acceptance to follow Christ. On October 31st, 2021, James and I watched Rohit be baptized in front of our whole church family. I love Jesus! He's so good.

In chapter 4, you met Clara. We saw how she lived a life full of anxiety and legalistic church duty, and then Jesus revealed Himself to her during a Bible study at work. You should have seen the look on her face as the good news of Jesus was presented to her. I felt like I was watching scales fall from her eyes. Jesus is so good! She then shared the gospel with her husband Josue, and he too became transformed by the grace of Jesus.

The lead pastor of my church, Pastor Tom, and I got to baptize Clara and Josue together in front of our church. Josue has been a faithful participant in my discipleship group for a few years now. He and Rohit and the other guys are a blast each week as we seek after Jesus together.

In chapter 5, you witnessed how the Holy Spirit led Clara to share the gospel with a dying ICU patient. Jesus used her to lead the critically ill man to Christ right before he departed from this world and entered eternity. Isn't Jesus so amazing that He made Clara His masterpiece by His grace, and then He prepared good works for her in advance that she would walk in them?

In chapter 6, you met my beautiful bride, Kelley. You heard her story of relationship betrayal and how Jesus used her brokenness to lead her to begin reading the book of Ephesians. Right away she saw in Ephesians 1 how she had been chosen by God the Father and then adopted into His family through the work of Jesus Christ. And then Jesus blew her away when she read about being dead in her sins apart from God's rich mercy to her in Christ. She saw how He made her alive together with Christ. Her identity and life trajectory completely changed. And then Jesus intersected her life with mine, and He has blessed us with three beautiful children. This book is dedicated to my bride!

In chapters 7 and 8, you met Jos. After losing his father he entered into a time of rebellion and gang activity and was even complicit in murder. But again, Jesus is beyond lavish in His grace. He allowed Jos to be exonerated of all charges. In that courtroom, Jos truly had a Barabbas moment. He was released by the judge and set free by the grace of Jesus. He came to forgive his dad and learned of his true sonship in Christ through reading Ephesians 1:5. Jos was once a cold and hardened criminal, but now in Christ, he is just about the kindest and most caring man I have ever met.

In chapter 11, you heard about my brother-in-law, Joseph, and his story. We saw that his struggle with pornography addiction was much deeper than a sexual urge. His addiction at its very root involved an identity crisis. He did not know who he was. But Jesus revealed Himself to him through John 4 and Jeremiah 2. Joseph came to understand the sinful, self-centered motivations he had all along for trying to get rid of his addiction. Instead, he came to realize that he was created for God's glory and that this Christ-centered motivation had to be his only motivation for overcoming pornography. Joseph encountered the very real presence of Jesus as he digested the truth about Christ's living water in John 4. Because of Jesus, to this day he has no desire to look at pornography.

In chapter 12, you met Ryan and heard about his persistent struggle with same-sex attraction. You saw how Jesus put different people in his path to lead him further along his journey. You saw how Ryan came to realize that Jesus is better than any sinful relationship his heart could desire. You also heard about the concept of redemptive experiences we can champion in the church for those who struggle with same-sex attraction. This is the heart of Jesus.

You also heard my story and struggle with same-sex attraction. You saw how Jesus used my dad to disciple me through this struggle to lead me deeper into the presence of Christ. The deep and rich father-son relationship I have with my dad is truly a gracious gift from Jesus.

Through my dad's counsel, my haunting thoughts became the very springboard and impetus to launch me into intimacy with Jesus. The Lord has been so very gracious to me. His grace is sufficient for Ryan and me.

In chapter 13, you met Amanda and Jordan. You saw how Jesus brought them together in marriage and how the gospel of Christ gave them a new lens with which to view one another. Instead of their marriage being transactional and quid-pro-quo, they serve one another by the grace of Christ. In fact, inscribed on the inside of Jordan's wedding ring is the following verse: "just as the Son of Man did not come to be served, but to serve, and to give His life a ransom for many" (Matt. 20:28 NASB).

In chapter 15, we saw how Jesus healed the woman with hemorrhage by restoring her, not only physically, but also socially, emotionally, and spiritually. We are the woman with the hemorrhage of sin in each of our lives. But Jesus has shed His blood to stop the ongoing flow of sin in our lives. Husbands and wives can receive this holistic restoration from Christ and then seek to be restorative to one another, as Jesus has done to them. This will display the gospel message to a broken world. Remember, marriage is not about you. It's all about Jesus. Our marriages are to be a real-life embodiment and display of the gospel of Jesus Christ to those around us.

In chapter 16, you met Matt. You witnessed the brokenness of his three failed marriages and subsequent divorces. You glimpsed how Jesus used my dad, David, to share the good news of Christ with him. We saw how he continually sought after an ideal marriage and family situation but always came up drastically short. And then we saw Jesus become the hero of Matt's story. We saw Matt realize that through all of the poor decisions he made, Jesus was standing right there with His arms open wide ready to embrace him. The heart of Jesus is staggeringly tender toward those who have been marred and broken by divorce.

Not only did Jesus redeem Matt from his brokenness, but He also infused a new purpose in his life to minister to those who are hurting and broken because of divorce or relationship trauma.

In chapters 18-19, we saw Lindsey and Joseph, my sister and brother-in-law, reveal how they disciple their children to follow Jesus. We witnessed the horrors of parenting when their son, Jackson, was bitten by a baby rattlesnake. As the situation grew more grave and dire, Lindsey called out to God and was met by wave after wave of His amazing attributes. He revealed who He is, His very heart to her. And the peace of Christ which transcends understanding came over her. And by the grace of Jesus, she awoke the next morning to find her son miraculously healed. Jesus is so good and so gracious.

We also saw how the gospel lens led Lindsey to be transparent about her brokenness with her children. This vulnerability allows Jesus to be the focus of our parenting as we lead our children to be transparent with us. The girl from across the street, named Ruby, ended up coming to Christ through the discipleship process Lindsey faithfully did with her children. Praise be to Jesus!

In chapter 21, you met Sean, and Lisa, his mother. We witnessed how long-term chronic suffering can be processed in light of the gospel of Jesus Christ. The lens of the gospel allowed Sean to look outside himself and reach out to Ricky, a patient who was having great difficulty coping with his medical situation. Jesus allowed Sean to share the good news of Christ with Ricky and his mother to sow gospel seeds into their lives.

In the gospel, we have a God who suffers horrifically in our place through Jesus Christ. He then conquers the grave to ensure that one day we will be with Him forever in a glorified body free of paralysis and pain.

In chapter 22, you met my dad, David, again. You saw how his missionary efforts in Zambia led to a tragic accident where Clement, his disciple, and apprentice in Christ, was killed. Following these events my dad found himself in a time of an affective fog after his 4 head surgeries where he experienced a blunted emotional state, thus plunging him into what he perceived as the silence of God or his "discipline of darkness." This persisted and was palpably felt to an even greater extent as the affective fog was lifted. Finally, Jesus brought my dad out of this, but for decades he sought healing for the soul wound of having the larger responsibility of another person's death.

It was not until being interviewed for this book that Jesus allowed my dad to connect the dots that the day of his arrest for causing death by dangerous driving was the same exact date as my sister, Lindsey's birthday, three years later. And the day of his exoneration was the same exact date as my birthday, seven years later. Through grasping these divinely orchestrated connections and going through the interview process with me for this book, my dad came to realize that all this time he was seeking healing for his suffering through the lens that this event was on him and about him. But by the grace of Jesus, the final door of healing was unlocked for him only when he saw through the gospel lens that his life is not about him and not about Clement either. It's all about Jesus (see Col. 1:16; 2 Cor. 5:15).

In chapters 23–26, I re-introduced you to Jesus. This book is all about Him. His heart is the lens of the gospel, and Jesus Himself is the focus of the lens.

Jesus is the crescendo of the symphony of Scripture. He is the thread running throughout all the beautiful tapestry of the Bible. He is the beginning and the end. He is the Alpha and the Omega. He is the one who prayed in the garden, sweating drops of blood, because He saw the petrifying panorama of God's wrath against sin opened to Him. He began experiencing Calvary before Calvary came.

He is the good shepherd who did not run when confronted by a mob of bloodthirsty men in Gethsemane. He laid His life down for His sheep. He took the place of murderous Barabbas. We are all Barabbas.

Jesus is the one who bore His own cross until He collapsed to the ground from a scourging that was meant to bring Him to the edge of death (see Matt. 27:26). He is the one who took the nails for us. He is the one who displayed His beautiful heart of forgiveness when He cried out, "Father, forgive them; for they do not know what they are doing" (Luke 23:34 NASB).

He is the one who disarmed and melted the heart of the thief on the cross next to Him with His ravishing mercy.

Jesus is the one who cried, "MY GOD, MY GOD, WHY HAVE YOU FORSAKEN ME?" (Matt. 27:46b). He was the one forsaken by His Father, so we who believe in Him would never be forsaken.

He is the one who absorbed the wrath of God to become the propitiation for our sins. He is the one who purchased forgiveness for *all* our sins: past, present, and future.

He is the one who caused the curtain of the temple to be torn in two from top to bottom to usher us into intimacy with God our heavenly Father.

Jesus is the one who declared, "It is finished" (John 19:30). Now, we who are weary and heavy-laden can cease from striving and rest in His eternal salvation.

He is the one who called Mary by name to reveal His resurrection to her first. With one word, Jesus opened her eyes and lifted her from terrible sorrow to inexplicable joy and hope.

He is the one who sought out doubting Thomas and revealed His great desire for our belief in His resurrection. Thus, He revealed His great desire to be with us for all eternity.

After being resurrected from the dead, Jesus is the one who sought out Peter. He restored and reinstated him by calling him by name three times expunging his three denials, and imprinting His forgiveness upon him. And then Jesus propelled Peter into shepherd leadership of the early church to preach the inaugural gospel message that brought three thousand souls to Christ.

Jesus is the one with all authority in heaven and on earth.

He is the one who changed history by calling us to join Him in His mission of making disciples of all the nations, baptizing them in the name of the Father, the Son, and the Holy Spirit.

Jesus is the one who is with us always, even to the end of the age.

He is the one who sent us the Holy Spirit after ascending to His Father. He is the one who gave birth to the church, His body.

He is the one who is our living hope through His death and resurrection.

Take this gospel lens. Put the heart of Jesus in front of your eyes. Look through and see every situation utterly different and transformed. Glimpse how those around you will never look the same because your heart now beats with Christ's purpose and joy. See that ". . . He died for all so that they who live might no longer live for themselves, but for Him who died and rose again on their behalf" (2 Cor. 5:15 NASB). Jesus, His very heart, is not only the lens of the gospel, but He's also the focus of the gospel lens.

He is breathtakingly beautiful to behold.

And one day, you will behold Him. One day, you will breathe your last breath. And you will walk into eternity. If you belong to Christ, this will be a blissfully rapturous moment for you. Imagine this moment with me now.

You take your final breath. In the blink of an eye, you enter eternity. You open your eyes and standing a stone's throw away from you is Jesus, the King of kings and the Lord of lords. His resplendent glory emanates from the white robe He wears. You behold Him. You drink in the moment. You take a step. Another step. And then you break into a sprint toward Him. You lock eyes with Him, undaunted by His majesty and invited ever closer by His gentle approachability. His gaze is piercing. His eyes are like fire but ever beckoning you to come. He sees into the depths of your soul and still loves you relentlessly. How do you know this?

As you draw near, your soul wells up in fullness of joy because you become acutely aware of His smile. He's smiling at *you*. His smile illuminates the totality of your being. You think to yourself, *Jesus is so kind. I've never known love and kindness like this before. I could drink this in for all eternity.*

You throw yourself onto the Son of God. He wraps you up in a wondrously warm embrace. He holds you to His chest. A love that was a mere abstraction on earth now becomes intensely tangible and intimately knowable. You are held by perfect love. His arms are omnipotently strong but gloriously tender. You realize every loving embrace you experienced on earth very dimly reflected the embrace Jesus now gives you. You are overwhelmed by His love for you. Tears begin streaming down your face. Your soul was made for this moment.

All of the sin and shame and heartache you knew so intimately on earth now become a distant and fading memory, never to be seen or felt again. All the pain you once knew is now like a ship sailing off into the sunset being incinerated by the sunbeams of Christ's perfect love and grace. You feel like your true self for the very first time. The healing, consoling, and restoring touch of Christ makes you gloriously new.

You let yourself melt in the arms of Jesus. You feel His heart beating inside His chest against yours. Thump. Thump. Thump. His very being pulsates with songs of delight over you. A nail-scarred hand warmly moves in circles on your back. And His deep, resonating voice fills your ears and swells your heart as He whispers:

"Welcome home."

CPSIA information can be obtained
at www.ICGtesting.com
Printed in the USA
LVHW081405141122
733099LV00004B/39